PRAISEWORTHY MUSIC

and

SPIRITUAL MOMENTS

DAVID GLEN HATCH

CFI
AN IMPRINT OF CEDAR FORT, INC.
SPRINGVILLE, UTAH

ISBN 13: 978-1-59955-993-3

Published by CFI, an imprint of Cedar Fort, Inc., 2373 W. 700 S., Springville, UT 84663
Distributed by Cedar Fort, Inc., www.cedarfort.com

LIBRARY OF CONGRESS CATALOGING-IN-PUBLICATION DATA

Hatch, David Glen, author.
Praiseworthy music and spiritual moments / David Glen Hatch.
pages cm
Includes bibliographical references.
Summary: A collection of personal stories and experiences of award-winning pianist David Glen Hatch.
ISBN 978-1-59955-993-3
1. Hatch, David Glen. 2. Pianists--United States--Biography. 3. Spirituality in music. 4. Music--History and criticism. I. Title.

ML417.H264A3 2012
786.2092--dc23
[B]

                    2012001013

Cover design by Angela D. Olsen
Cover design © 2012 by Lyle Mortimer
Edited and typeset by Michelle Stoll

Printed in the United States of America

10 9 8 7 6 5 4 3 2 1

Printed on acid-free paper

*"We recognize the universal power of music
to touch the hearts of men and women
everywhere and in all generations—
to inspire and encourage,
to sustain and lift, to comfort and bring peace."*

—President Gordon B. Hinckley

Praise for

PRAISEWORTHY MUSIC AND SPIRITUAL MOMENTS

For David Glen Hatch to write a book that is as captivating as his music and musicianship is a daunting task. The fact that he has done so with *Praiseworthy Music and Spiritual Moments* is a testament to his remarkable talent. His insights about music's power to uplift and edify will resonate with readers—musicians, and non-musicians alike. It's a terrific read.

—Orrin G. Hatch

If there is anyone qualified to talk about the ability of music to inspire, praise, uplift, and heal, it is David Glen Hatch. What joy to read the thoughts of his heart about a gift that has touched so many hearts! . . . With the insight he shares in these pages, you will never listen to music in the same way again. This is a book that belongs in every home where families yearn to invite the Spirit to dwell.

—Kathryn Jenkins, Managing Editor,
Covenant Communications, Inc.

In my long association with David Glen Hatch, I have marveled at his understanding of the power of inspired music . He is able to articulate in word and song this important message that many of us hold dear deserving our respect and admiration.

—Michael Ballam, Opera Tenor,
General Director, Utah Festival Opera

Riveting! David Glen Hatch has come as close as anyone I have known to clarifying the inexplicable power of music to unify, entertain, and uplift mankind. You've been moved by his keyboard mastery, and now will be deeply touched by his heartfelt explanations about how music can enhance the spiritual atmosphere in our homes during these troubled times.

—Janice Kapp Perry, LDS Songwriter

In his work on and off the stage, David maintains the highest level of artistic integrity. The artist's new book reveals not only a musician of considerable stature, but a man of intelligence, dignity and charm.

—Susan Haber, Director, Critics Choice Records,
Critics Choice Concerts

Dr. Hatch is a musician who has kept abreast of the developments of his own time, and the possibilities of using music as an international source and gift to the world. His accomplishments and activities are well documented and attest to the continuous activities he promotes as a performer, teacher, ambassador for music, composer, arranger, and citizen of the world of music. This significant document will be a source for reference by colleagues, many students, and admirers of this distinguished musician and professor.

—Dr. Paul C. Pollei, Founder/Artistic Director, The Gina
Bachauer International Piano Foundation

Entertaining and informative, this book by ideal pianist and musician David Glen Hatch is filled with engaging research, opinions, and anecdotes. A magnificent achievement!

—Matyas Antal, Associate Conductor,
Hungarian State Symphony Orchestra

"His unique blend of musical artistry and his vast performing and teaching experience combine to give David Glen Hatch a perspective which is rare among concert artists. Within the pages of this book, Dr. Hatch exposes the facets of music which have power to heal, comfort, motivate, and exalt the human spirit. . . . a compelling read!"

—Jerry R. Jackman, CEO,
Jackman Music Corporation

Contents

Acknowledgments

As always in such an undertaking as this, there are many to whom heartfelt appreciation must be expressed. Among the numerous individuals to thank for the encouragement, inspiration, and preparation I have received in discovering the magic of great music throughout my life are my exceptional wife, Paula, and our five gifted children: Erika, Denise, Ryan, Jessica, and Christopher.

To these incomparable family members, I express my gratitude for their lifelong support and energy in sustaining me in my quest for beautiful music-making. Each is most satisfying and beloved to me—family that has ever been my source of strength, motivation, and joy.

This book is also dedicated to my cherished parents, who were prompted early in my childhood to provide me with the best musical study and opportunities available while instilling a love for the gospel and encouraging my dreams of accomplishment.

Furthermore, inspired teachers and professors have shared their vast knowledge and example. Enthusiastic students have provided energy and exhilaration. Church leaders have given wise counsel about music. Musicians in the Church have unselfishly shared their talents and testimonies through music. I will forever respect and admire the numerous master composers and performers across the globe gifted in creating the world's musical masterpieces that have endured the test of time. And especially am I grateful to the Lord for giving us this marvelous miracle of beautiful music and for His gospel, which encompasses all worthwhile arts.

Last, for their constant encouragement and support of this book from the outset, I recognize and give thanks to Lyle Mortimer, president of Cedar Fort, Inc., and his staff. Particularly, my editors—Jennifer Fielding, Catherine Christensen, Heather Holm, and Michelle Stoll—pooled their extraordinary talents to bring forth the book I had envisioned, though exposed only through working with them. I am grateful for their painstaking assistance and pithy advice during the process. Further heartfelt gratitude goes to Jennifer, who generously shared her ideas as I worked, tirelessly reviewed my drafts, and conveyed her unique sense which supplied me with imaginative suggestions and saved me many times from the dangers of muddy prose. I also express appreciation to Angela Olsen, a specially gifted graphic designer who created this aesthetically pleasing visual product.

I am indebted to them all.

Foreword

F ortunately, I have kept a diary since my early teens. This weekly and sometimes daily activity, coupled with my good fortune of having been endowed with a peculiar memory, allowed me to effectively trace my life of music throughout the years of advancement toward attaining my personal musical goals and eventual professional career.

Besides the numerous, valuable aspects of music and its power that will be usefully considered, the following words will also provide readers with my primitive but truthful account of the struggles, the mistakes, the adventures, and the miraculous beauty and happiness over these, my many years as a professional artist and teacher.

Preface

From the outset, music has been my life—my eventual professional career. After several music degrees and years of local, state, regional, national, and international work and acclaim, I have recently felt a strong impression to share the valuable contents of this book regarding music that enhances the spiritual atmosphere in our homes and in lives everywhere during these troubled times.

Music is a very powerful expression of emotion through the medium of sound. It is unhindered by the mental barriers usually in place to filter all input and is directly applied to the soul in a manner that is startlingly effective. Music is the most powerful of all the arts because it stimulates, manipulates, and dissipates our moods through the emotions it transmits. It illuminates the power to unite, bless, heal, empower, inspire, praise, uplift, and teach. Possessing a dimension of its own, music often exceeds the spoken word in expressing moods and feelings of the heart and soul.

Praiseworthy Music and Spiritual Moments is a book for parents, families, and individuals who yearn to understand and feel the power of music in their lives. It is my desire within the following pages to provide musical insights and information with a gospel emphasis that will enrich lives in the pursuit of spiritual edification.

Chapter One

THE POWER OF MUSIC TO UNITE

"What love is to man, music is to the arts and to mankind. Music is love itself—the purest, most ethereal language of passion, showing in a thousand ways all possible changes of color and feeling; and though true in only a single instance, it yet can be understood by thousands of men—who all feel differently."

—Carl Maria von Weber

Although music signifies different things to different people, often extending to a deeply personal level, cultures around the world have appreciated, enjoyed, and incorporated some form of music in their everyday lives since the beginning of time. Music, as a part of culture, will most often have more roles to play than simply a source of auditory pleasure. Music is an extremely versatile medium of communication that has touched the human soul across all boundaries of time, space, and genre. Consider for a moment how bleak life would be with no music present. A philosopher once said, "Without music, life is a journey through a desert." Certainly music is one of the most essential and endearing gifts of God to man!

Music has the power to endow the listener with aesthetic or intellectual pleasure. It can be simple or complex, subtle or blatant. Fortunately, music is burgeoning around us daily in myriad forms—

1

in the sound of a train, waves crashing upon the shore, chirping crickets, croaking frogs, singing birds, a mother's lullaby, the very sound and rhythm of nature—which all touch the emotions. It is universally present through radio, television, audio systems, elevators, supermarkets, cinema, airports, dental and medical offices, teaching studios, places of employment, buses, taxis, aircraft, and concert performances. Wherever it is heard, music creates joy in the heart and brings refinement to the soul.

Music's form, style, texture, rhythm, and system of harmony are as varied as the personalities found on any given New York City subway train. From simple folk songs to religious chants, and from Carnegie Hall to the Broadway district, the range and diversity of human music is almost incomprehensible.

In a world of diversity where often there is a clash of values, social status, and personal convictions, music has a way of bridging gaps and bringing people together by leaping across language barriers and uniting people of varied cultural backgrounds and geographical locations. In each generation, music represents the aspirations, heartbreaks, emotions, and achievements of people living in that specific period. The feeling to be human and alive to the world around us and the desire to express life's experiences through music remains common to all mankind.

Music has the ability to reflect deep feelings and the power and dramatic effect to unify people and move them to action. Throughout history, for example, hymns of inspiration, classical masterpieces, love songs, marches, and songs about disappointment and tragedy have all stirred souls and unified hearts. Music can generate love of fellowman, especially while utilized to protest injustice and advocate for human rights. Stated best: Music sounds like feelings feel, and WE ALL FEEL!

Musicians—including musicologists, theorists, composers, conductors, teachers, professors, music therapists, instrumental manufacturers, music publishers, instrumental technicians, church musicians, amateur performers and concert artists—who choose to study, understand, teach, create, and perform music are all unified through the art and power of music. Furthermore, by being exposed to the world through the varied contributions of musicians, music makes a positive and lasting impact upon society in profoundly significant ways.

It has been said that the best way to understand and learn about people and their culture is to observe and listen to their art and music. Through my sundry concert travels, this has been an opportunity of mine which has often created closeness with my audiences. One such experience and certainly one of my most intense moments as a professional classical pianist took place because of a hymn! On this occasion it was demonstrated to me how the power and magic of music can unite people of diverse cultures.

Several years ago during a concert tour of Scandinavia, I was performing a sizable program of works of the masters in the gorgeous Sorgenfri Lutheran Cathedral (ninety percent of Danes are Lutheran) for an audience whom I had never before met. Yet it was here, while paying attention to the Spirit's voice, that an awkward moment with these unknown people was transformed into a transcendent experience that immediately unified those in attendance!

After my final piece, a Liszt Transcendental Étude, the capacity audience became rowdy—stomping their feet and applauding in unison—a cultural tradition of many European countries. I bowed and left the stage. With the audience demanding more after two curtain calls, I decided to perform an encore, the Schumann Arabesque. But the Spirit whispered that I should perform a different selection. Instead of the Schumann, a feeling came to me that I should perform my hymn arrangement of *How Great Thou Art*. I rejected the notion, however, because of my desire to perform the elegant Arabesque.

Returning once again to the stage with the crowd clamoring, I was determined to proceed with the classical encore, but a much stronger spiritual impression came over me to perform *How Great Thou Art*. Having learned my lesson from similar spiritual promptings in the past, I sat down and obeyed the instruction.

After performing the hymn arrangement, I stood and faced the audience. Not a sound! To my surprise, every person was standing in silent tribute, tears streaming down their faces. The spirit of love and unity enveloping all of us in that hall that moment is completely indescribable. Afterward, while visiting with audience members, I was informed of the reason these Danes had been touched in this way. The composer of this, the greatest Protestant hymn of all time—especially beloved by these Scandinavian people—was one of their own, the Swedish pastor Carl Boberg! Immediately, I began to understand the magnificent unifying process of music from those remarkable moments that evening. Feelings of love and reverence increased for all present as the power of this music that expresses faith and devotion to God became a uniting force between artist and audience that evening in that beautiful corner of the world.

Interestingly, the Lord already knew that my performance of this inspired hymn would be the closing benediction to the program and promote the spirit of unity and love between His children on that occasion! Such music spreads love, life, and spiritual joy among God's children living in this troubled, sinful, and chaotic world of ours. That night, the Spirit taught me about the power of music to unite. It was also a wonderful reminder to always listen to the Spirit and heed that voice.

Music has been called the inner or universal language of God, as it speaks to all men everywhere. I cannot speak nor do I understand German, Russian, Japanese, Italian, or Swahili, but when I hear music in these languages, immediately the music enters into my heart or my heart enters into the music. At that time, no outer communication is needed; the inner communion of the heart is enough. My heart is communing with the heart of the music, and in our communion we inseparably become one. Music, the inner language of Deity, communicates to the soul of man. It has been said: "Let us not try to understand music with our mind. Let us not even try to feel it with our heart. Let us simply and spontaneously allow the music-bird to fly in our heart-sky. While flying, it will unconditionally reveal to us what it has and what it is. What it has, is Immortality's message. What it is, is Eternity's passage."

First and foremost, music is the universal language of mankind. Before he went on his first concert tour of England, the great Austrian composer Joseph Haydn did not speak a word of English. He, too, understood the language of music and thus was not concerned. His family and friends, however, were troubled about the language barrier, but Haydn replied with confidence, "I don't need to speak the language, I speak the language of music and everyone understands this language. My language is understood all over the world."[1]

However complex, music is readily appreciated by the mind without the need for formal knowledge. Some listeners may not understand some music intellectually, yet they have no problem appreciating music as a whole. This is certainly true in The Church of Jesus Christ of Latter-day Saints. Three months after the Church was organized, the Lord, through the Prophet Joseph Smith, instructed Joseph's wife, Emma, to make a selection of sacred hymns for the Church: "For my soul delighteth in the song of the heart; yea, the song of the righteous is a prayer unto me, and it shall be answered with a blessing upon their heads" (D&C 25:12).

The First Presidency Preface to the hymnbook discusses important elements of music in our church meetings.

> Inspirational music is an essential part of our church meetings. The hymns invite the Spirit of the Lord, create a feeling of reverence, unify us as members, and provide a way for us to offer praises to the Lord.
>
> Some of the greatest sermons are preached by the singing of hymns. Hymns move us to repentance and good works, build testimony and faith, comfort the weary, console the mourning, and inspire us to endure to the end.
>
> We hope to see an increase of hymn singing in our congregations. We encourage all members, whether musically inclined or not, to join with us in singing the hymns. We hope leaders, teachers, and members who are called upon to speak will turn often to the hymnbook to find sermons presented powerfully and beautifully in verse. [2]

In a July 2001 *Ensign* article titled "The Power of the Hymns" by Elder Merrill J. Bateman of the Seventy, further inspired information was presented:

> In the process of singing together, a spirit of unity builds within the Saints. This occurs not only within a ward and stake but across the world. We can travel the earth from Sunday to Sunday, and wherever we are the music of the hymns will be familiar. Elder Dallin H. Oaks of the Quorum of the Twelve Apostles spoke of his first trip to Brazil to attend a regional conference. He states: "Over three thousand Saints gathered for a regional conference. The printed program listed the musical numbers, but the Portuguese words meant nothing to me. But when their beautiful choir began to sing, the music crossed all barriers of language and spoke to my soul." [3]

Second, music can reach the deepest areas of the soul. Where does music come from if not the soul? Animals do not sing; only the human being has produced the majesty of music, which emerges from the deep mysterious places of our soul. It can stir, it can call forth tears, it makes us swell with healthy pride and exuberance, it can instill joy, provoke our deepest thoughts, and make us want to sing and dance. Music is the soul's way to exhale, to express itself beyond words. It signifies the soul's longing, its sighing, its happiness, and its sorrow. We must always appreciate this miracle of human existence, this unique gift to all people, this flash of beauty and dignity in the soul of every human person.

> For the common things of every day,
> God gave man speech in a common way;
>
> For the deeper things men think and feel,
> God gave the past words to reveal;
>
> But, for the heights and depths that know no reach,
> God gave man music, the soul's own speech.

Third, music, unlike any other language, can express every emotion. Music's highest achievement is realized in those circumstances where words fall short of expression. Where words fail, music can continue to vocalize all that has ever needed to be said. At that time, other communication is not needed! Truly, music speaks spirit to spirit. Following a concert in Paris several years ago, a woman came to meet me backstage. Due to our language barrier, she simply touched her heart as tears streamed down her cheeks, and said one word, "Chopin." Instantly, I understood that my performance of the Chopin nocturne that evening had communicated deeply to her soul. It was this experience that taught me firsthand that music genuinely is the universal language. It is especially fitting that Frederic Chopin declared, "Music may be termed the universal language of mankind, by which human feelings are made equally understandable to all."[4]

Music may even predate human speech. Speaking of the genesis of music, the remarkable German romantic composer Robert Schumann once noted, "Perhaps it's precisely the mystery of her origin which accounts for the charm of her beauty."[5] Some researchers have theorized that the development of music among humans originated against the backdrop of natural sounds. Most likely, it was influenced by birdsong and the sounds other animals used to communicate.

Music employs the inner communication of the heart—our richest, deepest selves: our emotions, our language skills, our imaginations, our universal humanity, and the cultural aspects of our identity. Music has been viewed over the centuries, both literally and figuratively, as a form of language or speech less specific than the spoken word but possessing subtler shades of meaning and more expressive force.

I vividly remember how music became a unifying force to hundreds of lawmakers on September 11, 2001, when members of Congress gathered on the steps of the nation's Capitol in a show of unity, strength, and resolve, promising to "stand together" against the evil terrorist attacks of that horrific day. It is difficult to describe the innermost feelings of our people at that time. Mostly, there was shock, fear, panic, anger, and a sense of hopelessness. The thought of all the innocent people lost in Washington, New York, and Pennsylvania was incomprehensible. The sheer savagery and inhumanity of the attacks sickened and shocked the conscience. Americans across the nation were traumatized and experienced severe emotional pain. At that very time, however, these members of the House and Senate, seeing the black plume of smoke rising from the Pentagon across the Potomac River, became as one while spontaneously singing *God Bless America*.

One year later, in 2002, the House and Senate held a solemn joint meeting in New York's Federal Hall—only the second meeting of Congress held outside Washington in the past two centuries! These lawmakers had gone to New York City to again show their solidarity with our citizens. As they stood together shoulder to shoulder, the power of music again joined them as they held hands and sang God Bless America with a high school choir.

Most recently, on the tenth anniversary of these terrorist strikes, and with that same sense of harmony that pulled Congress together ten years earlier, these lawmakers, many waving small flags, again stood together at the Capitol to pay tribute to the victims and heroes of that day, joining a Marine Corps band as they sang this emotional patriotic song. Definitely, music can become a healing balm that unifies people in times of duress, pain, and heartache.

Music is an eternal unifying power—one of the most unifying elements in our lives! Thousands of strangers have had the same moment of discovery as we have—loving that certain music by an orchestra, band, singer, instrumentalist, or composer that becomes our current favorite. Although we may not always discuss music with others, it's often present—an unspoken unity between you and the rest of the world. It has been a part of every culture and society of mankind since the world began. In essence, the musical dimension of life is spiritual and has a purpose and potential to unite and to change the spiritual climate of the earth. Herein lies the power of music—to connect us on a level we might not fully recognize, as it is part of everything around us.

The Cuvilliés Theatre is a gorgeous rococo opera house I once had the privilege of visiting in Munich, Germany, where many operas were staged by the Bavarian State Opera, including the premieres of Mozart's *Idomeneo* in 1781 and Carl Maria von Weber's *Abu Hassan* in 1811. In the foyer hangs a gold placard that anonymously shares these discerning words: "Bach gave us God's words, Mozart gave us God's laughter, Beethoven gave us God's fire, and God gave us music that we might pray without words." Music uniquely connects us all together. Not only does music unite men, it was discovered from my harrowing evening several years ago in Lviv, Ukraine, that music can also connect us to God, who is there for us in times of distress.

That Ukrainian concert tour proved thrilling but exhausting for my students and me from the extensive traveling and performing crammed into a two-week period. Following my orchestral debut at Kiev's Mariinsky Palace with the Ukrainian National Symphony, we boarded a rickety overnight sleeper train to the attractive city of Lviv, with its glistening gold-domed and bright-colored Russian Orthodox churches dotting the landscape. After the successful concert at the prestigious Philharmonic Hall, a terrifying episode ensued— I was mugged!

Having been away from home for five days and not yet having the opportunity to call my wife, I knew she would be worrying. Therefore, at eleven p.m. with the students in their rooms for the night, I decided to make that call in the lighted city center at the bottom of the hill, since the hotel phones were inoperable to the States. Ignoring the Spirit's warning voice to NOT leave the hotel, I walked down through a pitch-black park to the international pay phone.

Immediately, while I was working my phone card, two men in their late twenties appeared from nowhere and flanked me on both sides of the telephone booth. The larger man in his broken English asked me—an easily-detectible tourist—if I was lost. I explained that I needed to make a call to the States and would then return to the Dnistesr Hotel at the top of the hill. He took the receiver from my hand, hung it up, and told me to follow them through the deserted streets.

Realizing I was in trouble, I began walking briskly in the opposite direction. To my dismay, the men kept up with me, walking faster and faster. The one who had spoken to me pulled a cell phone from his pocket and made a call. Within a minute, a car sped to the curb, and the men began pushing and pulling me toward the car as they tried to convince me that it was a taxi to return me to my hotel. But, with a pit in my stomach, I knew differently! Shrugging and pulling away from them, I tried to get away. For an hour, they pursued me relentlessly while I tried to stay within lighted areas, where an occasional person in view would unknowingly prevent my adversaries from touching me—not wanting to make a scene. Becoming disoriented in my walk back to the hotel, I mistakenly turned onto a dark avenue in the opposite direction with no way out.

A second "taxi" was called (another accomplice) and arrived at the curb, and again I was bullied and pushed toward the backseat. A strong impression came to me that these men wanted my money and would kill me if I was forced into the car. So, I again yanked myself away from their grip. The driver sped off in frustration, and the men again followed me in faster pursuit. Silently, I began praying like never before for deliverance from this horrific situation and in my mind began singing comforting Church hymns, including *I Am a Child of God*. This music comforted my heart and gave me peace, and I felt immediately connected to my Heavenly Father. While the music calmed me, the Spirit instructed me in managing the remaining ordeal.

I began reasoning with the abusers to let me return to the hotel since I had no money with me. But, greatly aggravated by my uncooperative attitude, the larger man grabbed my arm as we continued up a long, dark alley and produced from his pocket a fake police badge, explaining that he was a security officer trying to protect me from this dangerous city of crime. The Spirit spoke differently, however!

Again, I began to converse with him to find common interests to which we could relate. He told me of his wife and baby, and I shared my family situation—my wife and children whom I wanted to see again. But after several minutes of discussion and at the very moment the men grabbed my arms to force me away, a tiny, bent babushka (traditional Russian grandmother figure) appeared from a perpendicular alleyway. Not wanting to alert this old woman to the abduction, they immediately let go until she passed.

Freed from their grasp for those few seconds and having been a long distance runner my entire life, I began running at top speed toward the lighted intersection two blocks away. The men began to pursue me harder and harder, faster and faster, grabbing at me from directly behind.

I was running awkwardly in very heavy Skechers with one-inch rubber soles. Nearing the intersection while tripping over my feet from uncontrolled speed, one of the soles caught a slightly elevated cobblestone of the street, causing me to fly forward through the air and land sprawling onto the uneven pavement. Upon my fall at the intersection came the culmination of my plight—a modern-day miracle! Parked at the red light was a police officer who had witnessed the chase. The two men were apprehended, and the security officer drove me back to the hotel while cursing and chastising me, a foolish tourist—demanding that I never again find myself alone late at night in a foreign city!

Although I sustained significant injuries from my fall—bleeding knees torn open through tattered pants, cut elbows, badly scraped left hand, nearly broken right wrist, and damaged tendons that became excruciatingly sore and swollen and revealed several shades of bruises during the following days, I knew my prayers had been answered—the Lord had protected and delivered me! Yes, I was discouraged that the injuries to my arms and hands caused me to forego the next performance in Odessa, but I will forever marvel that the inspirational music in my head during most of that assault brought us together—the Lord and me—and kept me feeling comforted and hopeful during that mighty hour of terror.

In my view, music is one of the most unifying elements in our lives, as human emotions are universal, no matter the geographical location. Through exposing these emotions, music possesses the power to unify any group of people—their thoughts, beliefs, passions, ideals, and spiritual awareness. The spoken and unspoken sentiment to which almost every musician and music lover will attest is that the spiritual significance of music lies in the fact that it literally connects human beings with a pulse that transcends boundaries, culture, language, religion, gender, age, color, and politics in an area of commonality where men can experience their sameness. Of a surety, music has the power to unite. This I know!

NOTES:

1. Rosemary Hughes, *Haydn* (New York: Collier, 1962), 45.
2. The Church of Jesus Christ of Latter-day Saints, "First Presidency Preface," *Hymns*, ix-x.
3. Merrill J. Bateman, "The Power of Hymns," *Ensign*, July 2001.
4. Arthur Hedley, Chopin, ed. and rev. Maurice J. E. Brown (London: J.M. Dent, 1974), 189.
5. Joan Chissll, Schumann, rev. ed. (New York: Collier, 1967), 68.

Chapter Two

THE POWER OF MUSIC TO BLESS

"To engender and diffuse faith, and to promote our spiritual well-being, are among the noblest aims of music."

—C. P. E. Bach

Music, God's universal language, has the power to bless. It is a gift that fills our hearts each day of our lives with love and happiness and should be a source of communication among men. Praiseworthy music is marvelous—an emotional or spiritual experience for each of us with varying degrees of intensity. Listeners have a responsibility to strive to understand and appreciate musical works by finding joy, knowledge, and spiritual edification in them.

Two poignant quotes seem fitting. Martin Luther said, "Music is a master which makes the people softer and milder, more polite and more rational. It is a beautiful and noble gift of God." And Carl Schober once stated, "Study music in order to beautify your own heart, and beautify your own heart in order to make this world blessed for others."[1] To me, these considerations are apropos when contemplating the musical and cultural incidents that were cherished by my students and me during one of my concert tours in France.

Considered the land of romance, stunning France has always been one of my favorite European countries to visit. I adore the elegant language, the French cuisine, and the exceptional culture steeped in magnificent history and tradition! Through sharing stunning music in several concert performances over many years in the cities of Paris, Fontainebleau, Nice, Nancy, Lyon, Toulouse, Bordeaux, and Marseille, my life was abundantly blessed.

One could spend weeks in Paris and never glimpse the complete grandeur of this, one of the great cities of the world with its numerous iconic, world-famous landmarks: Napoleon's Arc de Triomphe; the Eiffel Tower; the Paris Opera House; Louis XIV's Palace of Versailles, with its hundreds of acres of forest, parks, and fountains; the Louvre; Montmartre and its artists; the stunning Champs-Élysées avenue; and the beautiful Seine River running through the city.

Although these cultural sites were breathtakingly magnificent, the musical highlights we experienced became even more magical and the absolute essence of our tour. The first exceptional happening was sitting and listening to a professional organist perform a glorious midday recital in the sixteenth century gothic Notre Dame Cathedral on its booming organ of 7,800 pipes. It was from this spectacular event that our group better understood how the power of music can bless lives. We realized that, after this spiritually moving musical occurrence, we would never be quite the same. Music... among the "Arts," possesses a brilliant power to bless lives.

Blessings of inspiration also came while exploring awe-inspiring paintings of the masters including the French Impressionists—Van Gogh, Matisse, Monet, Renoir, Degas, Rembrandt, and Da Vinci, to name a few. Later, our group had been moved emotionally and spiritually during various musical moments in our concert performances, these experiences caused me to remind the students that this was the power of music in action. After all, it was music that caused us to expend so much time and effort over many months in concert preparation that provided these amazing artistic opportunities in France. Not only did the power and inspiration of those performances enrich our lives, but it was also evident from the reaction of our audiences that those lives, too, had been blessed by the music.

In addition to the exhilaration that was present in our concerts in Paris and other areas of France, music relating to additional cultural stimulations became available. Each of us, for example, were very fortunate to visit and learn the historical background of the apartments and residences of Frederic Chopin, and explore the summer chalet of the famous journalist George Sand, where Chopin would spend his summers in the French countryside of Nohant. Wonderful nostalgia and inspiration flowed into our hearts for we knew that at each of these places Chopin had composed some of the world's most prolific and greatest masterpieces! This together with our attendance at a stimulating choir concert inside the Church of the Madeleine, the setting of Chopin's funeral in 1849, revealed the fact that music does have the power to bless!

Recently, while performing and presenting master classes at prominent music schools in Beijing and at the Shanghai Conservatory of Music in China, I witnessed hundreds of serious, dedicated young students studying, practicing, and rehearsing eight to ten hours daily to achieve the skills developed over several years to later bless the lives of listeners. Not only will this work ethic demonstrated by these young people be a blessing for their future audiences, but it was also an enormous benefit for my own American students who were with me at the time. They received insights to better understand their own possibilities and potentials through hard work in the development of their own pianistic talents and abilities.

Often during my travels, especially to Asian and Eastern European countries, I have observed that the musical arts are considered by school administrators, teachers, parents, and students to be as academically crucial as mathematics, science, and language. Unfortunately, this is rarely the case in the United States, where music courses are frequently slashed from school curriculums due to reduced funding and lack of interest by school administrators. Sadly, I have found that many educators in our American school system do not understand the vital role of music study as a critical component to academic achievement.

Nevertheless, having gained great satisfaction and enjoyment by working with two very bright and gifted Chinese pianists of the prestigious Shanghai Conservatory of Music, I felt additionally blessed on another occasion in Hong Kong. Following my college master class and Church concert at the Homantin Chapel attended by five hundred Church members, general public, missionaries, and investigators, a moment of instantaneous exuberance emerged.

Following my finale number, Liszt's Sixth Hungarian Rhapsody, the audience members were on their feet, demanding encores. As there were many members of the Church in attendance, my encore choices were two of my Church arrangements, *I Walk by Faith* and *Come, Come Ye Saints*.

After the lengthy applause, while feeling an abundance of the Lord's Spirit in that hall, spiritual approval unlike anything I had previously experienced occurred. All of the teenagers and younger children present stood and, in Chinese, began singing to me! They sang a most inspirational rendering of our beloved primary song, *I am a Child of God*. There were no dry eyes in the building during those special moments when everyone felt the outpouring of the Spirit and as I embraced many of those precious Asian Saints. It was a perfect end to an inspiring, thought-provoking day. To be sure, I will treasure for years to come the many fond memories and spiritual moments experienced in China, an incredibly unique country. I had been deeply touched!

Music has the power to bless those who live lives of righteousness and spirituality. Brigham Young made a fascinating statement about music when he said, "There is no music in hell, for all good music belongs to heaven. Sweet harmonious sounds give exquisite joy to human beings capable of appreciating music. I delight in hearing harmonious tones made by the human voice, by musical instruments, and by both combined. Every sweet musical sound that can be made belongs to the Saints and is for the Saints."[2] Though this is difficult to comprehend, what a tragedy it is that there will be those who live an eternity without music!

Music also has power to bless those in need temporally and emotionally. The proceeds from most of the numerous *Messiah* concerts were given to charities. Such charity performances prompted one biographer to say, "Messiah has fed the hungry, clothed the naked, fostered the orphan, benefited hospitals of the infirm . . . more than any other single musical production in this or any country." He also declared, "Perhaps the works of no other composer have so largely contributed to the relief of human suffering."[3] Handel had learned profound spiritual perspective when he realized that everything with which he had been blessed throughout his life had come from God.

It is highly inspirational that, in response to these bestowed gifts, he lived to provide charity for others less privileged! Likewise, though on a much smaller scale, throughout my travels to diverse areas of the world, numerous opportunities have been presented to me in using my music to bless lives through charity work. It is enlightening to witness the power of music as it provides temporal and emotional blessings to those in need. To this day, I cherish those efforts where the magic of music has not only been used to support others, but has also infused me with warmth, fulfillment, and joy. Here are some of those moments.

Nestled between the Alps and the Mediterranean in Eastern Europe is a gorgeous little country. Slovenia is small and often unfamiliar to tourists but uniquely picturesque and diverse. The charm and beauty of Ljubljana, its capital city, was something for which I was not prepared. Through murmuring forests, meandering alongside the river and over the stone bridges with flowers burgeoning with color; down old cart trails and past old homesteads, where one can smell tiny, old variety apples and pears in the autumn months; past lanes littered with little churches that stand on virtually every hillock, each of them representing a tiny jewel of art of the past centuries; walking narrow little streets of medieval towns, past old castles filled with stories of lust for power and fights between noble families; and on and on and on, Ljubljana is a multitude of incredible sights.

During our short visit to this clean and attractive city, while on our way to Romania and Bulgaria, my companion students and I provided a public concert at one of Ljubljana's music halls. What made this particular occasion memorable was that this performance actually became a charity concert. All income from ticket sales was donated toward purchasing a motorized wheelchair for Ram Vidra, a special young boy with cerebral palsy living in the area. Ram and his parents were most grateful for our contribution, expressing many times their heartfelt appreciation for this cause that blessed them. As a professional pianist of hundreds of performances, this was one of my most gratifying and fulfilling concerts, where not only beautiful music was shared with an appreciative audience, but in a more personal way, financial assistance was provided to a family in need.

In 2002 with a handful of prodigious students, different—but equally valuable—performance opportunities ensued in Australia and Tasmania as I embarked on a first-time concert tour of that vast continent of beauty and history 8,000 miles from home. One of the world's great cities, populated by more than four million people and renowned for its awesome natural beauty and world-famous buildings, including the "sailboat" architectural splendor of the Sydney Opera House on the charming Sydney harbor, Sydney, of course, won my heart.

In every city we performed—Sydney, Newcastle, Brisbane, and Cairns—we received splendid treatment by the gregarious and charismatic Australian people. When we arrived in Hobart (Tasmania's state capital and the second-oldest city in Australia behind Sydney), a publicity article in their newspaper, *The Mercury*, read:

> American piano virtuoso, David Glen Hatch, and some of his country's most promising young pianists will perform a variety of works at the Conservatorium Recital Hall tomorrow evening. Hatch also is a highly acclaimed teacher and is keen to foster young talent. He will perform three sets of pieces: several Scriabin Études, Schubert's Impromptus, op. 90, and the Liszt/Paganini Étude in A Minor. Hatch is graciously giving all proceeds from the ticket sales to the Conservatorium Piano Fund.

In the early afternoon following my radio and television interviews prior to that well-attended "Visiting Artists Series" conservatory concert, both I and one of Australia's leading piano professors, Beryl Sedivka, held a master class exchange. It was a privilege to work with three of her fine students, who played the second movement of Chopin's *E Minor Concerto*, Ravel's *Sonatine*, and Mussorgsky's *Pictures on an Exhibition*. Following the applause for the class, Ms. Sedivka hurried to the stage to express her great appreciation for my teaching, saying, "Dr. Hatch, my three students were exhilarated by your teaching style. Your vast pianistic knowledge presented was most illuminating. We are very grateful to you for the significant scholarship funds you have raised for conservatory students who otherwise could not pursue their talents due to the lack of financial backing. Thank you for coming!"

On another occasion, many lives were blessed through music. Naturally, Christmastime is a time for giving. As the spirit of Christmas fills the air each year, people everywhere desire to serve those in need. When contemplating how to use my music at this time of year to bless others less fortunate, strong impressions revealed that proceeds gathered at Christmas performances and from commercial recordings would be an excellent way to support local charity groups.

Consequently, the majority of the selections appearing on my three Christmas albums are programmed on my frequent local and regional Christmas concerts which have also included orchestra, choir, and vocal soloists. As an example, my favorite concert admission one year became a creative advertising ploy—one non-perishable food item per audience member. That December, we were thrilled to be able to give the proceeds—hundreds of pounds of canned goods and other needed items—to the Utah Food Bank. Upon their arrival at the concert venue, the food bank volunteers seemed rather astonished by the vast mounds of goods they gathered and hauled away in their large truck to be donated to the homeless and poor among us. For me and for those concert-goers who contributed these items, this became a heartwarming, fulfilling performance event.

Music's power to bless lives is significant. It is not necessarily based on musical talent, but on our ability to feel deeply. When our music expresses the true feelings and depth of our souls, it becomes music of the heart, which communicates to God and to all men everywhere. Personally, I have seen the marvelous effects of music bless lives in myriad ways—healing, teaching, inspiring, strengthening, and uplifting, to name a few.

Moreover, there have been countless times that music has sanctified my own life. For instance, I treasured six years on the Brigham Young University campus in Provo, Utah, presenting lecture/performances for thousands of delightful people who gathered from throughout the United States, Canada, and several other countries to be inspired and taught by professionals in their fields during Education Week. Repeatedly, from my various classes of piano selections combined with the spoken word—including such themes as "The Power of Music"—came the blessing of meeting hundreds of warm, supportive patrons. I was a recipient of copious notes, letters, and cards of appreciation and gratitude from which my musical life became forever enriched. It was at that time the realization came to me that my music actually mattered to others. The following is a sampling of communications from generous men and women who blessed my life by expressing gratitude for my music. Certainly, the blessing of music in our lives is reciprocal!

"Brother Hatch, I want you to know how much I have enjoyed your brilliant performances at Education Week. Thank you for sharing your God-given talent."

"Thank you, Brother Hatch, for lifting our lives to a new level! And, thanks for bringing your gracious spirit and enormous talent."

"Dear Brother Hatch, I attended three of your lectures and loved being there! The music was beyond mere words; it was 'God's voice through music.' Your words turned me to Christ. . . your music melted my heart. . . it came out my eyes. Later that week, I met a mother of one of your students who told me that you weren't simply a teacher, but an inspired mentor. Again, I was impressed. I'm writing to say THANK YOU for being an instrument in the Lord's hands. But, even though your talent is a gift from God, I don't want to ignore the fact that you have lived half your life, at times of great sacrifice, to become a master pianist, pedagogue and inspired musician. Again, thank you for all you have given your listeners."

"Dr. Hatch, thank you for a beautiful experience. Never before have I sat on stage at a concert. . . . . This was a blessing! Please continue to inspire, excite and soothe our souls."

"The following poem was composed by a professional writer/poet and class attendee during David Glen Hatch's presentation, Music: Soothing the Soul. Thank you for the inspiration, Bro. Hatch!"

Music

Music speaks to my soul,
Washing over me in waves of familiarity,
A language once remembered,
Now forgotten

Is rekindled
And awakens my soul
To a voice I once knew.
I feel joy, and healing

And renewal
To recognize
My maker
Once again.

Oftentimes, life is very lonely for the solo musician. We spend countless hours alone studying, practicing, and preparing for the next performance, fireside, master class, or lecture. On rare occasions, however, the blessing of collaborating with other fine musicians has been revelatory and immeasurably rewarding. At one notable time, I was invited by several LDS artists to join them in a concert for Church members with an open invitation to the public in the magnificent Bass Performance Hall in Ft. Worth, Texas. First, some background information is requisite to understand my place in such a concert.

Members of the Church frequently refer to me as an LDS artist due to my several marketed LDS and inspirational recordings over many years. Truthfully though, while it is a fact that I have arranged and improvised inspirational, patriotic, Christmas, Broadway/movie, and other contemporary music, I am not actually a true LDS artist, but primarily a classically trained international concert artist who performs the enduring piano compositions of the masters.

Much of the music of LDS artists is good, as it can lift, encourage, and bless the lives of church members, but it is music that is appropriate in only certain settings, just as we have different forms of art for different needs. Mostly, LDS artists perform shows where the music relates specifically to LDS audiences, whereas my professional performances are attended more readily by trained musicians and the general public who appreciate and understand classical music. Of course, this doesn't mean that serious, classical music is better than other musical styles simply because it takes more musical and technical skill to perform it. We need to understand that we can value music for its function and recognize fine and inspired music within each particular style.

The Bass Concert Hall is the crown jewel of Fort Worth, Texas, which boasts the nation's third-largest cultural district. The hall is characteristic of the classic European opera house form built entirely with private funds and is the permanent home to the Fort Worth Symphony Orchestra, Texas Ballet Theater, Fort Worth Opera, and the prestigious Van Cliburn International Piano Competition and Cliburn Concerts.

On this concert evening, unlike the other musicians who were at the hall to perform inspirational Christian music, I chose to perform classical music due to the magnitude of this beautiful and prestigious venue that attracts some of today's most renowned musical artists.

Although I was apprehensive in how my Liszt and Scriabin pieces would be received, I gained insight and understanding that evening that powerful music of the masters, including my classical performances for that event, can move people, no matter their musical training.

At length, it was my turn to approach the stage, after considerable applause for the several LDS selections presented prior to my classical contributions. At the conclusion of my playing, and to my astonishment, the audience gave an immediate standing ovation.

The exhilaration I experienced by performing with other solo musicians, the acquisition of knowledge and comprehension that showcasing inspired, fine-art music of the masters can generate an enthusiastic response from its listeners no matter their level of musical training or understanding, and the fact that my music that evening was greatly appreciated and enthusiastically received, became a tremendous blessing of validation in my life at that time.

On other occasions, individuals have sometimes been blessed through the medium of music by experiencing certain miracles. This became apparent most recently during my travels and performances in the Sicilian cities of Palermo, Siracusa, and Catania, and in Athens, Greece, where the Roman- and Grecian-influenced charm and magic of these cultures became immediately captivating.

To my great disappointment, the Athens concert, held in the gorgeous state-of-the-art ACS performance hall, was poorly attended. For weeks prior to our arrival, I had been most enthusiastic about this particular performance as hundreds of RSVPs had been received from months of enormous publicity throughout the city. It was expected that the one-thousand-seat hall would be filled to capacity, including three hundred American families associated with the US Embassy who had been personally invited for this cultural event. By 5:00 p.m. on the day of the concert, however, all public transit operators went on strike, making it impossible for most people to travel to the performance venue. Though this entire situation was extremely disheartening for me, having spent months of planning and preparation with enthusiastic anticipation, the performance was well received by the sixty-five member audience. So, rather than this classical program becoming what I had envisioned as the tour's inspirational highlight, I rapidly learned that the Lord had other plans of inspiration for my presence in Greece!

Today, the Church is in its infancy in this beautiful country. Learning months previous to my arrival that I would be performing in Athens, the mission president through, his public affairs missionary couple for the entire region, invited me to present a musical fireside for the small Athens branch the evening prior to the concert. I had prepared the fireside text, sent it to the translator beforehand, and, on the appointed date, delivered the message entitled "The Power of Music" for a small chapel of approximately fifty people— members, friends, missionaries, and a handful of investigators—on the second floor of an office building in central downtown.

To facilitate my translator's work as he spoke into headsets of those who needed translation, I followed the text very closely. To my surprise, however, when bearing my concluding testimony, the Spirit directed my thoughts away from the musical theme, and words began to flow regarding our living prophet and twelve Apostles of the Church! I found myself speaking emphatically and with great conviction about this aspect of the gospel. It wasn't until the following evening, however, while standing in the concert hall greeting audience members after my classical performance that I would understand the significance of that abrupt departure from the written text.

One of the full-time elders took me aside and shared a miracle for which they had prayed and that had transpired from the musical fireside the previous evening. With excitement in his voice, the missionary explained to me that he and his companion had brought an investigator to hear my message, and the investigator had invited a close friend, who, though completely uninterested in organized religion, had come only to hear the music of an "international pianist." Afterward, however, he told the missionaries that he had been "blown away" by my declaration of there being a living prophet and twelve Apostles on earth today directing the affairs of the "true church of Christ." He was amazed to hear of this reality, as this was the main issue causing his disenchantment with all religions—that no church professed the same organization that existed in the primitive Church of Jesus Christ. Consequently, the missionaries now had a new investigator who, at that time, was most enthusiastic about a living prophet directing the affairs of Christ's Church on earth—the Church of Jesus Christ of Latter-day Saints. Shortly thereafter, I learned that this young man had become a member of the Church.

A second spiritual occurrence in Athens made me realize yet again that the Lord is in charge of our lives. After my fireside presentation, while my students, chaperones, and others in attendance socialized over a table of delicious refreshments prepared by the relief society sisters, the senior missionary couple over public affairs for the country whispered that they needed to share with me in the adjacent kitchen area what they deemed a miracle related to my performances in Athens.

With great emotion, the senior elder began speaking, expressing that my presence in Greece was an answer to many prayers. He explained that several months previous to my arrival, the mission president had called him and his wife into his office to share a letter I had written. My letter had been sent to inform the mission and two branches of the Church in that area of my coming to Athens as an invited guest artist to perform in one of their music halls in June and that I would be pleased to also provide a musical fireside for the Saints if that might be of interest to them.

The missionary couple then explained that for months prior to reading my letter, they had been praying to know what to do as assigned public affairs missionaries to provide exposure for the Church in Greece. Since publicity didn't seem natural or appropriately beneficial, this couple became frustrated for a long period of time until, finally, my letter was shared with them—a letter from an international concert pianist and member of the Church.

As the mission president handed my letter to this couple to read, he said to them, "I have no time to entertain this proposal from Brother Hatch, but if you feel this is something that would assist you in your public relations work, feel free to contact him." Ecstatic, they claimed this event gave them the opportunity of introducing the Church by mass media—radio, newspaper, television, and so on—by attaching my name and concert appearance for the general public with an enormous publicity blast throughout the city.

I became most humble and grateful to hear from this senior couple and several of the young single missionaries that from their many efforts to promote this musical performance, the name of the Church had become more recognizable to many of the citizens of Athens and surrounding areas. Young elders claimed that often while tracting, the recognition of the Church's name made it easier for them to be invited into homes.

Having experienced many difficulties that had plagued my efforts to solidify an international concert in Greece with the country's current troubles, I recognized that the miracle of this performance opportunity to bless countless lives had been provided by the Lord!

On another occasion in Beaumont, Texas, my classical program at the beautiful turn-of-the-century Jefferson Theater was performed for an overflowing crowd. When my host family drove me to the venue, a first-time surprise awaited me. On the exterior marquee in flashing lights it read, "International Pianist, David Glen Hatch, in Concert." It was fun to see my name in lights for the first time!

Publicized as a musical event for the general public, this concert was sponsored by the Beaumont Stake of The Church of Jesus Christ of Latter-day Saints as a missionary event titled "A Come unto Christ Concert." Although this was primarily a classical concert, I was also asked to perform inspirational Christian music and to speak to the audience. Basically, the Spirit moved me to teach gospel principles to the crowd, bearing testimony of the restoration of the gospel, the prophet Joseph Smith, and The Book of Mormon, the keystone of our religion. After speaking about each concept, I would return to the piano and perform spiritual music that enhanced the gospel concept I had taught. That evening, the Lord's Spirit was profuse as it had been on so many other similar occasions and again provided me with another spiritual highlight of music blessing lives. Following the performance, a Baptist family, who had been invited to the concert by members of our Church, tearfully approached to speak to me. They said,

> Dr. Hatch, we came here tonight expecting a professional piano concert by an international artist. But that which we received was much more than that. We have never felt the Spirit of Christ as prevalent on any occasion as we have here tonight. We met the Mormon missionaries recently, and after feeling the power of the Spirit in tonight's presentation, we recognize that The Church of Jesus Christ of Latter-day Saints is true. We will be setting a date for our baptism with the elders upon our return home this evening. Thank you for a beautiful, spiritual evening of music-making and inspirational words. It has changed our lives forever!

There is one last experience I wish to share. I am often grateful to be able to provide performances that benefit orphans, impoverished children and people who are in great need. These are always special times when many lives are blessed through music! This is why I routinely accept offers to travel to foreign countries throughout the world, even when it sometimes means playing on a rented upright piano in Barcelona, Spain, or getting away from a pair of muggers on a dark night in Lviv, Ukraine!

Recently, I returned from Chile and Peru, where my performances for outstanding humanitarian organizations have forever blessed my life in immeasurable ways. In Santiago, for example, my VIP concert—an exclusive charity event sponsored by the Embassy of Monaco—brought in substantial funds from dignitaries of twenty embassies, ambassadors, consuls, and high-ranking government officials. These contributions are presently blessing the lives of hundreds of burned children in their treatments at the pediatric burn victim facility, Coaniquem, directed by one of the world's top plastic surgeons, Dr. Jorge Rojas Zegers.

Music truly has the power to bless and heal our lives, the ability to uplift our souls, the means to remind us of the magnificence within—to brighten our mood and to lift our spirit! Anyone of strong faith who is spiritually prepared with sensitivity and understanding to accept the gift and power of music in their lives will be richly blessed—not only in significant, but in miraculous ways!

NOTES:

1. *The Musician's Diary* (New York: McAfee Music, 1979), 189, 256.
2. John A. Widtsoe, *Discourses of Brigham Young* (Salt Lake City: Deseret Book, 1925), 242–243.
3. Gerald Abraham, *Handel: A Symposium* (London: Oxford University Press, 1954), 63.

Chapter Three

THE POWER OF MUSIC TO HEAL

"Music is the medicine of an afflicted mind; a sweet sad measure is the balm of a wounded spirit; and joy is heightened by exultant strains."

—Henry Giles

Martin Luther, the German priest, professor of theology and iconic figure of the Protestant Reformation said, "Music is one of the fairest and most glorious gifts of God, to which Satan is a bitter enemy; for it removes from the heart the weight of sorrow and the fascination of evil thoughts."[1]

Throughout the ages, it has been observed that music and sound have always had the power to heal the body, mind, and spirit. Believed to have been written during the reign of Solomon in the Bible, the following account between two legendary kings of Israel appears significant: "And it came to pass, when the evil spirit from God was upon Saul, that David took the harp, and played with his hand; so Saul was refreshed, and was well, and the evil spirit departed from him" (1 Samuel 16:23). One of the greatest gifts of God to man, music can be a powerful catalyst in the healing process.

Paradoxically, before I could share beautiful music and its healing powers with others, an incident occurred in my childhood that first found me in need of physical healing myself. At age three, my family was enjoying a summer evening in a canyon near our home. While my parents were preparing to cook our dinner in an open fire pit in the ground, I tripped and fell hands first, palms down into the fire's white-hot coals. Still today, I recall that excruciating pain and screaming and thrashing on the backseat floor of my parents' car as we raced down the mountain road to the hospital. My hands sustained the worst of the injuries—third degree burns. The doctors, having had extensive experience with prior burn victims, seemed certain my hands would shrivel and scar for life. However, that was not to be the case. Instead, my horribly burned hands were miraculously healed by a priesthood blessing pronounced by my father. Today, many people, including myself, marvel at this modern-day miracle.

As I matured over the years, I began to better comprehend this profound spiritual experience of faith that had occurred in my young life and the tutoring I'd received regarding the reasoning behind this miracle. There is no doubt that Heavenly Father knows each of us personally, by name. He loves each of His children and desires only the best for us. I am convinced that He healed my hands so that my life could be devoted to sharing beautiful and uplifting music—many times used as a process for healing—with my fellow men and women throughout the world.

Modern research similarly supports music's healing power. Don Campbell, author of *The Mozart Effect*, cites many examples in which sound and music are used to help patients suffering from everything from anxiety to cancer, from high blood pressure to chronic pain and mental distress. Music has been proven highly effective for enhanced health, relaxation, and mental stimulation and has shown that it has the power to heal the body, strengthen the mind, and unlock the creative spirit.

Among numerous other examples of music being used for healing purposes, Campbell relates the following:

> It was the beginning of Act One of a live broadcast of Rossini's The Barber of Seville from the Metropolitan Opera House in New York. Lorna was driving home on a rainy afternoon when a truck rear-ended her just before the woman playing Rosina was to sing.
>
> "The impact was sudden and stunning," recalled the self-possessed New Jersey professional. "But even as I entered a world of

shock and pain, I found a world of bliss and order. I listened to the whole aria and the next fifteen minutes of the opera as ambulance people and fireman tried to free me from the wreckage of my car." State emergency crews later told Lorna that she had been unconscious until she was strapped in a cot in the ambulance, but she remembered listening to Rosina's voice throughout the ordeal. "My spirit stayed with my body," she says. "This music kept me alive. I was able to listen and stay conscious, alert, and at peace with the music. I never thought I was injured because the music was so alive. I just kept listening, listening. From the beginning of that aria, I knew I had to finish the opera of my life."

I have encountered many stories like Lorna's and have asked myself: Is music actually healing us, pulling us through crises, reorchestrating our abilities? By developing our listening skills, are we able to awaken our spirits and activate our immune systems, thereby restoring our injured bodies and scattered minds? The Mozart Effect is not a panacea, but it holds a key with which each of us can open ourselves up, to hear the world more efficiently—and to heal.[2]

My understanding of the power of music to heal was reconfirmed several years ago while performing throughout fascinating Japan. I spent time visiting exotic landmarks of this country including Tokyo's Tower (higher than the Eiffel Tower in Paris), Imperial Palace Gardens, Shinto temples, Osaka's Cosmo Tower, Todaiji Temple with the world's most enormous Buddha—so huge that a person could climb through its nostrils!—and a shogun castle where, two hundred years ago, lived ninjas/samurai. In the course of the tour adventures, I became very ill with a 105 degree fever the very day of my significant concert in Osaka.

I was extremely sick with a perspiring fever, body chills, and feeling weak physically with no desire or ability to eat. Understandably, I became very concerned. I knew that because of the extensive publicity over several months and pre-sold tickets by the hundreds, the concert that evening must proceed as scheduled.

The Izumisano Municipal Culture Hall in Osaka's precinct surrounded by beautiful Osaka bay at its north and the Izumi Mountains at its south, is a high-tech, state-of-the-art concert hall—a remarkable performance venue! Upon arriving at the hall, I petitioned Heavenly Father that a healing process begin promptly since

I felt as if I would faint at any moment. Hesitantly, I stepped out onto the brightly illuminated contemporary stage and bowed to the elegant, all-Japanese audience.

Surprisingly, as I began the Mozart Adagio in B Minor on the beautiful Steinway concert grand piano, my playing progressed into a musically sensitive performance, which sparked the mental confidence necessary to continue the program at a superior level. Within minutes, I felt my high fever dissipate, and with renewed strength and energy, I completed the concert successfully with a rousing rendition of a physically demanding Liszt rhapsody.

Afterward, while I was greeting the public, a music critic from the local newspaper agency expressed his admiration for my playing and informed me of his concert review that would appear in *Osaka Shimbun* two days later. Of the many positive comments, the article concluded with this statement, "In addition to his program of vitality and impressive finger technique, Hatch's musical poetry in the Mozart Adagio was exquisite."

Relieved that the concert was over, I immediately recognized that my prayers had been answered. During my playing of the program, the fever had left my body. I also realized that the adrenaline associated with concert performing coupled with a strong desire to communicate the beauty of the compositions with my listeners could have enhanced the healing process. On a more personal level, I now understood better how music can be used in the process of healing. I was, however, still grateful to return to my hotel room, where my condition improved to normal while I slept deeply until late the following morning.

Of a surety, music has power to heal people. Music therapists have shown that music may be a cure for modern-day tensions and disharmony. In fact, this study was in existence anciently. Pythagoras—who extensively studied the interrelationships between mathematics, music, medicine, and astronomy—believed that a daily "dose" of music could lead to greater harmony between a person and the universe. Music is a gift from God to inspire, uplift, and heal the human spirit.

Two years ago, I personally encountered evidence of emotional healing. Following a four-stake musical fireside for the greater St.

Louis area at the Frontenac Chapel, I experienced one of the great spiritual highs of my life. The missionary theme for the nine hundred attendees filling the cultural hall and spilling onto the stage— including LDS member families, numerous investigators, and non-member friends—was The Worth of Souls. During the entire musical evening of hymn arrangements and classical numbers, the Spirit directed my remarks. One of the Stake leaders mentioned to me afterwards that the Spirit was so prolific during my presentation that he noticed it produced a constant flow of tears and much sniffling among those throughout the congregation.

After the presentation, I greeted many Saints, church leaders, friends, investigators, and missionaries and listened to an experience that left me speechless and spiritually moved. A very emotional man in his late sixties, who had patiently waited in line for over an hour and a half to visit with me, finally approached me to relate the following story, which I recorded in my journal immediately upon my return to the mission home later that evening:

> Brother Hatch, I felt that I must tell you of my profoundly spiritual experience here tonight during your fireside presentation. One year ago, our little seven-year-old grandson drowned [he began sobbing as he continued]. I was the one who found him and I was unable to revive him [he had been holding on to this guilt all that time].
>
> Brother Hatch, my grandson's very favorite song in the world was *I Am a Child of God*. Every time he'd hear it, he'd stop what he was doing and listen quietly and always tell us, "This is my very favorite song ever!"
>
> Well, when you performed your arrangement of it tonight at the closing of your testimony [he again stopped for a few seconds to gather his composure], I want you to know that my grandson was here! I felt his strong presence sitting beside me on this pew as you played his "favorite song." I finally knew that all was in order and that I could now be at peace. Thank you Brother Hatch.

Instantly, with moist eyes, I finally recognized the significance of an earlier prompting. Just minutes before the fireside had begun; a strong impression came to me to change my final musical number from what had originally been planned. Then, after hearing this grandfather's account, the Spirit testified to my mind that this had been the reason for the change. It was extremely moving for me to witness the miracle of music comforting a grieving grandfather—another testament that music is sacred, powerful, and inspired from God who is its creator through his musical children here on earth. I squeezed his hand and thanked him for sharing this sacred experience, knowing that his feelings of agitation and guilt over the past year could finally subside.

Another personal experience from which emotional healing was exhibited—and that had a deep effect on me—came during a significant performance on the east coast. It taught me the truth that music can be a healing balm. The poet, Giles, expressed it this way, "Music is the medicine of an afflicted mind and breaking heart."[3]

Following the 9/11 terrorist attacks on American soil, in an effort to comfort our sorrowing people, I was invited to record a nationally distributed, patriotic album with piano, orchestra, choir, army band, and three vocal soloists, and then perform the selections from that recording in a live concert at the Arlington National Cemetery Amphitheater in Washington, DC. This concert was given in 2002 on the one-year anniversary of this tragedy for several busloads of family members of those victims. In addition to performing these sensitive, reflective, and poignant piano arrangements, my pride soared as one of the singers, my own gifted daughter Erika, sang an emotional rendition of *Morning Breaks on Arlington*, written by my cousin, Senator Orrin Hatch of Utah, that brought the tender audience to tears. After these inspiring performances that peaceful September afternoon, we were greeted by several of these families, who, still tearful following the program, generously thanked the performers for this significant and touching patriotic music that had lifted and comforted their grieving hearts that day. This occasion became one of the most humbling musical happenings of my life.

When a person realizes a need to remove a stressful or adverse situation from their life, listening to powerful or inspirational music can completely change the mindset. Music has been used for thousands of years as a way to restore energy, to reduce anxiety and depression, and to help with the natural healing process. Negative attitudes, depression, and feelings of guilt often cause stress levels that produce illness. Furthermore, classical music has been proven to promote a positive attitude and to improve retention rate and learning abilities while studying. Specifically, scientists explain that classical music scores from Mozart, Beethoven, and Bach release certain types of neurons into the brain which help the body relax. This generates more receptivity to learning and absorbing new information.

When experiencing depression, individuals have been fascinated to learn that listening to uplifting music instantly elevates the spirit! That is sound healing, an exceptional way of nourishing the soul. Listening to certain sounds has the power to open our subconscious, slow our heart rate and breathing, and transport us into a relaxed and optimistic state. Music is widely becoming recognized as a valuable tool for health and healing, whether physical or emotional. Arthur Schopenhauer once said, "Music is a shower-bath of the soul, washing away all that is impure."[4]

This past Christmastime, an incident in my personal life taught me the enormous value of music as a profound source for healing.

The Temple Hill Orchestra in Oakland, California, extended an invitation to me to participate in their annual Christmas concert. Performing with them in the auditorium on the temple grounds became a huge honor. To be honest, I wasn't expecting the excellent quality of playing from the orchestra that I heard during our first rehearsal early that Saturday morning before Christmas. Actually, the orchestra sound was rather stunning. I was excited to learn that many of these musicians were professionals who performed with important groups throughout the Bay Area, including the Oakland Symphony, which created in me a renewed enthusiasm for the Sunday evening concert.

As I walked onto the stage for the first number, greeted by a jam-packed hall of 1,600 cheering fans and audience members, I experienced a great adrenaline rush. The spirit was strong, the orchestra sound marvelous, and my playing was at its highest level. From the moment I received the unusual standing ovation at intermission, I knew this would be a very special, memorable evening!

The carols of the season and of Christ are magical and often spectacular in their musical scope. And, although the program consisted primarily of Christmas arrangements, there had also been previous requests that I perform some classical selections, which seemed to electrify the audience. Following my *Silent Night* "chime" arrangement, encores, and standing ovations at the conclusion of this spirit-filled concert, a profound spiritual incident occurred in a reception area while I was greeting people and autographing programs—an experience that was pivotal to this entire performance weekend!

A woman who had stood in line for over an hour finally reached me. Her shaking hands and eyes brimming with tears betrayed her feelings. Gathering her composure, she said,

> Dr. Hatch, about fifteen years ago someone gave me one of your musical fireside CDs titled *I Walk by Faith: Believing in Christ and Yourself,* to which I listened over and over and over. When I read the publicity that you would be here as the guest artist tonight, I had to come and in person tell you something I should have told you those many years ago—that your music and motivating words on that CD completely changed my life. As I was extremely suicidal at that time, you must know that your music and message gave me hope, assurance, and a renewed faith in Jesus Christ. I am a recovering alcoholic since that time and have never been happier in my life. Thank you for saving my life, Dr. Hatch. I will be forever grateful.

With her tears now flowing freely, we hugged, and then she walked quietly away. Some moments in our lives are unspeakably precious, even sacred. From this one such moment, I will never be quite the same!

In the minds of many Americans, the spiritual condition of our nation for the past several years has been an overwhelming concern! Since history provides hope for another spiritual awakening in the United States, Dr. Dale A. Robbins, in his editorial "Don't Give Up On America," expressed the following:

> Today we face what seems to be a hopeless condition in America. Gross immorality has engulfed the land. Crime has taken over the streets. Drunkenness and drug abuse is everywhere. God has been rejected by most of our citizens—virtually kicked out of our government and our schools. A few years ago, Billy Graham issued a profound warning, that 'If God doesn't soon bring judgment upon America, He'll have to go back and apologize to Sodom and Gomorrah!' It seems that the United States has drifted far from its rich religious heritage. Let's not give up on America, but let us embrace God's great promise of prayer: He said, 'If my people, which are

called by my name, shall humble themselves, and pray, and seek my face, and turn from their wicked ways; then will I hear from heaven, and will forgive their sin, and will heal their land" (2 Chron. 7:14).

Yes, today America looks hopeless and needs to be healed of its moral and spiritual decay. Recently, significant music has been written in an effort to restore the spiritual climate of our nation. As an example, Senator Hatch wrote another insightful and deeply moving song titled, Heal Our Land, which I have frequently performed with accomplished singers, including at the Arlington concert in 2002. In this touching piece of music, the lyrics written by the Senator express similar sentiments that should be meaningful to all Americans regarding spiritual and emotional healing.

Heal our Land

Heal our land.
Please grant us peace today, and strengthen all who lack the faith to call on Thee each day.
Heal our land, and keep us safe and free. Watch over all who understand the need
for Liberty.
Heal our land, and guide us with They hand.
Keep us ever on the path of liberty.
Heal our land, heal our land, and help us understand that we must put our trust in thee if we would be free.

Heal our land.
Please help us find our way, for in Thy word we find our strength if we look up each day.
Heal our land, and fill us with Thy love. Keep us upon the path of truth that comes from Heaven above.
Protect us by the power of Thy rod,
And keep us as one nation under God.
Heal our land, heal our land, and guide us with Thy hand,
Keep us ever on the path of liberty.
Heal our land, heal our land, and help us understand
that we must put our trust in Thee
if we would be free.

It is music like this that often facilitates motivating and encouraging people back on the right path. There is always hope in being healed if God's people will come together and serve the God of this land who is Jesus Christ. Therefore, let us embrace God's great promise to us: "For behold, this is a land which is choice above all other lands; wherefore he that doth possess it shall serve God or shall be swept off; for it is the everlasting decree of God. And it is not until the fullness of iniquity among the children of the land, that they are swept off" (Ether 2:10).

Much of this change for healing, of course, will fall on the shoulders of younger generations. During one of my travels to perform in the Pacific Northwest and Canada, I was asked to present a university recital for six hundred people in a chamber concert hall in Seattle, as well as two enjoyable Church musical firesides—one for the youth and one for the adults of the Yakima and Puyallup Stakes of the Church. It was expressed to me by church leaders that many in attendance at each presentation were greatly moved by the music. Likewise, each performance was a deeply enriching experience for me as I visibly noticed an enhanced demeanor in my congregations.

In addition to these professional musical and spiritual moments in Washington State, another highlight of this trip emerged in Canada—no, not at the classical concerts with standing ovations, but at another youth fireside in Calgary for three hundred Canadian young people. The previously given theme for my presentation involving music and spoken message for that occasion was "Achieving Success in Life." These bright, gifted, and enthusiastic youth appeared touched by my musical presentation, keeping me afterward for over an hour to visit and ask questions about my career, music in general, and various other aspects of their lives. In a time when many young people settle for much less than the best while thinking they have it all, this group of youth renewed my hope in the young people of today. They agreed that, to their peers, everything is in the here and now with no sense of precedent, respect for the past, or obligation to the future—that often, the entire human experience is devalued.

With sincerity, this outstanding group expressed to me that their lives are often difficult—most seemingly inundated with morality issues of all kinds. With so many disturbed, misguided, and deceived youth of our time, this outstanding gathering of young people acknowledged that responsible parenting and activity in the Church gave them direction they would not otherwise possess. The time I spent with these good and faithful teenagers of the Church gave me encouragement and hope for a better world in the future.

Incidentally, during my musical performances and candid remarks directed to these teenagers, many of them became highly emotional and thanked me for my honesty and inspiring counsel that they seek higher levels of living, continue to embrace moral values and conduct at all costs, and to be true to self in the midst of sin and adversity. Later, when it was communicated to me that my music had made a difference in their lives—a genuine impact for good upon this group of young people—naturally I felt much gratitude, fulfillment, and humility.

For several weeks afterward, I continued to receive thank-you notes and letters from several of these stellar youth, expressing love and appreciation for my musical fireside and the time I spent with them. Some had written that my presentation "put them back on track" and, in a sense, helped them feel a healing presence. From this refreshing encounter, it is my strong opinion that inspirational music and inspired dialogue moves young people in a positive spiritual direction, and in so doing they become a most valuable, worthwhile asset to society and of great assistance in building the Kingdom of God on earth. I will always appreciate, enjoy, and revel in the goodness and exuberance of our youth—many of those with whom I have had the pleasure of spending much of my time during my professional career!

It has been said time and again that music can make a person happy or make a person cry. It also can make us dance or make us relax. But most importantly, scientists have proven that music can heal. Not only does music help those who are sick, but it also does wonders to those who are well. Apart from the scientific research, music is a kind of medicine that everyone requires. In this way, it may be used for treating sadness or in exalting one's happiness. Accordingly, each of us should take enough daily dosage of music in order to improve our physical and emotional health—starting now!

As Martin Luther also stated, "Music is the art of the prophets—the only art that can calm the agitations of the body and soul; it is one of the most magnificent and delightful presents God has given us."[6]

While music therapists use a mix of music and traditional techniques to show that music's power to heal is well known and documented to help patients, neuroscientists are uncovering the scientific basis for music's healing powers and starting to understand how music helps rewire a brain affected by illness, injury, or emotional trauma. Thus, since there's no doubt that music affects people deeply and powerfully, in today's world we find music being used in hospitals, clinics, surgery centers, dentist's and physician's offices, and so on. Specifically, the pulse of music affects the body's natural rhythms instantaneously with its healing powers that are capable of soothing the nerves, calming the mind, lowering the body's blood pressure, boosting the immune system, focusing the mind, comforting a broken heart, and overcoming depression by enhancing joy in life.

The healing power of sound has been revered for thousands of years and has an exceptional way of nourishing the soul. The strains of a piano sonata can bring calm to the soul, while a stirring chorus may rouse our faculties. Truly, not only can our moods change when listening to elevating music, but we can also be healed physically, spiritually, and emotionally. This is power—the power of music to heal!

NOTES:

1. *The Musician's Diary* (New York: McAfee Music, 1979), 156.
2. Don Campbell, The Mozart Effect (New York: HarperCollins Publishers, 2001), 60.
3. *The Musician's Diary* (New York: McAfee Music, 1979), 138.
4. Ibid, 202.
5. Dr. Dale A. Robbins, "Don't Give Up On America" (Grass Valley: Victorious Publications, 1995), 23.
6. The Musician's Diary, (New York: McAfee Music, 1979), 79.

Chapter Four

THE POWER OF MUSIC TO EMPOWER

"Music is not a mere pastime. Its effects are both powerful and beneficial, not only upon the cultured few, but upon the uncultured many."

–Hugh Haweis

Music reveals deep feelings and moves people to action—hymns, marches, songs about love and disappointment stir people's souls. The power of music has been used throughout history to protest injustice and advocate for human rights. Musicians often perform music that makes an impact upon society.

Jazz originally celebrated the Black community and incorporated social protest. Jazz masters such as Nina Simone, Charlie Mingus, and John Coltrane frequently composed music as anthems for humanity. Folk and popular music have been widely used in social movements from labor to war protests around the world. Performers from Woody Guthrie and Pete Seeger to Bob Dylan, Joan Baez, and Bruce Springsteen are well known for their songs for social justice.

In the 1960s, rock musicians participated in anti-war and social protests, and in recent years, in addition to lyrics of protest, rock music has been central to global fundraising concerts such as Live Aid. Early rap music captured the sense of rage and alienation reflected in the world of poor urban Blacks and has since incorporated anti-drug and feminist messages. A new level of social responsibility is emerging in today's underground hip-hop movement. Even as far back as the eighteenth century, certain humanity was sought among the masses. For instance, "In the classical world, Beethoven's *Ode to Joy*, finished in 1824, has achieved worldwide popularity as an anthem for human rights."[1]

Throughout the history of the Christian church, congregational song has been an important part of the worship service and for much of early Church history, the primary instrument utilized was the unaccompanied human voice.

"It is widely recognized that the Last Supper was a Passover meal and that the Jewish Passover liturgy included special hymns drawn from the book of Psalms. These hymns were known as the Hallel Psalms (meaning "Praise" psalms), and consisted of Psalms 113–118."[2]

After identifying the bread in remembrance of His "body" and the wine in remembrance of His "blood," the Lord, Himself, was prepared for His greatest test through music's influence, for the scripture records: "And when *they had sung an hymn*, they went out to the Mount of Olives" (Matthew 26:30; Mark 14:26, emphasis added).

Our Eternal Lord and Savior Jesus Christ sang! In this hour of meditation and emotional stress, the Savior was comforted through music's healing balm and sang with His disciples. Whatever hymn was sung that evening included Jesus singing—our omniscient and all-powerful God, the Creator of perfect pitch . . . singing! The Creator Himself using creative expression! This music no doubt empowered his agitated soul at that time while he approached His impending atonement and death. There was no large audience there, just He and the disciples, but He sang. Knowing He was on His way to Calvary, yet He sang. Knowing the road of persecution was just merely hours away, still He sang. What an incredible experience that must have been to be able to sing a hymn with Christ!

There is great power in sacred music, especially if it is used to express our gratitude to the Lord for His countless blessings in our lives. Sacred hymns direct the soul toward feelings of gratitude. Sacred music, in particular, like the hymn the Savior used on that occasion, is used to worship God by singing songs of praise and thanksgiving. In the Doctrine and Covenants, He tells us, "If thou art merry, praise the Lord with singing, with music, with dancing, and with a prayer of praise and thanksgiving" (D&C 136:28).

Elder Oaks has counseled that "sacred music has a unique capacity to communicate our feelings of love for the Lord . . . Many have difficulty expressing worshipful feelings in words, but all can join in communicating such feelings through the inspired words of our hymns."[3]

One of the most intense examples of music's ability to empower the individual comes from the life of Ludwig van Beethoven, the German composer, pianist, and central figure in the transition between the classical and Romantic eras in Western Music.

No composer has demonstrated the kind of determination to "endure" and the strength to overcome his insurmountable obstacles as did Beethoven. Remaining one of the most famous and influential composers of all time, Beethoven began losing his hearing in 1796, at age twenty-six. In 1802, at the young age of thirty-two, he was completely deaf. But Beethoven rose above his adversity to compose some of the world's most enduring music that often shared deeper insights about musical communication. It is hardly imaginable that he would become one of the most celebrated musical masters in the history of the world without the sense of hearing, a sense that most would consider absolutely crucial for a musician. "It is astonishing to consider that many of his most revered works were written by a man who never heard them with his own natural ears."[4]

As a brief background to his malady, Beethoven's physician, Dr. Schmidt, recommended seclusion in the countryside for a period of time to remedy this problem. Therefore, Beethoven retired to the quiet village of Heiligenstadt (a village I have visited and which today is part of Vienna, Austria) for six months.

It was there that Ferdinand Ries, one of his students from Bonn, Germany, went to see him and later described both his apparent deafness and his moods. Ries wrote, "I called his attention to a shepherd who was piping in the woods on a flute made of a twig of Elder. For half an hour Beethoven could hear nothing. He became extremely quiet and morose."[5]

We learn of Beethoven's grief from the famous document that was found in his bedroom among his papers after his death in 1827, known as the Heiligenstadt Testament. He wrote this letter on October 6, 1802, to his brothers Carl and Johann at Heiligenstadt. It reflects his despair over his increasing deafness and his desire to overcome his physical and emotional disorders in an effort to complete his artistic purpose. Beethoven kept the document hidden among his private papers for the rest of his life, and most likely never showed it to anyone. Here is a portion of this document:

> You men who think or say that I am stubborn and anti-social, how greatly do you wrong me. You do not know the secret cause which makes me seem that way to you. Think that for six years now I have been hopelessly afflicted, made worse by senseless physicians, from year to year deceived with hopes of improvement, finally compelled to face the prospect of a lasting malady.
>
> What humiliation for me when someone standing next to me heard a flute in the distance and I heard nothing, or someone heard a shepherd singing and again I heard nothing. Such incidents drove me almost to despair. But, it seemed to me impossible to leave this world until I had brought forth all that I felt was within me. So I endured this wretched existence! Oh, Divine One, thou seest my inmost soul; thou knowest that therein dwells the love for mankind and the desire to do good. But, little more and I should have put an end to my life. Music, and music alone deterred me.[6]

From this writing, it is apparent that music had a powerful effect upon Beethoven and drove him to fulfill all his musical aspirations in spite of temptations to end his life. From his severe pain, grief, and adversity came the inspiration for some of the supreme musical masterpieces known to man. Like Beethoven, there are those more recently who have better endured personal challenges through inspired music that empowers, calms, and comforts troubled souls.

Although the following happening certainly cannot be compared to the absolutely devastating adversity that Beethoven experienced and overcame in his day, it does exhibit further principles of music's ability to empower in times of difficulty. A few years ago I spent much time and energy over a period of months preparing five of my award-winning teenage students in perfecting ensemble piano pieces to be presented at the Annual WPPI (Well-Prepared Piano Institute) Jr. and Sr. Piano Teams International Competition held in

Las Vegas, Nevada. From the award results, the unfortunate fact was reinforced in my mind that the finest pianist/musician is not always selected as the competition winner. As with many other endeavors of life, political unfairness sometimes plays a role in the outcome.

To my recollection, the older of my two sets of students were one of twelve senior piano teams of five pianists each participating at this competition. Each group performed three rounds of competition—two preliminary and one final. The founder of the competition and director of the Piano Institute were one and the same individual. This woman had, of course, created the competition rules, which, among others, included, "in the case of a tie in the final round of competition, the director will serve as the tiebreaker, independent of the four adjudicators."

My students were brilliant. After their initial playing, the audience knew this group, Pianists Extraordinaire, was the one to beat! Although most of the other piano teams hadn't memorized their repertoire (since it was not a competition requirement), my group had. In contrasting their polished, memorized playing of *Aragonaise* by Georges Bizet and *Serenade* by Franz Schubert to the performance level of the other groups, it was obvious that my students had prepared more refined artistic ensembles of energy with technical and musical perfection. In the opinion of most audience members, only one other senior team played near this level of proficiency but without memorized repertoire. Clearly, my students had the advantage going into the finals.

The final performance of my student group, *Dance of the Tumblers* by Rimsky-Korsakov, was impeccably performed with remarkable musicality, strong rhythmic drive, technical precision, and solid memory. During the judges' lengthy deliberation, several competition-goers, even those supporting other groups, congratulated me on my outstanding student pianists and remarked that no other piano team appeared as polished—and that obviously we would be receiving the first-place prize, a new Kawai grand piano for our studio!

Shocking to audience members was the announcement of the winning team from Arizona who, we later learned, was composed of members of this director's institute in that state and had been trained by one of its teachers. Although it was evident that having the Utah piano team win first prize rather than one affiliated with WPPI would be embarrassing to the director and her staff, in frustration I decided to investigate this farce as my students and many in the audience were highly dissatisfied.

Being well acquainted with one of the distinguished adjudicators, I privately sought his explanation of this conflicting outcome. Reluctantly, he revealed that in the judges' collaborative session held to determine the winning team, concealed pressure from the competition director had been placed on the panel, insinuating that her institute and its teachers' reputations for training the best pianists should be regarded. Hence, the judges called a tie to be broken by the "tiebreaker"—the director herself—who, of course, declared the Arizona team the winner. My gifted students were heartbroken. I was frustrated with the blatant disregard for an impartial outcome! But, from this incident, I decided it was important to stress to my students that from some of life's difficult challenges, we can learn and implement many character-building principles. As we discussed some of these, I became increasingly proud of these young people who, though feeling very let down, showed graciousness, composure, and emotional maturity!

They noticeably gained some positive reinforcements that would bless their lives in years to come by realizing it is important to always maintain civility when wronged, to realize that overcoming trials can make us persons of immense power, and that life's obstacles can shape our values and perspectives by making us more aware and sensitive of others. Furthermore, we together validated that the influence of great music, which is an expression of God's love, will never let us down as the competition had done. Instead, it can be the means of expressing all our innermost feelings—sorrow, hope, love, turmoil, tranquility—when words fail.

After the discussion with these spectacular young musicians, each expressed to me in their own way that the love they had developed toward the music—the competition pieces—coupled with the wonderful rehearsal experiences of working together as a team over a period of months to musically shape and technically polish this repertoire gave them remarkable coping skills during this trial and deception.

Now, without sounding self-righteous, there was an incident in my personal life where I learned that my obedience in serving an LDS mission empowered me during future musical decisions and successes. At my last piano lesson before entering the mission field, I apprehensively explained my mission decision to my prominent Jewish piano coach. Simply put, without describing her adverse reaction in graphic detail, I encountered tremendous wrath and verbal disapproval! She seemed infuriated for various reasons, including the fact that I was leaving after I had just won first place in the high school division of the prestigious Utah State Fair Competition, which win gave her great pride in our work together and caused her to enthusiastically entertain lofty future ambitions for me.

She told me that if I really left to serve the two-year mission, I needed to know that a professional performance career would no longer be attainable. In essence, she explained that this would be the case as I would be away from my studies and practice for far too long during the most critical years of career development.

Although disheartened to hear of this probability from my experienced piano professor, I served the mission, enjoying two of the best years of my young life, finally returning home in April, determined to pursue a music career against the odds. At that post-mission time, I was blessed to have a motivating professor during my undergraduate work at Brigham Young University—a gifted piano pedagogue and exceptional mentor to this day!

Although I was eager to advance quickly in my pianistic studies, it was startling to me that my mentor would have me so soon prepare to enter the distinguished collegiate division of the highly regarded Utah State Fair Piano Competition that following August! Having been away from the instrument for 26 months (I had savored a two-month mission extension), I explained to him my very strong reservations about my ability to reach that high performance level in only four months; having been away from my practicing for over two years, I was extremely "out of shape" pianistically! Furthermore, it was common knowledge that among those thirty talented competitors, I would be competing against two or three very practiced and accomplished young men who had decided against serving missions during those same two years in order to keep their careers alive by remaining at school to work on the instrument several hours daily while progressing in their university degree programs. It seemed obvious to me that they clearly had the advantage in this premier piano competition!

My teacher paid no attention to my reasoning. Instead, he simply insisted that I would compete in the competition that following August, expressing to me that it was a matter of feeling empowered to achieve this goal.

As a result, my energetic six to eight hours of daily practice continued for the subsequent four months. To encourage me in this work, my remarkable professor gave me a key to his studio so that I could use his piano each morning for several hours before his arrival at eight or nine in the morning to begin his teaching day.

I vividly remember arising in the early morning hours in an effort to be at the Harris Fine Arts Center by four or five. Because I sometimes arrived earlier than the custodians who opened the building, I would nap in the car until they came. This practice schedule continued throughout the summer months until the competition day arrived. Finally, upon entering the building where the event was being held, I felt satisfied with my preparation, though I was still anxious about competing with some of the finest collegiate pianists in Utah, including those who, instead of serving missions, had been working on the piano at home the entire time I had been working with people in Pennsylvania.

It was a magnificent feeling to realize that my teacher and I had persevered in this goal when it could have been easy to give up along the way. His numerous weekly and sometimes daily lessons on the competition repertoire had been stimulating. His daily words of counsel and encouragement had given me hope, incomparable vision, determination, and excitement during my preparation to compete! The adjudicators called out my competition number. As my teacher and I walked to the performance pianos on stage, I heard a distinct voice communicating to my mind, "David, there is a reason you will win this competition today. You were obedient in serving a mission while other young male competitors here today were not. They will be humbled when they learn a great lesson about obedience from your example. Always share this testimony of spiritual and temporal insight and success when opportunities present themselves throughout your life."

It is impossible for me ever to forget my innermost feelings at that time. The principle of obedience gave me an added measure of confidence in my pianistic playing that day. The performance of Franz Liszt's *Totentanz* for piano and orchestra (the orchestral reduction played by my teacher on a second piano) that came from my hands that afternoon was completely stunning. I had never played it more flawlessly before that time! Audible gasps came from the audience at the conclusion of that performance.

A required second contrast piece, the expressive middle movement of J. S. Bach's *Italian Concerto*, followed. The best way to describe these two performances is to say that I was in awe watching as my hands traveled across that keyboard with skill and precision that were unfamiliar to me. Certainly that playing was not totally my own. I felt not only spiritual and physical assistance, but tremendous empowerment from the music—all blessings from a Divine source, our Heavenly Father! I'll forever remember how profoundly humbled I was upon hearing my name announced as the collegiate winner at the conclusion of that competition later that afternoon.

While mingling with the many other contestants and audience members following the announcement of the winners, those young men of whom I've briefly made mention were noticeably speechless for some time. Finally, one of them approached me and said, "Congratulations, David! Have you any idea what you've done? You've barely returned home from your mission and beaten those of us who stayed behind to practice for the past two years!" I believe they began to understand the Lord's ways. I did!

Richard Wagner, the great nineteenth-century German composer and conductor, once made the statement, "Whatever the relations of music, it will never cease to be the noblest and purest of arts . . . its inherent solemnity makes it so chaste and wonderful, that it ennobles whatever comes in contact with it."[7]

We can all become empowered by music, whether by listening to it or as participants in the performing process. Listening to music can provide opportunities for an individual through their own musical experiences. Music can address how people interact with and affect their environment. Music can encourage social interaction among people, from listening to it or performing it. The interaction may take the form of talking about thoughts and feelings, contributing to group experiences, cooperating with others, or responding to others' needs.

In speaking of music and its ability to empower, here is an email that I received recently from a former student. In order to understand these feelings he expressed to me, here is a brief background on this young man. Now a college-aged student, he has been clinically depressed for most of his young life and struggles daily in his pursuit of accomplishing his life's dreams. To be sure, his music studies have basically been the only component of his life that has brought stability and inner strength during very dark days. He wrote:

> Dear Dr. Hatch,
>
> I would like to thank you for the great influence you have been in my life. Today had been one of those extremely stressful days. I couldn't really think straight and was just feeling basically down about everything.
>
> Then, I went to the piano. I tried practicing scales and warm-up exercises but struggled to high degrees. I tried reviewing pieces that I had learned with you but that activity also proved burdensome. I then tried composing; same thing! Finally, while going through our big basket of music here at home, I found the books of hymn arrangements that you had written.
>
> It had been forever since I had picked up one of these and I started playing from the book. Though my sight reading wasn't the best, I went through every arrangement in the two books I have. By the time I had finished reading all of them, I had spent over three hours on the piano. I began to feel much more calm and inner-confidence than before. I couldn't be more grateful for the wonderful gift that you have shared with me and the world. Having those pieces at hand has really lightened my load. I am trying to keep up with all of the things you have taught me to do musically. Thank you for the two years that I was able to study with you. That time was the greatest experience that I have ever had with music.

It is my opinion that musicians often get caught up in their own desires. Sometimes, we focus too much on ourselves and not on the needs of other people. If people, including musicians, stop dwelling on themselves and concentrate on making contributions to society—filling in "gaps" that are needed in a person's life—they will not be as apt to consider their own flaws. This increases self-confidence, which provides the ability to contribute with maximum efficiency. The more musicians contribute to the world the more inner strength they gain from being rewarded with personal successes and recognition in their various musical pursuits.

In concluding this chapter, I feel impressed to share a personal triumph that conveys my perspectives regarding music and empowerment. Last year, to my complete surprise, I received an invitation by the president of the European Piano Teachers Association (EPTA) to be a guest artist and teacher at the Second World Piano Conference held in Novi Sad, Serbia. What an honor to be asked to provide a lecture/performance and master class for an international audience of music conservatory and university professors and piano aficionados in addition to the other sixty-two conference presenters—some of the most distinguished pianists and piano pedagogues in the world.

Although excited to receive such a request, I was extremely nervous to classify in the same league with these exceptional world-class musicians and international pianists. I worried about adequately representing myself, my teachers, colleagues, and students. But then the focus on me was replaced with the objectives presented by this sensational organization that appeared in the conference booklet. It became apparent that this wasn't about me as I began to read and study the following: "The objectives of the Association are: connection and coordination of work of piano teachers, promotion of piano pedagogy and performing, influence on development of piano productive and reproductive art, affirmation of piano teachers and their activities and results on domestic and the scene abroad, affirmation of talents in piano performing and updating of piano pedagogy and performing."

Immediately, it came to me yet again that the musician is not larger than the music itself. The musician is only a humble servant of the music and a vehicle to communicate it to the heart and soul of the listener. As I prepared my presentations with this in mind, I felt energized while realizing that this was a tremendous opportunity that I had been given to share the gifts God had given me with those in attendance; and in doing so, all lives would be blessed, especially mine.

Following my morning lecture/performance, I received a handwritten note from one of the audience members, a piano professor from Eastern Europe. He said,

> Dr. Hatch, your lecture topic, Pianistic Fundamentals of Musical Communication and Artistry, was most captivating with new and refreshing ideas. Thank you for the fascinating insights into the realm of artistic communication which I am eager to implement in my studio upon my return home.

The second day it was pleasing to work on significant piano pieces with four Serbian students from the Isidor Bajic Music Conservatory before a large audience of peers, teachers, and other music professionals. After the two-hour master class, I again received a congratulatory message from the professor of one of the students who had performed for me.

> Dr. Hatch, thank you for a brilliant class. I was astounded, as I have never observed such energy and skillful teaching from anyone. It was remarkable to witness a masterful pianist use his perfected teaching skills in such an effective way. Not only were we given sound musical advice, but your presentation was highly entertaining. Perhaps you noticed that each of the students who played for you wore a huge grin when stepping down from the stage. They were very enthusiastic and knew they had been taught well. Many thanks for inspiring us here today.

The beauty and power of music transcends time and space and encourages the best in people. It is a universal truth, just as love is its inspiration. Consequently, it is highly rewarding to be involved in a performance and teaching career where numerous musical opportunities are presented that empower me to continue to provide encouragement and to build others in the art of beautiful music-making. In Serbia, I strove to do my best work, and, apparently, those present in my classes were lifted in that teaching process.

Notes:

1. Mary Worthington, "Voices of Change: Artists Speak Out" (Alton Creative: Nov. 2002), 2.

2. Michael Barber, "What Did Jesus Sing at the Last Supper?" *The Sacred Page*, April 2009, 24.

3. Dallin H. Oaks, "Worship Through Music," *Ensign*, November 1994, 9.

4. Marden Pond, *Virtuous, Lovely, of Good Report* (Provo: Music Enterprises, 1990), 194.

5. George Marek, *Beethoven: Biography of a Genius* (New York: Funk & Wagnalls, 1969), 194.

6. Friedrich Kerst & Henry Edward Krehbiel, eds., *Beethoven: The Man and the Artist, as revealed in His Own Words* (New York: Dover Publications, 1964), 81–82.

7. *The Musician's Diary*, (New York: McAfee Music, 1979), 96.

Chapter Five

THE POWER OF MUSIC TO INSPIRE

"Music should kindle the divine flame in the human mind."

—Ludwig van Beethoven

In the early years of my performance career, I enjoyed giving a community concert in Birmingham, Alabama. The South is truly different than other areas of the United States. I learned firsthand that the so-called southern hospitality of people in that region is genuine. These southerners are warm, sincere, kind, helpful, and friendly.

With numerous members of the Church in attendance that evening, I will never forget the unique circumstances regarding the encore piece that I played following that substantial classical program. Having been extremely busy studying and passing spring semester finals, my preparation for this concert had been limited. I had scarcely enough time to sufficiently prepare the complete program, which had been submitted months earlier, let alone to include encore pieces!

After the Prokofiev *Eighth Sonata* finale, the applause of the near-capacity audience would not stop. After three curtain calls, I was chagrined not to have an encore to play. As I walked off stage the first time, the Spirit spoke to my mind, "David, perform the arrangement of Come, Come Ye Saints." Feeling pressure and nervousness about not having an encore to share, I considered these thoughts to have been created by my own emotions rather than direct communication from the Spirit. But with a second curtain call, I again heard similar words in my mind whispering, "David, perform the *Come, Come Ye Saints* arrangement." Again I left the stage and, because of pride, justified not performing the arrangement following this professional classical concert, as it would be laughable to the many expert musicians, pianists, and music professors from the local university in attendance that evening. But the applause continued! What to do? While walking out on stage a third time, the Spirit pressed me harder than before, "Perform the hymn arrangement and DO IT NOW!" From this experience I learned that when the Spirit speaks, MOVE!

Sheepishly, I sat down on the piano bench without announcing the encore, which quieted the audience. I began to perform the arrangement of *Come, Come Ye Saints*, a musical interpretation of the story of our people—the Mormon pioneers—which had been revealed to me a short time previously during my graduate school years. The auditorium was breathlessly quiet during that music, with the Spirit present so powerfully that no one dared make a sound at its conclusion. Then, after what seemed to be a very long time, the auditorium exploded with applause—especially from the Church members present. The impact of this music and the reason it was to be performed that evening became apparent moments later while I greeted audience members in the lobby.

One emotional woman approached me and introduced herself as a member of the piano faculty from the university. Then, quickly glancing around to ensure that her colleagues were not within earshot, she awkwardly asked me, "Mr. Hatch, I'm sorry to admit that I'm not familiar with the encore piece you performed. It sounded a bit like Chopin with elements of Schumann. What was it?"

My response that it was not a classical piece greatly surprised her. I explained that it was an arrangement of a very special hymn of my Church entitled *Come, Come Ye Saints*, and that I had performed it for the many members of The Church of Jesus Christ of Latter-day Saints in attendance that evening who would appreciate this musical benediction. To my astonishment the music professor, wiping tears, replied, "If that's the Spirit that is felt in the Mormon Church, then I must be part of it!"

A few years later I received the joyful news that this woman, the piano professor, had become a member of the Church and was serving at that time as the Relief Society president of her ward. In addition to its marvelous power to inspire, how remarkable it is that music possesses the power to dramatically alter lives in magnificent ways.

Musical motivation in our lives should deepen our thoughts and feelings toward virtue and beauty and make us more sensitive to others, to ourselves, and to the Spirit. Good, influential music can encourage receptivity to the light of Christ, the source of all righteous inspiration.

During my travels, I'm usually asked to present firesides for local units of the Church in cities where my concerts are held. These are often Spirit-filled meetings that are held to strengthen the Saints and to support the missionary efforts of the area. Four years ago, however, in beautiful Tuscany—while feeling immense sadness and complete distraction from spiritual things due to the loss of my money belt that contained cash, credit cards, and my passport—my mindset was not one ready to provide a spiritual presentation. But knowing that I could not disappoint those who would be making the effort to attend the fireside, I dropped to my knees and poured out my soul to Heavenly Father for comfort in this mighty hour of need to give me peace, strength, and a disposition to convey the Spirit while enduring an evening of great pain and heartache. Promptly, He answered my prayer as I witnessed a spiritual evening never to be forgotten!

In that chapel in Pisa, Italy, my music and the spoken word, with the assistance of a translator and the Spirit, resulted in a visibly emotional evening for many of those Italian Saints. I clearly recall being directed several times during the fireside to speak thoughts and gospel concepts that had not been prepared initially. (Later, I would learn that this had caused my translator slight anxiety, as he was also diverted from the prepared text he had studied beforehand.) Afterward, I would learn that, through my message, the Spirit communicated with someone in that congregation who needed to be spiritually charged.

When I finished and walked down off the stand, Brother Maurizio Ventura, public relations director for the Church for that Tuscan area, embraced me firmly. Then, with emotion in his voice he whispered, "Brother Hatch, I want you to know that your musical presentation of special inspirational music and moving words was most powerful! Many of our people were moved to tears. But, more importantly, the man sitting next to me, our former branch president of years ago, who for eight years has been totally inactive, leaned over to me at the conclusion of your final number, *How Great Thou Art*, and told me that he had felt the most powerful spirit he'd ever experienced in his life and would be returning to church to worship once again as an active Latter-day Saint!" Needless to say, it was deeply humbling to realize that the music and Spirit present in that meeting caused this spiritual rebirth.

Not only does great music inspire God's children, but master composers have frequently received inspiration for creating great music. To these gifted musicians, inspiration was not only desirable, but an integral part of their writing process. In my view, every composer needs inspiration to produce inspired music. Brahms once declared that "the powers from which all truly great composers like Mozart, Schubert, Bach and Beethoven drew their inspirations is the same power that enabled Jesus to work His miracles."[1] Besides, "when composers find the Spirit, composers from the other side of the veil join forces with them and inspire them with music—works that live forever, inspiring limitless others to good works, and building the Kingdom of God."[2]

Although Brahms was reluctant to discuss this sacred subject matter concerning the source of his creative genius, insisting that his remarks not be published until many years following his death, it is significant that his thoughts and beliefs were very close to truths of the restored gospel. Brahms often referred to John 10:30 about becoming "one with the Father." Moreover, it was his conviction that when he felt inspiration in his compositional work, he was becoming one with his Creator. Of this, Brahms affirmed:

> When I feel the urge I begin by appealing directly to my Maker and I first ask Him the three most important questions pertaining to our life here in this world—whence, wherefore, whither?

I immediately feel vibrations that thrill my whole being. These are the Spirit illuminating the soul-power within, and in this exalted state, I see clearly what is obscure in my ordinary moods; then I feel capable of drawing inspiration from above, as Beethoven did. Above all, I realize at such moments the tremendous significance of Jesus' supreme revelation, "I and my Father are one." Those vibrations assume the forms of distinct mental images, after I have formulated my desire and resolve in regard to what I want, namely, to be inspired so that I can compose something that will uplift and benefit humanity—something of permanent value.

Straightway the ideas flow in upon me, directly from God, and not only do I see distinct themes in my mind's eye, but they are clothed in the right forms, harmonies and orchestration. Measure by measure, the finished product is revealed to me.[3]

With such spiritual purpose, then, there is little wonder that the Lord blessed this special man with musical gifts to inspire mankind. When Brahms heard the voice of God, he let it speak through his music.

Likewise, hymns create a feeling of reverence and revelation. Elder Jay E. Jensen of the Quorum of the Seventy shared,

When the Seventy and Presiding Bishopric are invited to meetings with the First Presidency and the Twelve, we are reminded to arrive early and reverently listen to prelude music. Doing so invites revelation and prepares us for the meeting. President Packer of the Quorum of the Twelve has taught that a member who softly plays prelude music from the hymnbook tempers our feelings and causes us to go over in our minds the lyrics which teach the peaceable things of the kingdom. If we will listen, they are teaching the gospel, for the hymns of the Restoration are, in fact, a course in doctrine![4]

As well as sacred music that is essential in breeding reverence in our lives, inspirational secular music can motivate the senses. Never in all my years of concert travel have I been more inspired by music or by its cultural and historical background than during the weeks I spent entrenched with the flabbergasting music scene in Russia in the late '90s!

The magnificence of Russia's artistic culture—pianistic, instrumental, and orchestral tradition—remains for me completely unsurpassed! Because the stunning music and musical history of this tour exhibited much power to inspire, it seems only fitting to communicate many of those experiences relating to some of the world's leading musicians—composers and pianists since the late eighteenth century.

As a framework, my performance tour began in St. Petersburg (formerly Leningrad) with its five million people, where my wide-eyed students absorbed intriguing musical and cultural sights day after day. Founded in 1703 by Peter I, it became the city of the famed Russian czars thereafter. This Peter the Great married Catherine II of German descent and together, the two introduced western classical music to Russia. Also, adoring the layout of Amsterdam, the couple endeavored to duplicate the ambiance of this city with canals and waterways spanned by 330 bridges. The gorgeous city, then, became known as "Venice of the North" named after Venice, Italy. But, foremost for our group in this prominent city was, of course, visiting and receiving a personal tour of the famous St. Petersburg (Rimsky-Korsakov) Conservatory of Music with its illustrious inspirational history of music-making.

First, the piano chair graciously allowed us to listen to the playing of some of the student examinations in the famous recital hall, having arrived during their week of semester finals. My students were astounded by the professional pianism they heard by these conservatory students of comparable ages, which gave me the opportunity to explain aspects of the incredible "Russian School of Piano Technique" with its extreme demands. I was pleased that this dialogue seemed to greatly inspire a stronger work ethic within my students upon our return home. The musical inspiration and adventure that proceeded at the Russian conservatory was breathtaking! We walked the aged wooden hallways where Russia's most renowned teachers, pianists, and composers once walked, taught, and performed!

The piano professor unlocked a private area and kindly allowed us to enter and peruse the conservatory's restricted collection of fascinating items, such as original musical scores, photos, manuscripts, awards, busts, statues, portraits, and plaster hand casts of some famous musicians as Anton Rubinstein (the first conservatory director), Prokofiev, Glinka, Shostakovich, Rimsky-Korsakov, and Tchaikovsky.

Following my first concert of Scriabin Études and Rachmaninoff's *Étude-Tableaux* on a beautiful nine-foot Bluthner grand and two-hour master class at the Russian music college for 650 adults and students, we visited the Alexander Nevsky monastery and basked in the celebrated history at the grave sites of these above-mentioned Russian musical giants and two others, Borodin and César Cui. Visiting this famous place where many of Russia's most renowned musicians and famous writers as Dostoyevsky and Tolstoy are laid to rest became for my group a cultural and historical highlight of the tour. Learning of the cultural background that created the inspirational artistic efforts of these brilliant men became a motivating factor in my young pianists, who returned home with a newly discovered desire to achieve greatness in their own musical pursuits. In this sense, it becomes obvious that the power of music to inspire is far-reaching.

Musical inspiration continued in the great city of Moscow. After months of correspondence, finally I met my distinguished contact person for this city, delightful composer and pianist Aleksandr Rakviashvili, who arranged my concert and piano master class at the House of Composers in central downtown.

After observing me in action, Aleksandr praised my performances and teaching, which brought forth an indescribable musical opportunity later that week. To thank me for my work, he somehow procured admission tickets for all of us to attend the sold-out Tchaikovsky International Competition! For sure, that extraordinary privilege, which will be shared later, demonstrated magnificently the power of music to inspire!

During my master class, not only did I experience abundant inspiration while working with Elena and Igor, two excellent piano students from the world-renowned Moscow Conservatory of Music, but afterward appreciated the comments from their professors that my teaching and performance demonstrations had inspired them. Then, quite shocking to me was having these piano professors offer me a teaching position on their piano faculty, inquiring seriously of the feasibility of my moving to Moscow by the following school year.

Furthermore, the gracious twenty-eight-year-old Igor who one year previously had won the Szymanowski International Piano Competition in Poland, asked to speak with me privately. He said,

"Dr. Hatch, while you motivated me in perfecting my repertoire during today's master class, I felt a strong impression that music has much power to inspire! Highly respecting your musical instincts, knowledge, and teaching style, I would be grateful if you would accept me as a student. If so, my desire is to move to America and have you prepare me for international competitions over the next five years." Of course I was flattered and our interaction has been wonderful since that time.

Great inspiration continued as our group enjoyed tremendous opportunities to explore the musical legacies of famous Russian musicians, composers, and world-famous music conservatories, including the Gnessin School of Music for gifted children that boasts alumni such as Aram Khachaturian, Evgeny Kissin, Vissarion Shebalin, Nikolai Demidenko, and Boris Elkis and the Prokofiev School of Music. The director of the Prokofiev School, Alexander Kanevsky, gave us a tour through the facility, including the spacious performance hall where renowned Russian musicians such as Richter, Rostropovich, and Firkušný had performed. My students enthusiasticly played Prokofiev's boyhood upright piano, enjoyed his photos, and examined his original piano and orchestral manuscripts—including the original manuscript of his legendary *Third Piano Concerto*, arguably the finest of all twentieth-century concertos!

The momentous day remained stirring as we continued to the flat (now a museum) of Alexander Scriabin in the old part of the city where we had the chance to inspect his fascinating paraphernalia—pianos, concert clothing, photos with friends (Rachmaninoff and Stravinsky), a 1915 recording of his personal piano playing, and various concert programs he had presented. The stimulating afternoon was spent driving eighty kilometers (seventy-five miles) through drizzling rain past charming Russian villages and well-kept farmland to the beautifully wooded, rural community of Klin and the home (also a museum) of Peter Tchaikovsky, the most celebrated Russian composer of all time. Increased appreciation for the life and contributions of this master composer came while viewing his original opera, symphony, ballet, and piano manuscripts, playing his grand piano in the music parlor, and seeing his photographs, bed, and the desk where he composed. To be in his home where

Tchaikovsky received inspiration while composing some of the world's most celebrated musical masterpieces enhanced our awareness and gratitude for truly great, praiseworthy music.

Specifically, the most inspirational moment at the Tchaikovsky homestead was sitting in the atmospherically dim concert hall adjacent to his home and listening to two of his most beautiful compositions—first movements of the (final) *Sixth Symphony in B Minor (Pathetique)* and the *First Piano Concerto in B-flat Minor.* As trained musicians and pianists, we felt incredible admiration for his compositional feats, realizing that those listening moments of sheer ecstasy would never be forgotten! A culminating musical inspiration of the day came during our evening back in Moscow where we were exhilarated by an incomparable performance of Tchaikovsky's *Swan Lake* by the Bolshoi Ballet. This inspired music and the technical perfection of the dancers was sensational in every respect. From this day of musical and artistic magnificence became a defining moment of the tour. My group had been infused with sheer motivation, encouragement, and strong desire in the acquisition of musical expertise—to inspire as we had been inspired through the power of music!

Finally, this spectacular Russian musical experience would not be complete without one concluding pinnacle of musical opportunity that, for our group, eclipsed all others—attending preliminary and final rounds of the most prestigious quadrennial Tchaikovsky International Piano Competition in the Grand Hall of the Moscow (P. I. Tchaikovsky) Conservatory of Music on two consecutive days. The hall adorned with huge, oval-shaped color portraits and artist renderings of the world's greatest composers; the Russian State Orchestra on stage to perform with the concerto soloists; an enormous illuminated photo of Tchaikovsky secured directly overhead; and piano enthusiasts from around the world crowded body-to-body into seats, aisles, and balconies created an atmosphere of magic and inspiration forever to be remembered!

After the cello, violin, voice, and piano competition finals the last evening, we witnessed the presentation of awards to the winners in each division. We were thrilled with the announcement of the piano gold medalist, the young Russian Denis Matsuev; we had listened to the power of his stirring renditions of Tchaikovsky's

Concerto no. 1 and Rachmaninoff's *Third* in the final round of competition.

Of the tremendous insights gained in Russia concerning music's power to inspire, I concur with Sergei Rachmaninoff when he said that music is enough for a lifetime, but a lifetime is not enough for music. Music's magic cleanses the understanding, inspires it, and lifts it into a realm it would not reach if left to itself. Ultimately, these many years later, I have contemplated frequently on those days of musical inspiration during my international concert tour of Russia: They forever constructively transformed my musical life.

Now, because of the historically important relationship that music bears to religion, and because of music's power to inspire those who worship in the church setting, it deserves a more basic and serious consideration than some churches give it. Several years ago, this concept was expressed to me in a phone call I received from Dr. Robert H. Schuller of the famous Crystal Cathedral, a Protestant Christian mega-church located in Garden Grove, Orange County, California.

As the Cathedral's founder, American televangelist, pastor, and author, it was thrilling to me to be personally invited as a guest artist during the Christmas holidays at his church, the architectural landmark and home for the international Crystal Cathedral Ministries, including a congregation of over 10,000 members and the internationally televised *Hour of Power*. The name "Crystal Cathedral" describes the building's size and appearance, but it does not denote it as a "cathedral" in the traditional Roman Catholic, Anglican, or Lutheran use of the term.

Since I was well aware that his ministry recognizes national and international guests on those weekly television broadcasts throughout the year, this offer was a flattering gesture by Dr. Schuller, who scheduled me to perform with the Cathedral orchestra on his *Hour of Power* program one Sabbath morning that December. From my album *Christmas Treasures*, Dr. Schuller selected his favorite piano and orchestral arrangements of traditional Christmas pieces that would be performed twice during live Sunday morning services. My rehearsals with a very fine cathedral orchestra for my *Joy to the World*, *O Come All Ye Faithful*, and *Angels We have Heard on High* arrangements were enjoyable and dynamic.

Following my playing with the orchestra during the services, Dr. Schuller asked that I join him at the pulpit of the enormous church before those thousands of people. With thoughtfulness, he also presented my wife, Paula, who was with me at the time, to the television viewers and to those seated in the cathedral audience. He proceeded to interview me, asking questions about my musical career, the importance of quality music in our daily lives, and of my amiable relationship with my cousin, United States Senator Orrin Hatch of Utah, informing me of his interest in this association since he and Senator Hatch were close friends, having worked on past projects together. After my answers, Dr. Schuller acknowledged that the power of my music had greatly inspired their entire congregation that morning—the reason he had felt prompted to invite me there to participate in those services, he said. Then he gave his strong endorsement of my Christmas album. Holding up the recording jacket for all to see, he concluded with these words, "From the power of his inspirational performances here this morning, we know that obtaining this beautiful Christmas music will enhance the holiday spirit in our homes, for David plays with tremendous warmth and passion."

In a recent entry on the "LDS Composers" Facebook page, Marden Pond asked, "What makes any specific piece of music endure?" After contemplating that question, it is my opinion that from pleasing musical material, inspiration, knowledge, understanding, and insight of music's substance makes the music long lasting. Most "easy-listening" popular music in our culture requires little if any special knowledge or effort to be understood. Most people recognize, however, that music of the masters has enduring power due to its compositional depth and substance.

Many people today understand the interesting phenomenon in our society that much of the music of our time is pedestrian and rarely stays in fashion beyond half a century, whereas western classical music is a combination of many styles of music which has a long history of over seven hundred years. Shallow music loses its popularity because it shares no significant musical core of lasting value. Instead, the inspiring music of the gifted classical masters—such as J. S. Bach, Beethoven, Brahms, Handel, Mozart, Schubert, Chopin, Liszt, and Rachmaninoff, to name a few—has endured for centuries because it inspires listeners through musical richness and intelligence that often radiates from Deity. Speaking of classical music specifically, it can be divided into six periods of different stylistic characteristics:

> **Medieval**—This period was famous for Gregorian chant—mainly religious music—and was established before 1400.
>
> **Renaissance**—Secular music, madrigals, and art songs are the essence of this period, spanning the years 1400–1600.
>
> **Baroque**—Intricate ornamentation is the style of this period, starting in 1600 and existing through 1750.
>
> **Classical**—Characteristics of the period are balance and structure, beginning in 1750 and ending in approximately 1810.
>
> **Romantic**—Emotional music is the beauty of this period, which spanned the years 1800–1890.
>
> **Twentieth-century**—This limitless music started about 1890 and has progressed to the present.

From these eras of music history, it is my strong belief that some of the world's greatest musical compositions were previously composed in heaven. God then used his musical geniuses on earth to bring these master works to us through their inspired re-creations of them. The following occurrence is a perfect example of this perceived idea.

Ruined by health and fortune and very discouraged because his operas were not being well accepted, baroque composer George Frederic Handel decided to return to composing religious music in 1741. He had written a few oratorios previously, including *Saul, Israel in Egypt, Judas Maccabaeus, Solomon, Samson,* and *Joshua.* But his most enduring oratorio was to be the *Messiah,* based on the scriptures of the Bible and written in the astonishingly short period of twenty-three days during 1741.

Handel hardly stirred from his room during that time. His man-servant would bring a meal, only to find the previous one untouched. When Handel had completed the second part of this work containing the *Hallelujah Chorus,* the servant found him with tears running down his cheeks. Looking out the window above his desk the composer said, "I did think that I saw all Heaven before me, the choir and the great God himself."

Now what did Handel hear that heavenly choir singing? I submit that they were singing that magnificent section of this oratorio known to us as the *Hallelujah Chorus*, and that Handel simply copied it onto manuscript paper as he heard it being sung. In my opinion, this composition was given to man through Handel for the praising of God. History records that when the king heard the majestic work, he was so moved by it that he respectfully stood in silent tribute, a tradition still held by modern-day audiences.

Perhaps I'm convinced of Handel's vision of the *Hallelujah Chorus* from this oratorio because of personal revelation I once received, though on a much smaller musical scale. My first album of inspirational music was recorded in 1980 on the Covenant label. It was explained to me by the president and managing directors of this company—all of them members of The Church of Jesus Christ of Latter-day Saints—that the first hymn arrangement on the album (entitled *Mormon Hymns)* should be *Come, Come Ye Saints*, which is essentially the theme song of the Church. When this project began, I was a graduate student at the Conservatory of Music at University of Missouri–Kansas City.

I well remember suffering one summer afternoon in a hot and humid conservatory practice room without air conditioning trying to achieve an inspirational arrangement of this hymn, which is written to an old English folk melody. For hours I worked without success. The melodic content was difficult. The changing rhythmic meters became frustrating. There was simply no inspiration with which to proceed. Finally, I decided that a satisfactory piano arrangement of this hymn was not possible—at least from me.

Telephoning the producer, I explained that I was unable to work with this hymn, as it seemed impossible to arrange effectively—stylistically, melodically, and rhythmically. To my surprise he insisted that I continue the process until an appropriate and artistic arrangement was completed, since Church members would be purchasing the album expecting that hymn to be included. Consequently, I went back to work in that muggy practice room and suddenly realized, while sitting on the piano bench discouraged, that I had not yet prayed for guidance. Quickly, I dropped to my knees and asked for assistance from Heavenly Father to help me create an inspired piano arrangement of this hymn. Immediately, as I arose from that bench, my mind was flooded with an inspired piano score of this sacred hymn of the early pioneer Saints. Incidentally, this arrangement that finally surfaced is the same one that I performed in Alabama that had touched and initiated the conversion of the university music professor.

I cannot assume credit for this arrangement, for it is not mine, nor is it my pianistic style. Rather, it is a brilliant musical rendition that had come from a divine source—God himself! As I began to play the piano keys, I realized that the music was telling a story— the magnificent story of our people. From that day to this, the heaven-sent arrangement has not changed. Performing it frequently throughout the world for the past three decades, I have seen it bring tears, generate spiritual insight, move Saints to action, and produce small miracles in the lives of LDS Church members and others in my audiences. From this experience with personal musical revelation, I rapidly learned that our Heavenly Father not only inspires His musical children on earth with musical masterpieces, but that He, himself, is a remarkable musician and pianist!

Christoph Gluck, the great opera composer from the early classical period, said, "I regard music not only as an art whose object it is to please the ear, but as one of the most powerful means of opening our hearts and of moving our affections."[5]

Music and the spiritual life must go together; one complements the other. Music helps the spiritual seeker to delve deeply in order to acquire the highest satisfaction from life, from truth, and from reality. In return, the spiritual life helps music to offer its capacity to the world through the light of the soul. On another performance occasion, music and its power to inspire was witnessed by many!

It is normal for me to receive appreciative feedback from audience members regarding performances they term inspiring. However, unexpected compliments from a newspaper critic were revealing, following my performance of Russian composer Anton Rubinstein's *Piano Concerto no. 4 in D Minor* with the Westminster Orchestra held in the Assembly Hall on Temple Square in Salt Lake City, Utah, as part of the Temple Square Concert Series.

I recall feeling discouraged after the initial rehearsal with the orchestra. The conductor apologized for certain time restraints that had prevented sufficient rehearsal work to prepare the difficult composition adequately, explaining that other orchestral repertoire had also required attention simultaneously for other performance events during that same period of time.

Knowing that this enormous tour de force requires great technical, musical, and ensemble demands of both soloist and orchestra in order to give a brilliant presentation of the piece, I prayed for divine intervention that all the musicians would receive spiritual assistance in the final performance. Assistance came in profusion, and we were stunned with the outcome—a stirring performance that can best be described from the written words of the critic's music review that appeared in the local newspaper the next morning: "Hatch's dazzling technical prowess coupled with powerful, sensitive playing of the concerto noticeably elevated the orchestra's level of performance."

With these words came great humility. Not only did numerous audience members express to me that they had been greatly inspired by the performance, but by striving to do my best playing and seeking the Lord's assistance for all of us that evening, orchestra personnel also shared with me that the piano performance had inspired their playing of the gripping concerto rendition that evening at a level of performance far above any previous rehearsal together. The music had shown the power not only to inspire the concert audience, but also the performing musicians themselves!

Knowing its enormous power to inspire, our Father in Heaven uses music on very special occasions in history, such as the birth of Jesus Christ (Luke 2:13–14), His death (Matt. 26:30), the prophet Joseph Smith's martyrdom (History of the Church, June 27, 1844), Emma Smith's injunction regarding the hymns (D&C 25:11–12), and Christ's Second Coming, which will be proclaimed by music. (Zeph. 3:17).

As has been mentioned, it is widely recognized that most of the inspirational music masterpieces have come from the past. In determining a plausible explanation for this fact, I find it rather fascinating when comparing many of these phenomenal classics as they are considered by the world's music professionals—such as Beethoven's *Fifth* and *Ninth Symphonies*; Schubert's last three piano sonatas, numbered 958, 959 and 960; Chopin's *Fantasy in F Minor*; Brahms'

Requiem; Bach's *St. Matthew Passion*; and Mozart's two-act opera *The Magic Flute*—that the numerous listing of such music was either written or discovered within fifty years of the Restoration in 1830! This is an exciting reality when considering that this was also the Age of Enlightenment, a time when the Lord was flooding the earth with knowledge, light, and truth, not only at Hill Cumorah, but in science, literature, art, and music. Hence, God's voice can be heard in music that inspires as well as in the scriptures.

Elder Bruce R. McConkie referred to music as the "language of the gods" and that inspired music is eternal, given of God to further His purposes. The prophet Brigham Young taught that "great music is a special means of communicating with God," and J. Reuben Clark, Jr., of the LDS Church's First Presidency (1933) agreed when he said, "A man can get nearer to God by music than any other method except prayer."[6]

From my recent classical concert presented at the distinguished Ghione Theater in Rome, an unexpected but encouraging happening developed. It was an honor to have been invited to perform in this gorgeous deep red and gold posh hall located near St. Peter's Basilica, which offers an annual performance scheduling of impressive Italian and international artists. Due to the hectic bumper-to-bumper rush-hour traffic that evening, however, our bus arrived at the hall far too late for any stage rehearsing—the doors having already been opened for public seating.

Quickly, I donned my tuxedo in an off-stage dressing room and hurried on stage to the Steinway concert grand, where I bowed to audience applause at barely the appointed start time. In frenzy and exhausted from a demanding touring day, it was surprising that my concert repertoire was performed well at all that evening. Excitement ensued while I was greeted by several Italian city officials and dignitaries who showered me with compliments for the performances and requested to take photos with me.

Weeks earlier, I had been notified of the possibility of the Vatican organist being in attendance. In anticipation, I met this distinguished individual, who congratulated me, expressed that my music had greatly inspired him, and introduced himself as James Goettsche, personal Vatican organist of His Holiness, Pope Benedict XVI.

Mr. Goettsche explained that the Pope had also planned to attend the concert—a pianist himself who favors the music of Mozart—but was unable to be there due to unforeseen security concerns. Yet, the audio engineer explained that he had recorded the concert and would have it aired directly into Benedict's Vatican apartment later that week. That which was to follow would become, for me, the highlight of this tour!

Having been informed beforehand of the likelihood that I'd encounter the Pope's personal organist at my concert, I presumptuously prepared a gift before flying to Italy that June, hoping he would consent to deliver it for me to the Pope while informing Benedict that it came as a gift from the international American pianist who had performed at the Ghione Theater. I had written my personal testimony inside the two front covers of both German and Italian editions of the Book of Mormon, as Benedict is German, but speaks and reads Italian. By giving both books, the excuse he could possibly give to not read the book due to a language barrier was eliminated. Because he had a personal association with the Pope, I was pleased that Mr. Goettsche seemed delighted to accommodate my special request.

After my return to the States, James Goettsche contacted me to report that he had delivered the books to Benedict after he had listened to my concert performance in his apartment. The Pope shared his feelings about the music that had moved and inspired him and created an interest to know more about the "expressive performer." Hence, the Pope graciously accepted the copies of the Book of Mormon, expressed appreciation for my gift, and said he would read the German edition. To my understanding, this was the first time Benedict had received a personal copy of the book, which he seemed to more readily accept, having been specially touched by the music of this pianist—music that had produced a desire to better understand the spiritual implications and strong emotions that emanated from the performance and that deeply penetrated his soul.

Listening to music of J. S. Bach, Haydn, Beethoven, Mozart, Mendelssohn, Schubert, Tchaikovsky, and Rachmaninoff, among others, transports me to places where the outside world no longer exists, while enveloping me with feelings of pure bliss and relaxation.

To be sure, these musical experiences are indescribable! Inspirational music inspires the heart and mind, creates energy within, and provides an excellent means to remaining positive throughout the day while living in a troubled world. Definitely, music possesses a power to inspire!

NOTES:

1.   Peter Latham, *Brahms* (New York: Collier, 1962), 112.
2.   Reid Nibley, "Facing the Music: The Challenges Ahead for Mormon Musicians," in *Arts & Inspiration*, 1980.
3.   Arthur M. Abell, *Talks with Great Composers* (New York: Philospohical Library, 1955), 5–6.
4.   Jay E. Jensen, "The Nourishing Powers of Hymns," *Ensign*, May 2007, 12.
5.   *The Musician's Diary* (New York: McAfee Music, 1979), 134.
6.   Michael Ballam, "Music's Great Power can Uplift and Inspire—or Promote Evil," *LDS Church News*, Aug. 1991.

Chapter Six

THE POWER OF MUSIC TO PRAISE

"Music, in the opinion of many, ranks second only to faith and religion; and apart from its power, its effect, and its many advantages, we may justly regard it as belonging to heaven rather than to earth, awakening and stimulating, as it does in our hearts, a desire to praise the Almighty with psalms and thanksgiving."

—Michael Praetorius

Ever since King David wrote his many psalms, musicians of faith have attempted to praise God through musical gifts He has given them. Paul and Silas, in jail in Philippi, "prayed and sang praises unto God" at midnight (Acts 16:25). And the people of Jared, crossing the great deep, "did sing praises unto the Lord" day and night (Ether 6:9). Russell M. Nelson taught:

> The Book of Mormon teaches that one's desire to sing praises to the Lord comes with one's complete conversion to Him. Alma asked this penetrating question: "I say unto you, my brethren, if ye have experienced a change of heart, and if ye have felt to sing the song of redeeming love, I would ask, can ye feel so now?" (Alma 5:26)[1]

As Christians who love the Lord, Jesus Christ, and the powerful, inspired music that has been given to man as a gift from God, we desire to praise His name forever; for certainly, as has been shown,

70

the inherent beauty of great music can itself draw us closer to Christ. Much is said in the scriptures about praising the Lord with music; therefore, we must always seek discernment in our musical choices since not all music is praiseworthy or suitable for worship or virtuous living.

At the dedication of the temple in the days of Solomon, "the priests waited on their offices: the Levites also with instruments of music of the Lord, which David the king had made to praise the Lord . . . and the priests sounded trumpets before them, and all Israel stood" (2 Chron. 7:6). The dedication of the Kirtland Temple was accompanied with remarkable manifestations of the Spirit with the hymn *The Spirit of God* being sung immediately following the dedicatory prayer. Of this experience, Joseph Smith reported, "A noise was heard like the sound of a rushing mighty wind, which filled the Temple, and all the congregation simultaneously arose, being moved upon by an invisible power." The words of the traditional Hosanna Shout, in which the entire congregation participated at this time, are repeated in the chorus: "Hosanna, hosanna to God and the Lamb!" It was an extraordinary time enhanced by this powerful, praiseworthy music.[2]

On one occasion, Igor Stravinsky—one of the eminent Russian twentieth century composers—exclaimed, "Music praises God. Music is as well or better able to praise Him than the building of the church and all its decorations; it is the church's greatest ornament."[3] Moroni also tells us that in church meetings, "as the power of the Holy Ghost led them whether to preach . . . or to sing, even so it was done" (Moroni 6:9). Thus, it is clear that our spiritual lives are intensified through uplifting, music of praise.

Michael Moody of the Church Music Department said,

> Appropriate music for sacrament meeting is music that contributes to the spirituality of the meeting and inspires or strengthens the members in their desire to live the gospel. Although some music may have merit for other occasions, if it does not achieve these results it is probably inappropriate for sacrament meeting. The following guideline is given in the *Handbook for Church Music*, 1975, page 18.
>
> "Those responsible for selecting music for Church meetings should make certain that music and text are sacred, dignified, of

high quality, in harmony with the spirit of Latter-day Saint worship, and suitable to the occasion and circumstances. The text should be doctrinally correct. Since there is so much worthy music, it is not necessary to select music of questionable propriety. The Church Music Department does not dictate what may or may not be used, but offers only general guidelines in this matter. Final determination should be made by the presiding priesthood leader in consultation with appropriate music personnel."

Another area of concern seems to be the use of instruments. The *Handbook for Church Music*, page 17, includes a statement on this subject:

"Organs and pianos are the standard instruments used in sacrament meetings. Other instruments, such as orchestral strings, may be used when appropriate, but the music presented must be in keeping with the reverence and spirituality of the meeting. Brass and percussion instruments generally are not appropriate."

Of course circumstances vary, and it's possible that a given piece of music might be appropriate on one occasion but not on another. For example, if a family is speaking in sacrament meeting before leaving the ward, "Ye Simple Souls Who Stray" might not be the best choice for a closing hymn! The way a piece of music is presented can also make a difference. For example, an appropriate selection performed in an irreverent manner would render it inappropriate. Those who select and perform music need to use good judgment in applying the general guidelines to specific situations. The question should not be "How far can I go?" but rather "What will be the most effective and the most appropriate?"

Music for our church meetings should strike a responsive chord in the hearts of Latter-day Saints. Although we vary in our musical preferences and are conditioned to appreciate different kinds of music, there is one kind of music that ought to be a common denominator for all members of the Church—the hymns. When I say "the hymns" I don't necessarily mean all hymns—I mean hymns (and even songs and anthems) that are characteristic of our worship services—hymns that are known and loved by the Saints, like "How Great the Wisdom," "High on the Mountain Top," "I Need Thee Every Hour," and "Redeemer of Israel." Hymns are such an integral part of our worship experience that we learn to respond to them spiritually. They speak to all, and they bring the Holy Spirit with them.

Those responsible for music in our services should see that the musical selections are well suited to the occasion. But we not only need good music for our meetings, we also need good listeners. If the music is in tune but the hearer is not, there will be no harmony and no response to the music. Sometimes we as listeners "tune out" because the music isn't to our personal liking—perhaps too "highbrow" or too "low brow" for us. When we do this, we deny ourselves an opportunity to partake of the inspiration that could be there for us. We who listen should be involved, not in making musical judgments, but rather in participating with glad hearts in the spirit of worship.[4]

In a Church Educational System fireside address given at Brigham Young University, Elder Merrill J. Bateman of the Seventy taught,

> Music is one of the most effective forms of worship. In our hymns, we praise God, and give thanks for His love and mercy. I am impressed with this statement by Elder Jeffrey R. Holland of the Quorum of the Twelve Apostles: 'Sacramental hymns are … like prayers and everyone can give voice to a prayer!' Although I had thought of some hymns as prayers, I had not thought of each sacramental hymn in that form. And yet it is! Like the chiasmatic writing structure of old, the sacrament, the central feature of our key weekly meeting, occurs near the center. In an important way, it is the climactic feature of the service. As the priests break the bread, the entire congregation is given the opportunity to voice their prayerful thanks through music. Sacramental hymns focus our attention on the Lord, His atoning sacrifice, and the gospel plan.[5]

Another Church Educational System fireside address on May 4, 2008, at Brigham Young University was presented by Elder Russell M. Nelson of the Quorum of the Twelve Apostles. On that occasion he said:

> The purpose of music in our Church services is not for performance but for worship. Prayerfully selected compositions and excellent performances are appropriate in our worship services when and if members feel a spirit of worship and revelation. Church music should support the Lord and His work and not attract attention to itself.[6]

We should not only worship and praise God in Church services, but it is of great importance that music be used in the praising of God in everyday life! "If thou art merry, praise the Lord with singing, with music, with dancing, and with a prayer of praise and thanksgiving" (D&C 136:28). When we praise, we are expressing our admiration for God; we are lifting Him up in exaltation. Praise is the act of celebrating the Lord. Praise is a way of life, the very heartbeat of our relationship with God.

The Bible teaches that we can and should praise our God through musical instruments and singing. "Shout for joy to the Lord, all the earth, burst into jubilant song with music; make music to the Lord with the harp, with the harp and the sound of singing, with trumpets and the blast of the ram's horn - shout for joy before the Lord, the King" (Psalm 98:4–6). And, in Psalm 150:3–5 we read, "Praise him with the sounding of the trumpet, praise him with the harp and lyre, praise him with tambourine and dancing, praise him with the strings and flute, praise him with the clash of cymbals, praise him with resounding cymbals." In this way, music becomes a powerful influence for good in our lives and sets the stage for many things spiritual. Essentially, praiseworthy music can assist us in entering the presence of God.

Furthermore, for those of us who have achieved enough to be involved and to occupy a significant role in perpetuating the musical arts, giving our very best requires that we work to please the Lord, not men. Many years ago during a devotional service at Brigham Young University, Elder Boyd K. Packer shared sincere and insightful counsel on this matter.

> There have been a number of efforts to take sacred gospel themes and tie them to modern music in the hope of attracting our young people to the message. Few events in all of human history surpass the spiritual majesty of the First Vision. We would be ill-advised to describe that event, the visit of Elohim and Jehovah, in company with rock music, even soft rock music, or to take equally sacred themes and set them to a modern beat. I do not know how that can be done and result in increased spirituality. I think it cannot be done.
>
> When highly trained artists insist, as they occasionally do, that they receive spiritual experiences in tying a sacred gospel theme to an inappropriate art form, I must conclude that they do not know—not really—the difference between when the Spirit of the Lord is present and when it is not.
>
> Very frequently when our musicians, particularly the more highly trained among them, are left to do what they want to do, they

perform in such a way as to call attention to themselves and their ability. They do this rather than give prayerful attention to what will inspire . . . they are not content to use the hymns and anthems of the Restoration, for such a presentation, they feel, will not demonstrate their full capacities. When pressed to do so, they may grudgingly put a hymn on the program. But it is obvious that their heart isn't in it, for the numbers they select themselves seem to say, "Now let us show you what we really can do."

So in the Church, for the most part, we do without because the conductor wants to win the acclaim of the world. He does not play to the Lord, but to other musicians. The composer and the arranger want to please the world. The painter wants to be in style. And we find that there have marched through this grand parade of mortality men and women who were sublimely gifted, but who spent all, or most, in the world and for the world. And I repeat that they may well one day come to learn that "many men struggle to reach the top of the ladder, only to find that it is leaning against the wrong wall."[7]

It is vitalizing to realize that some musicians and performers are driven to work without the external motivation of applause and wealth! It is apparent from an examination of Schubert's life that he was motivated to praise God by simply developing his God-given musical gifts, whether recognized or not. He even went to bed with his glasses on because he wanted to begin composing the minute he awoke. What enthusiasm for life! During one of my international concert tours to Europe, I visited the two very modest homes in Vienna of the great Austrian composer Franz Schubert—his birthplace and the meager home where he died. He never knew affluence, but of any composer in history, Schubert had the gift for melody. Considering that he died at the young age of thirty-one, the prolific output of his musical genius is most impressive. He once said, "When one piece is finished, I begin another."[8] The endearing melodies found in his symphonies, sonatas, chamber music, and choral works were virtually ignored by the world at that time. Yet, this lack of public attention had no adverse effect on Schubert.

From history, we learn that Schubert possessed a strong faith in Christ, which sustained him through years of unrewarded labor. His audiences were not the concertgoers or even his musical friends and colleagues, but the Lord Himself. From his life's circumstances, we can learn a great lesson about true perspective: In pursuing excellence in the development of our own unique gifts and talents bestowed by God, a righteous motive would be to strive to do our best for Him—not for worldly success—for, no matter how respectable our work may appear to our associates, the intentions we bring to it will be measured by God himself! In the Bible we read, "Man looketh on the outward appearance, but the Lord looketh on the heart" (1 Samuel 16:7). There is another aspect of praise that is pertinent to this discussion. Not only does music have the power to praise, but when musicians receive praise and encouragement, their level of performance and other musical contributions are often improved significantly. Having worked in the music teaching profession for four decades, I have witnessed on numerous occasions the difference an encouraging word has made to struggling students, amateur performers, and music professionals. It is inspiring when camaraderie and praise is found in a musician's circle of influence.

When people are encouraged, they are given reasons to pursue their goals and dreams and eventually develop the self-confidence to make it happen! When we are affirmed, it's empowering. It becomes contagious, and we begin to encourage others. Accordingly, it is a fact that when we build up others, we are built up!

The story is told of an elderly man who approached the famous nineteenth-century poet and artist Dante Gabriel Rossetti. The old man had some sketches and drawings that he wanted Rossetti to peruse, and then reveal if any were good or at least showed potential talent.

After examining the first few carefully, Rossetti knew these were worthless, showing no signs of artistic promise. But being a kind person, he explained to the old man as gently as possible that the pictures were without value and exhibited little talent. He was sorry, but could not lie to the man. Although disappointed, the visitor seemed to respect Rossetti's judgment. After apologizing for taking up Rossetti's time, he asked if he would quickly look at a few more drawings of a younger art student.

Rossetti looked over the second group of sketches, immediately becoming enthusiastic over the talent they revealed. "These," he said, "are excellent. This young student has great talent and should be given every encouragement in his career as an artist. He has a great future if he will work hard and stick to it." Seeing that the old man was deeply moved Rossetti asked, "Who is this fine young artist; your son?"

"No," said the visitor sadly. "It is me—forty years ago. If only I had heard your praise then! For you see, I became discouraged and gave up—too soon."[9]

Though the author of this story is unknown, this is a wonderful example of how important encouragement can be in a person's life. We may not always know when an individual needs praise or we may not see the result of it, but giving encouragement may be one of the most powerful tools each of us has to positively change our world.

Specifically, when musicians bestow and accept encouragement and praise, everyone is elevated in the process. For me, this valuable insight has been gained from years of performing and teaching. Particular details relating to my more recent conservatory master class and professional concert in Sofia, Bulgaria, effectively communicate this perception. The guest artist invitation to present this piano master class and concert during Sofia, Bulgaria's prestigious 2008 Annual International Music Festival (Sofia Weeks) was a great honor that brought me remarkable musical exposure.

At the Pantcho Vladigerov School in Sofia (National Music Conservatory of Bulgaria), I listened to performances of four gifted young pianists, one of which had recently won a European international competition. After working with these excellent conservatory students in a master class setting and having several of my prodigious students with me, we began a musical exchange. These conservatory students, their teachers, and my American students enjoyed a music dialogue session through the assistance of a translator that quickly became a highlight for these young pianists who enjoyed learning of the similarities and differences in the two music traditions.

What meant more than the profuse compliments showered upon me by the foreign students and their conservatory professors (including the school director), were the heartfelt comments of my four adult chaperones—all parents of my students. After my enthusiastic master class, these parents expressed to me their gratitude for the inspiration they experienced from my class, humility for the opportunity their children had to study with a most knowledge-able professional, and compliments for the rapport I had noticeably developed with the Bulgarians while motivating in the teaching process.

For me, this praise from those with whom I work so closely each week provided support to continue the contributions in my life's work. As with students, it is equally satisfying and highly encouraging when professionals are validated and appreciated for their influences. Then, the ongoing challenges of a teaching and performing career seem well worth the sacrifices and time commitments required.

Scheduled for the subsequent day was the distinguished performance at Chamber Hall Bulgaria, a beautiful concert hall in Sofia's city center. The performance for the large audience of classical music enthusiasts, conservatory piano and music professors, festival participants, and other serious musicians was of the highest level. Sometimes, it seems that when audiences are of this musical caliber, I am driven further toward higher musical excellence.

The exhilarating evening was a special one, with the Bulgarian audience's exploding applause, cheering, and shouts of approval following my performance of each piece. Finally, after two concluding encore numbers, Debussy's *Clair de Lune* and Chopin's *Nocturne in E-flat Major*, a standing ovation with additional applause persisted for several minutes while the director presented fresh flower bouquets. It is not possible to capture in words my feelings for this professional evening of success and praise from this emotional crowd!

Immediately, audience members flooded the stage to congratulate me and to praise my "electrifying performances"—their words, not mine. Furthermore, while showering me with high compliments, Svetla Mateeva, music editor of Bulgarian National Radio, swept me away from the noisy crowd to the lobby for an interview that would air nationally at the end of the week. She seemed visibly moved and expressed having been "overtaken by my exquisite pianism." After the fifteen-minute interview filled with intriguing questions from this national radio personality, she thanked me profusely for my time and took my address to send me a transcript of the edited piece upon its completion.

Additionally, the photographer and the music critic from the Sofia City News Agency were both in attendance to take photos and to gather pertinent information to write a concert review, which appeared one week later in the Sofia newspaper, the *Bulgaria Gazette*. Among the commendations, the article read,

> The inspired concert performances by Professor Hatch . . . from works of Rachmaninoff, Bach, Chopin, Debussy, Scriabin and other beloved composers caused the hall filled with professional pianists, musicians and the public to burst into applauses throughout the evening! . . . Of the beautiful piano playing of all the distinguished pianists this music critic has heard, Hatch's performances were of the highest artistic level.

While contemplating these words, a flashback of decades of unrelenting labor, tenacity, and sacrifice came to mind. How wonderful it was to be reassured of my talents and abilities following this Bulgarian concert evening of praise and appreciation for my work.

Teachers and parents of promising musicians especially have an enormous responsibility in this regard. To encourage musicians through years of rigorous work in pursuing and developing their gifts of singing, writing, teaching, or performing music is vital in bringing them to a point of self-esteem, professionalism, musical enjoyment, and satisfaction. Encouragement also becomes a driving force that challenges those students with confidence in their musical skills to forge ahead as they routinely encounter new concepts, techniques, and skills in their training as accomplished musicians.

As a professional teacher, it has always been my objective to provide my students with not only exceptional music education and stellar performance skills, but to be for them a positive and encouraging mentor in their pursuit of musical excellence. In my view, master teachers have a decisive obligation to share their expert knowledge and experience with future generations. Teaching becomes a considerable responsibility of nurturing and developing successfully trained musicians that will preserve the musical arts. Ultimately, then, encouragement is the key to unlocking the music inside of these students and to later spotlight their learning and experience that brings them to a new place of meaning and purpose in the world.

In Germany several years ago, I visited the Bayreuth Theater that Richard Wagner (1813–1883) built expressly for his enormous twelve-hour opera trilogy, *The Ring*. Today there are thousands of lovers of Wagner's musical genius, although it wasn't always recognized! It is said of that time that his musical style was too advanced for audiences and, therefore, appeared ludicrous. Only the finest, most scholarly musicians of the day could truly understand his efforts, but most of them were indulging their own careers.

One remarkable exception was the Hungarian pianist and composer Franz Liszt. Considered the greatest pianist of his time, Liszt was convinced of Wagner's brilliance as a musician and determined to publicize that fact. For instance, one evening while Liszt was enjoying an orchestral performance of the overture to Wagner's opera Tannhauser, he saw from his box seat the audience's minuscule applause at the end of the piece. An unsatisfactory response to him, he stood, raised his hands, and clapped violently. Of course, recognizing the famous pianist, the audience turned and excitedly cheered him. But Liszt motioned back to the stage, demanding the music be performed once again. Following his lead, the crowd clamored for an encore. The orchestra repeated the overture, to which this time there was a huge outburst of applause. Liszt's praise of the work proved powerful!

On a second occasion, Liszt learned of an upcoming concert of Wagner's music to be performed in his native Budapest. But as before, there was not much audience appeal, and tickets weren't being sold. (Of course, it didn't help that the local press discouraged attendance at the concert.)

One day, one of his friends explained the situation to Liszt, who didn't understand why his fellow Hungarians couldn't learn to appreciate Wagner's music. To salvage a possible fiasco, Liszt quickly devised a plan to remedy the problem. The adored piano virtuoso announced, "I will play Beethoven's Emperor Concerto at the same concert," and within twenty-four hours the Wagner concert was sold out![10]

Liszt's praise of Wagner's compositions and musical genius was highly successful. In fact, prior to Liszt's death, he would hear critics assert that Wagner's compositional gifts had eclipsed his own. But rather than be jealous of Wagner's newfound fame due to Liszt's supportive efforts, he was thrilled to see genius rewarded and acclaimed! Most likely, had it not been for Liszt's praise and encouraging spirit, Wagner's music would not be known, performed, or praised as it is today!

On a lighter note, there was a slightly humorous situation regarding music and praise that I encountered a few years ago in Atlantic City, New Jersey, while attending a Miss America Pageant. Over the years, many of my college and university female students have won not only local and state talent awards, but also Utah and Missouri State titles in the Miss America Organization. I've had the pleasure of twice attending the National Miss America Pageant, held at the Boardwalk Convention Hall in Atlantic City, New Jersey. My most recent student becoming Miss Utah (who incidentally became a top-ten finalist later that week) made a request of me to travel back with her family and friends in order to coach her during her dress rehearsal on the pageant stage.

I arrived at the hall early the morning of her scheduled rehearsal as the audio technicians were setting up their equipment. A sound engineer yelled out into that vast hall, asking whether any of the few of us there played the piano and could run to the stage to perform on the nine-foot instrument for a thorough sound check. Of course I was volunteered by those present! I sat down and played a Russian étude of virtuosity. As I concluded, there was huge applause and shouts of approval from the small early morning crowd. The engineer yelled out to me, "David, it's too bad you're not competing in the pageant! If you were, you'd win hands down!" Though a bit embarrassing, we all enjoyed a good laugh over his outburst for my playing whether or not the praise was sincere, as I realized yet again the power of music to move people in significant ways.

The power of music to praise is magnificent. But mostly, as has been mentioned, music exists to praise God. Like the psalms of King David of old, we, too, can praise our God through music; or like Moses who thanked God in song after being delivered from the Egyptian army: "Then sang Moses and the children of Israel this song unto the Lord, and spake, saying, I will sing unto the Lord, for he hath triumphed gloriously. . ." (Exodus 15:1), we can praise, glorify, and worship through music.

While we are in the attitude of praise, music can penetrate our minds, affect our hearts, and change our behaviors. We know that God is a lover of good music and that music is a witness to the power of God. Praiseworthy music has the power to embed words deeply into our minds, to capture the beauty of God's grace and love, and to evoke feelings beyond the range of ordinary words. Praising through music is an outward manifestation of our gratitude to God for all things. As Christians, we would be wise to follow the counsel of the Apostle Paul, "Let the word of Christ dwell in you richly in all wisdom; teaching and admonishing one another in psalms and hymns and spiritual songs, singing with grace in your hearts to the Lord" (Colossians 3:16)

NOTES:

1. Russell M. Nelson, "The Power and Protection of Worthy Music" (Brigham Young University fireside address, May 4, 2008).

2. Karen Lynn Davidson, *Our Latter-Day Hymns* (Salt Lake City: Bookcraft, 1988), 30–31.

3. Patrick Kavanaugh, Spiritual Moments with the Great Composers (Grand Rapids: Zondervan Publishing House, 1995).

4. Michael F. Moody, "I Have a Question," *Ensign*, December 1976, 56.

5. Merrill J. Bateman, "The Power of Hymns," *Ensign*, July 1998, 16.

6. Russell M. Nelson, "The Power and Protection of Worthy Music" (Brigham Young University fireside address, May 4, 2008).

7. Boyd K. Packer, "The Arts and the Spirit of the Lord," (Brigham Young University fireside address, February 1976).

8. Maruice J. E. Brown, *Schubert: A Critical Biography* (London: Macmillan, 1958), 45.

9. Oswald Doughty, *A Victorian Romantic: Dante Gabriel Rossetti* (London: Frederick Muller, 1949), 136.

10. Patrick Kavanaugh, *Spiritual Moments with the Great Composers* (Grand Rapids: Zondervan Publishing House, 1995).

AT BARTOK'S FORMER RESIDENCE in Budapest, Hungary, David stands with the statue of Bela Bartok.

DR. HATCH BOWING with his gifted students at the conclusion of their concert in the John Calvin University Performance Hall in Geneva, Switzerland.

DAVID'S CONCERT AT Izumisano Concert Hall in Osaka, Japan.

VALENTINE CONCERT—SYMPHONY HALL—SALT LAKE CITY
February 11, 1995
SELECT WINNERS AND FINALISTS
(from 1978–1994)
of the
GINA BACHAUER INTERNATIONAL PIANO COMPETITION
Dr. David Glen Hatch is the ninth pianist from the left side
(Photo by: Rolf W. Kay)

DAVID IN CONCERT in Ljubljana, Slovenia.

QUARTET FINALE of Dr. Hatch and students at their Fundacion Canal Concert Hall performance in Madrid, Spain.

AFTER HIS CONCERT PERFORMANCE, David enjoys the beautiful fountain at the Conservatory of Music in Kiev, Ukraine.

VISITING WITH JAMES GOETTSCHE, Pope Benedict XVI's personal Vatican organist, after David's Ghione Theatre concert in Rome, Italy.

DAVID WITH BUDAPEST SYMPHONY CONDUCTOR, Mátyás Antál, during a concerto rehearsal.

DR. HATCH'S CONSERVATORY master class presentation in Donetsk, Ukraine.

DAVID STANDING with the Franz Liszt monument outside the
Liszt Academy of Music in Budapest, Hungary.

DR. HATCH at the prestigious Shanghai Conservatory of Music
where he presented a master class and concert.

ATTENDING THE FINALS of the prestigious Tchaikovsky International Piano Competition in the Great Hall of the world-famous Moscow Conservatory of Music.

DR. HATCH WORKING WITH a student during his master class at the Second Annual World Piano Conference in Novi Sad, Serbia, 2010.

DR. HATCH VISITING the grave of Frédéric Chopin with his students in Paris, France.

AWAITING THE FIRST FINALIST to appear on stage during the Tchaikovsky International Piano Competition in the Great Hall of the Moscow Conservatory of Music.

DAVID PLAYING THE GORGEOUS Steinway Concert Grand in the rotunda of Steinway Hall in New York City.

DAVID RECORDING with the Budapest Symphony Orchestra in Hungarian Radio Symphony Hall for an internationally promoted CD.

WITH HIS TRANSLATOR, Dr. Hatch works with a conservatory student in his Santiago, Chile, master class.

DAVID STANDING OUTSIDE the Crystal Cathedral in Garden Grove, California, following his internationally televised Christmas performance with the cathedral orchestra.

AS AN INVITED GUEST ARTIST, Dr. Hatch presents a lecture/performance at the Isidor Bajic Music School during the Second Annual World Piano Conference, 2010.

DR. HATCH AND HIS STUDENTS visiting the world-renowned Chopin Conservatory of Music in Warsaw, Poland.

DAVID AND THE CONSUL OF MONACO, Daniele Biancheri-Quintana, following his V.I.P. Concert in Santiago, Chile.

FOLLOWING DR. HATCH'S MASTER CLASS with these students at the Second Annual World Piano Conference in Novi Sad, Serbia.

AT A PRESS CONFERENCE for David's charity concert in Piura, Peru.

DAVID BEING HONORED by the mayor of Siracusa and the President of the Province following one of his concerts in Sicily.

ALEXANDER KANEVSKY, director of the Prokofiev School, and David together at the school entrance in Moscow, Russia.

DAVID IN PERFORMANCE at the recital hall of the renowned Villa Bertramka in Prague, Czech Republic.

GREETING CHURCH MEMBERS and investigators following a stake musical fireside in Buenos Aires, Argentina.

DR. HATCH with his award-winning Japanese student in Tokyo.

DAVID WITH HALL ADMINISTRATORS and publicity personnel following his concert in Rio de Janeiro, Brazil.

SHANGHAI CONSERVATORY STUDENTS who played for Dr. Hatch's master class.

DAVID IN CONCERT at the University of Hawaii in Honolulu.

DR. HATCH AND SELECT STUDENTS following a performance exchange in Beijing, China.

AT THE "SOUND OF MUSIC" gazebo in the gardens of Hellbrun Palace on the outskirts of Salzburg, Austria, David gives a performance for tourists.

DAVID AND LIFE-SIZE STATUE of Norwegian composer Edvard Grieg at Troldhaugen (Grieg's homestead).

DAVID PERFORMING A V.I.P. CHARITY CONCERT for Coaniquem, a humanitarian organization specializing in the treatment of pediatric burn victims. Of the hundreds attending were twenty embassies and several government officials.

AT MICHELANGELO SQUARE overlooking Florence, Italy, following David's concert for the city's cultural arts series.

AFTER DAVID'S MATINEE performance in the Troldsalen
Concert Hall, Bergen, Norway.

DAVID, CONDUCTOR VLADIMIR SIRENKO, and the Ukrainian National
Symphony during a Prokofiev concerto performance at the Mariinsky Palace
Amphitheater in Kiev, Ukraine.

DR. HATCH AND HIS STUDENTS who participated
on his concert in Osaka, Japan.

DR. HATCH AND STUDENT QUARTET performers in a finale of
Sousa's Stars & Stripes Forever, at his concert in Madrid, Spain.

REHEARSING FOR a concert performance in Madrid, Spain.

FORMER AWARD WINNERS of the Gina Bachauer International Piano Competition in concert at Abravanel Hall, Salt Lake City, Utah. (David is the eighth performer from the left.)

In a performance of Prokofieff's Third Piano Concerto during the Ft. Collins National Concerto Competition. Dr. Hatch's student was announced as the second place winner.

Selected as Utah's artist to represent Steinway's specialty pianos, David performed on the unique instruments in the lobby of Symphony Hall for a Channel Five News broadcast during Salt Lake City's Winter Olympic Games.

DR. HATCH WITH STUDENT Jackie Hunt (center)—Miss Utah, 2001, a top ten finalist in the Miss America pageant, Atlantic City, New Jersey.

DR. HATCH VISITING MACHU PICCHU with his students during a concert tour of Peru and Chile.

JOANNE BAKER, A DISTINGUISHED PIANO
PEDAGOGUE in the United States and David's teacher
and mentor at the UMKC Conservatory of Music.

SYDNEY, AUSTRALIA
(Sydney, Newcastle, Brisbane, Cairnes,
Australia & Hobart, Tasmania Tour 2002)

DR. HATCH AND SELECT STUDENTS enjoying Sydney Harbor during his
international concert tour to Australia.

DR. HATCH AND STUDENTS VISITING the famous Christ the Redeemer Monument in Rio de Janeiro, Brazil, while performing in parts of South America.

DAVID WITH U.S. SENATOR ORRIN HATCH of Utah and several well-known LDS Artists following their Bass Concert Hall performance in Ft. Worth, Texas.

DR. HATCH AND STUDENTS visiting the Parthenon in Athens during a concert tour of Greece and Sicily.

APPRECIATING THE AUDIENCE at the conclusion of Dr. Hatch's concert at the new performance venue, Teatro Municipal de Las Condes, in Santiago, Chile.

DAVID DURING a studio recording session.

FIRST ANNIVERSARY PATRIOTIC CONCERT for families of 9/11 victims at Arlington National Cemetery Amphitheater, Washington, DC.

DAVID'S CONCERT FINALE at the ACS Performing Arts Theater in Athens, Greece.

HATCH, CONSERVATORY DIRECTOR (far right), and students who performed in his master class—Sophia, Bulgaria.

GREETING AUDIENCE MEMBERS and signing autographs following David's concert performance in Sao Paulo, Brazil.

DR. HATCH AND SELECT STUDENTS entering Scotland during his international summer concert tour of the British Isles.

DAVID STANDING BESIDE the Tchaikovsky monument at the entrance of the Moscow Conservatory of Music.

AT THE PROKOFIEV MUSEUM, in the Ukrainian village of Krasne, Prokofiev's birthplace, David sits in the lap of the enormous, bronze statue of Sergei Prokofiev.

DAVID'S PIANO PROFESSOR at Brigham Young University and lifetime mentor, Dr. Paul C. Pollei, Founder/Artistic Director of the Gina Bachauer International Foundation Competition.

DR. HATCH WITH STUDENT AMMON BRATT, second place winner in the Four Corners Regional Piano Competition, Durango, Colorado.

DAVID STANDING in his performance and teaching studio in Orem, Utah.

Chapter Seven

THE POWER OF MUSIC TO UPLIFT

To uplift is to raise, to elevate, to lift. Consequently, the power of music to uplift raises or exalts to spiritual or emotional heights. Music nourishes our spirits by lifting our hearts with courage. Many will remember the heartache of the Prophet Joseph Smith in Carthage Jail the night and morning prior to his martyrdom. Joseph asked his friend and brother in the gospel John Taylor, who was with him at the time, to sing the hymn *A Poor Wayfaring Man of Grief*, a touching hymn about the Savior. In fact, he asked him to sing it several times.

On June 27, 1844, Joseph Smith was in jail in Carthage, Illinois, with his brother Hyrum, John Taylor, and Willard Richards. Hostility was growing, mobs threatened violence, and the prisoners knew their lives were in danger. John Taylor told of the scene in the jail cell:

> All of us felt unusually . . . languid, with a remarkable depression of spirits. In consonance with those feelings, I sang a song that had lately been introduced into Nauvoo entitled, 'A Poor Wayfaring Man of Grief.' . . . After a lapse of some time, Brother Hyrum requested me again to sing that song. I replied, 'Brother Hyrum, I do not feel like singing'; when he remarked, 'Oh, never mind; commence singing, and you will get the spirit of it.' At his request I did so.[1]

Journals from Church history evidence that this beautiful music calmed the Prophet Joseph's troubled spirit, soothed his soul, and comforted him as he approached his impending death.

This musical choice by the Prophet Joseph becomes a fitting example to us all, that our Heavenly Father has blessed each of us with an ability to use our spiritual judgment in selecting the best artistic atmosphere in which to become engaged. Our musical decisions will either uplift us or move us slowly away from the Spirit. In this case, where the Prophet was facing the most disturbing time in his life, he selected music that would provide him with peace and assurance as he encountered this grim last evening of his mortal life.

Hymns are an essential part of our church meetings and will certainly uplift us spiritually in our daily lives. They invite the Spirit of the Lord and often do this quicker than anything else we may do. Elder Jay E. Jensen tells the following story:

> Two missionaries teaching an older couple in their home in Peru were interrupted by the arrival of the couple's son, his wife, and three children. The elders explained who they were and what they were doing. The son was suspicious of the missionaries, resulting in an awkward moment. The junior companion prayed silently, "Heavenly Father, what do we do?" The impression came to sing. They sang "I Am a Child of God." The Spirit touched the hearts of this family of five. Instead of two converts, all seven became members, influenced initially by a hymn.
>
> …The hymns of the Restoration carry with them the spirit of conversion. They came as a result of sacrifice. Hymns like "Praise to the Man," "Come, Come, Ye Saints," "Ye Elders of Israel," "We Thank Thee, O God, for a Prophet," "Redeemer of Israel," and many others reinforce the great truths of the Restoration—such as the divinity of the Father and the Son, the plan of redemption, revelation, latter-day scriptures, the gathering of Israel, the holy priesthood, and ordinances and covenants. These nourishing hymns create an atmosphere that invites the Spirit, which leads us to conversion.[2]

Joseph Addison (a contemporary of J. S. Bach)—English essayist, poet, and playwright—said, "Music is the only sensual gratification in which mankind may indulge to excess without injury to their moral or religious feelings."[3] If that were true in his day, it is certainly not in ours. In our day, degrading music is widely available! This degenerate music contains hard rock beats and melodic and harmonic discord with lyrics depicting drug use, blatant immorality, violence, drinking, alternative lifestyles, Satan worship, and so on. There is especially great danger in music that is skillfully written and performed but can present to our minds deceitful and destructive messages from Lucifer, the father of lies. While prophet of the Church, President Heber J. Grant warned that "the more beautiful the music by which false doctrine is taught, the more dangerous it becomes."[4]

Furthermore, music that promotes evil can literally destroy the individual. Elder Boyd K. Packer cautioned, "Music, once innocent, now is often used for wicked purposes. In our day music itself, has been corrupted. Music can—by its tempo, by its beat, by its dissonance, and by its intensity—dull the spiritual sensitivity of men . . . young people, you cannot afford to fill your mind with the unworthy hard music of our day."[5]

Music is an important and powerful part of life. It can be an influence for good that helps us draw closer to Heavenly Father. However, it can also be used for wicked purposes. Unworthy music may seem harmless, but it can have evil effects on your mind and spirit. Choose carefully the music you listen to. Pay attention to how you feel when you are listening to it. Don't listen to music that drives away the Spirit, encourages immorality, glorifies violence, uses foul or offensive language, or promotes Satanism or other evil practices.[6]

In a Priesthood Bulletin in August, 1973, the First Presidency stated this counsel:

> Through music, man's ability to express himself extends beyond the limits of the spoken language in both subtlety and power. Music can be used to exalt and inspire or to carry messages of degradation and destruction. It is therefore important that as Latter-day Saints we at all times apply the principles of the gospel and seek the guidance of the Spirit in selecting the music with which we surround ourselves.[7]

These inspired words of that First Presidency encouraging each of us to surround ourselves with music that exalts, inspires, and uplifts, coupled with wise counsel of other Brethren presented here, reminds me of a thrilling performance invitation I received several years ago. Prior to the death of Gordon B. Hinckley, fifteenth president of The Church of Jesus Christ of Latter-day Saints, at age ninety-seven, it was my privilege to perform with the Mormon Youth Symphony in the prominent and legendary seven-thousand-seat Tabernacle on Temple Square in Salt Lake City, Utah, built between the years 1864 and 1867. On that appointed concert evening, the Tabernacle was packed!

Having recorded a CD with these accomplished musicians a few years earlier, I was invited to perform some of those recorded selections on this live concert program. It was a breathtaking sight to walk out to the piano positioned at the front center of the stage before a full house of five thousand audience members. After taking my entrance bow, my levels of energy and enthusiasm became even greater when I noticed that seated only ten rows from the piano were the prophet and Sister Hinckley! What an honor it was to have that opportunity to perform for the President of the Church and his sweet wife.

Afterward, President Hinckley, expressed with emotion that his favorite piece on the program had been my piano/orchestral arrangement of Janice Kapp Perry's *We'll Bring The World His Truth (Army of Helaman)*—one of the inspired LDS contemporary songs of our time. The melody and lyrics of this selection had touched him deeply with sincere meaning, for it had caused him to reflect with great love on the thousands of missionaries he had called to serve the children of our Heavenly Father throughout the world.

This incident with the prophet being moved and uplifted by my performance of Sister Perry's music reminds me of a similar occurrence where this music touched many hearts of the Saints attending a sacrament meeting in Bergen, Norway, two years later. The day following my successful Saturday matinee performance at the famous Troldsalen (Trolls Hall) concert hall (built in 1985 on the wooded property adjacent to Edvard Grieg's famous Norwegian homestead, Troldhaugen), these Norwegian Saints sang this same *Army of Helaman* as their closing sacrament meeting hymn with more fervor, intensity, and emotion than I had ever before experienced from any congregation of church members anywhere! Each of us in that quaint chapel could feel the Spirit of the Lord in profound abundance. Later, I learned that the majority of these Norwegian Saints were converts who had been taught and blessed by the service of full-time missionaries in their country. Some had sons serving in the mission field at that time, which brought their emotions very close to the surface. As a consequence, how deeply moving it was to be sitting in that spirit-filled room and to witness these precious, humble Saints being greatly uplifted by this powerful music while singing with tears of joy the following words that had become most meaningful in their personal lives:

> We have been born, as Nephi of old,
> To goodly parents who love the Lord.
> We have been taught, and we understand,
> That we must do as the Lord commands.
>
> We are as the Army of Helaman,
> We have been taught in our youth.
> And we will be the Lord's missionaries
> To bring the world His truth.

While leaving that church meeting on that warm and beautiful Sunday afternoon, it came forcibly to my mind that I would never be the same! From the spiritual edification I felt during that closing music, I know that the power of inspirational music has the ability to uplift mankind to soaring heights. It certainly did for me!

Daily life can be stressful. Problems and trials are inevitable. We are surrounded with issues of concern ranging from small to gigantic. Whatever may be our roles in life, each of us is exposed to economic, financial, personal, social, or emotional challenges. A father sometimes worries about how he can support his family financially. A student can have problems with consistent, heavy studies. An employed person can become discouraged with the daily burden that comes with daunting work assignments. Of course, there are often larger and more difficult issues than these—sickness, terminal illness, death, bankruptcy, or other serious problems that can be life-altering.

Many of us are regularly consumed by sad feelings and emotions. Sadness can bring negative effects to our lives—more pain and sorrows. Although music cannot solve our problems, it can help us escape sad thoughts and refocus on good ones. Good music does for us what almost nothing else can do! It has the mysterious power to lift sad souls, to feed our inner life, to raise our consciousness, to enrich the spirit, to generate memories, to bind wounds, to stir the imagination, to positively affect health, and to infuse the being with joy. Listening to music is therapeutic in managing problems by diverting negative energies, making it easier to cope with daily stress and concerns. Music gives us strength and can be our best friend!

Some of the greatest, most exceptional music of the masters has survived and been brought forth providentially through some of the hardest, toughest, and saddest times known to man. Such was the case in Poland, a revered country that brought to the world stellar musicians—Ignacy Paderewski (1860–1941), the Polish pianist, composer, diplomat, politician, and the second Prime Minister of the Republic of Poland; and more importantly, one of the most brilliant and ingenious composers and pianists of all time, Frederic Chopin (1810–1849).

My performance experiences in Poland during June 2003 relate perfectly with the contents of this chapter concerning the power of music to uplift. After spending our first day learning from our knowledgeable tour guide, Yolanta Postrzygacy, the daunting history of her Polish people from the time of Chopin through the Second World War, we understood more clearly how this phenomenal musical culture could, through the will of the human spirit, rise from ashes.

Our first memorable and uplifting happening was attending a Sunday afternoon piano concert in the famous Woliński (Królewskie) Park. The stunning concert of Chopin's music was shared by outstanding student pianists from the renowned Warsaw Conservatory of Music. The atmosphere for such an occasion was ideal in this beautiful park that exhibits the well-known monument of Chopin sitting under a willow tree, as a symbol of Polish resistance to communism. This towering memorial stands beautifully beside a large reflecting pool of water that is surrounded by myriad deep-red rose gardens.

Inspiration followed while lecturing and performing to a large audience on the stage platform of the eminent Holy Trinity Lutheran Cathedral, where a young fifteen-year-old Frederic Chopin himself had played almost two hundred years ago! But, most notably, two additional occasions enthusiastically confirmed music's great power to uplift. Interestingly, the lifting spirit was generated by the historical background from which the genius of Chopin's music sprang!

First, a morning spent in Żelazowa Wola—a tiny countryside village (population 65) and birthplace of Chopin—was completely elevating. Twenty-nine miles from Warsaw, we basked in its picturesque Masovian landscape and numerous winding streams surrounded by willows, hillocks, and flying storks (Poland's national bird). We witnessed the exact spot where Chopin was born, located in the preserved annex of the former home of the Chopin family, which is surrounded by a park where concerts of his music are given in the summertime by pianists from all over the world.

Totally exhilarating was visiting the world-renowned Warsaw Conservatory of Music and Chopin's apartment, where he wrote many of his greatest compositions—including his piano concertos and op. 10 études—before moving to Paris at age 20. While in Paris, Chopin became involved with the French aristocracy, teaching many of their children—approximately 150 over the twenty years until his death.

We perused his original manuscripts and listened in awe to parts of his two concertos composed in this one-room studio, which created an atmosphere that suddenly became ethereal, solemn, and mesmerizing. It seemed inconceivable that we were in this uplifting place where Chopin had lived, composed, and performed recitals for small groups on his two rented Pleyel and Erard grand pianos.

Like many of us, I listen to music to lift my mood when I'm down or to brighten an already radiant day. As elevating music raises the spirit of man, it is highly beneficial to our emotional, physical, and spiritual well-being to reliably take advantage of its power to release anxiety in today's noisy, high-stress world and to encourage the downhearted among us. When we listen to good and praiseworthy music, we will feel happy, enchanted, inspired, wistful, excited, empowered, comforted, and heroic. Few would question the power of music to uplift and rejuvenate.

As we learned from our inspirational morning spent in Chopin's flat in Warsaw, motivating and invigorating moments can be ours by relaxing and reflecting upon the day's events within a lush, comforting, soundscape of music drawn from various world traditions.

As listeners in the twentieth century, there is a ubiquitous treasure-trove of stylistic choices we can make! Wholesome, heartening music can come from medieval, renaissance, and classical Europe, Celtic, American folk tunes and spirituals, popular music, jazz, ragtime, dixieland, Broadway musical, film music, Christian inspirational, and a variety of other genres.

Often, not only do we not recognize the great impact of uplifting music in our lives, but many musicians also rarely comprehend the elevating influence of their musical talents upon others. For instance, one summer concert tour had me performing throughout the British Isles. I'll never forget the outcome of my performance in London for a large non-denominational audience, hosted by the Wandsworth Stake of The Church of Jesus Christ of Latter-day Saints. Of this event and unbeknownst to me, a newspaper article written by a music critic appeared in print the following morning. Then, to my complete surprise, this same music review had been published months later in the Church's *Liahona* magazine in Europe with a copy for me arriving in the mailbox at my home in the States! This was my first time reading it. The following is a condensed version of the review.

HATCH EXPLODES AT STAKE CENTER

Members of the religious community who gathered on Wednesday evening, 14 June at the Wandsworth Stake Center of The Church of Jesus Christ of Latter-day Saints ... were treated to a dazzling display of virtuosity on the pianoforte by David Glen Hatch, a pianist who has generated a large following of listeners worldwide. Despite suffering from jetlag, Dr. Hatch delighted the audience with a programme of gems from the classical repertoire. There was such depth of interpretation that you could have heard a pin drop.

Hatch's masterful experience of programming was completed by a powerful yet sensitive rendition of his touching arrangement of "Come, Come, Ye Saints" which brought the evening to a moving finale. The audience responded with a standing ovation which the artist truly deserved. Those who were unable to attend this event missed an uplifting musical evening that moved many present to tears.[8]

Music is music, and though we may speak or write a million words about it, nothing will change the fact that in the end it must stand or fall by its ability to uplift us, to move us, to stimulate us, to entertain, to perplex, to illuminate, to delight, or to enlarge our capacity for spiritual experience. As beneficiaries of these capacities of music in our lives, however, I deem it important that we have a keen understanding of our responsibility as listeners.

It is only too easy to be seduced by the sound of music without making any attempt to grasp its purpose. Classical music, for instance, often requires great skill and understanding. A great composer is a master of a highly specialized language, and it is silly to imagine that we are likely to comprehend that language unless we are prepared to make some effort commensurate with the intensity with which it states its message. For example, we live in an age when music is in danger of being devalued, since much of our listening is done through machines.

Nothing can reproduce the emotional power of the live performance, although radios, televisions, iPods, CD players, DVD players, and studio audio equipment do not complain if we treat them rudely. These remain sufficiently impersonal as we talk while they are playing. We adjust the volume to our convenience of the moment. When the telephone rings, we may cut off Mozart in mid-flight. While there may be no other argument in favor of preserving live artists, it seems to me that at least they justify their existence by ensuring that we do not forget our etiquette during their performances; though we may dislike the music, we respect the presence of the performer.

Looking at the audience at most classical music concerts in the United States today, one sees a crowd that is largely middle aged, verging on the geriatric. But, in fact, it is refreshing to note that more young people today are playing classical instruments than ever before, according to conservatory enrollments. Even more surprising is that the classical music world has never been healthier, with all ages returning to the genius musical compositions of the past masters whether as listeners or performers! Common reasoning that is given as an explanation for this music's rebirth is that it is educationally promoting, highly motivational, and deeply enriching.

Moreover, I find it appropriate to suggest some of the characteristics that I believe will assist us in becoming better listeners, as these will enhance the power of music to uplift. In general terms, an effective listener will appreciate every moment in the composition that has some special significance, not in an analytical sense, but as part of the whole interwoven tapestry of music. As the work progresses, an involved listener will respond to every sudden twist of harmony, to the subtleties of the scoring, to the deliberate balance of phrase against phrase. He will know precisely when the composer is stretching the musical parameters of his time, and appreciate those brief moments when he can detect the first signs of ultimate maturity. The joys of the performance itself will be incidental, a shared love and appreciation communicated to the listener from the musical presentation of the artist.

Accordingly, during my concert tour to three South American cities—Buenos Aires, Sao Paulo, and Rio de Janeiro—not only were the cultural highlights in this land of warm, friendly people truly magnificent, but the acquisition of exceptional performance incidents delivered to respectfully attentive, sensitive, and engaged listeners gives credence to these viewpoints.

Following my Stake fireside in Buenos Aires, for instance, hundreds of emotionally-charged Argentine Saints were so moved by the distinct spirit present that evening that none wanted to leave the building. For two hours afterward, I visited with these humble followers of Christ, each radiating love and gratitude for my presence and the musical fireside message they claimed had been most spiritually uplifting. And, as in this case, the Spirit can communicate to the heart through music without the listener necessarily realizing the various musical components involved in the composition. One special sister handed me a note she had written in English, which communicated her thoughts and feelings of that uplifting evening. It read:

Dear Brother Hatch,

My name is Silvia Rodrigo. My five daughters and I have been members of the Church during the last ten years. The first present we received from our missionaries besides the Book of Mormon, was a CD of wonderful music, beautiful arrangements of our dear and sweet hymns. And during those ten years I have loved you even without knowing you. Today my Heavenly Father gave me a loving present—the opportunity of listening and watching you at the same time. Thank you for making this Sunday a most uplifting one. With all my love and my family's love, too.

To be honest, I was quite stunned after receiving several similar expressions of love for my music that evening since, for only the second time in my performance career, the available instrument in that chapel was an electronic Yamaha keyboard that did not produce adequate piano sound, sufficient volume, or a pedal mechanism amenable to the spiritual music performed. Having worked on the techno-instrument beforehand, I was very concerned that the spirit of the music would be lost, adversely affecting the spirit of the fireside. But when the Spirit of the Lord is present, miracles exist, no matter the adverse conditions!

Miraculously, while performing the first hymn arrangement, the electronic keyboard sounded like a legitimate instrument. Shocked with the obvious transformation in the sound and touch of the keyboard from how it had responded earlier left no doubt in my mind that God provides miracles in times of need. Never before or since has His presence been felt more abundantly than during this emotionally uplifting meeting in Argentina! Tears flowed freely throughout the chapel and from the permeating presence of the Spirit and love of Christ, all hearts and minds were elevated that evening.

It would be ungrateful of me if I neglected to mention that in addition to the marvelous performance opportunities, these musical tours also provide uplifting cultural highpoints. Those on this excursion included visiting Evita's sarcophagi and the famous La Boca district, enjoying the musical delights of a captivating Tango folklore show by Argentine professionals, and feeling the majesty of the powerful Iguassu Waterfalls on the border of Argentina and Brazil. After these visits and following a successful concert attended by six hundred individuals in the gargantuan city of Sao Paulo, Rio de Janeiro—our final destination—brought further elevating "highs." Music is the most wonderful way to spiritual realization, and there is no quicker or surer way of attaining spiritual perfection than through music.

It was quickly apparent that our tour guide in Rio di Janeiro, Sarah, was spiritually inclined. A very refined, kind, and special person, she spent several days showing us the renowned tourist attractions of Rio, including the spectacular hike and tram ride to the top of Corcovado (Hunchback) mountain to the massive, internationally acclaimed 150-meter tall "Cristo Redentor" (Christ the Redeemer) monument with its breathtakingly picturesque view below! With His arms outstretched and overlooking Rio, the magnitude of this site was completely inspirational!

From our quickly developing friendship with Sarah (due to spending many touring hours together), it became known that although a spiritual person, she was not a member of any church. Now, a person need not be religious to feel the spiritual power of music, for it reaches into a part of the human experience that has no ties to religious preferences. Sounds that literally vibrate through the physical bodies of both the musician and the listener have transformative qualities that contribute to the awakening and development of the mind to sublime states of spiritual awareness. In an instant, music can uplift any soul and awaken within a spirit of prayer, compassion, and love. It is my belief, therefore, that the Spirit prompted me to invite Sarah to my classical concert the next evening to be held in the spacious cultural hall of the largest LDS building in the city.

Surprised but excited to see her enter with the numerous other concertgoers, I immediately introduced her to the stake Relief Society president, who quickly picked up on the "missionary opportunity." For the next ninety minutes she sat with Sarah, who afterward expressed to her that the music had spiritually renewed her in such a way that it created intrigue with our religion. She had many questions, and a rapid conversation ensued.

When I appeared from the dressing room after the performance, Sarah gushed over my playing, expressly detailing her favorite classical pieces and confessed that she had been moved to tears during the touching encore number, my chime arrangement of *Silent Night* (it was holiday time, though summer in South America).

The next morning on the tour bus, Sarah inquired about the Book of Mormon that had been mentioned by Church members at the concert the prior evening. I became enthusiastic, since we had already planned to give her a copy of the book as a gift upon our departure. I always try to travel with Books of Mormon in the languages of my performance areas. Sarah was visibly touched, expressed gratitude, and gave hugs when receiving two of my inspirational CDs and the Portuguese edition of the book with signatures and short notes of appreciation from our group written inside the front cover.

Aware of our guide's interest in the Church and of her spiritual tendencies, I asked the stake Relief Society President to please fellowship Sarah and to have the missionaries contact her immediately. Throughout the rest of that year, I wondered about her progress with the missionaries and possible acceptance of the restored gospel. To my joy, after sending a Christmas card the subsequent December to that president, a glorious response was returned—Sarah had been baptized, along with her daughter! Sometimes, from such associations derived from the power of uplifting classical music, lives are forever changed.

Personally, I know something of this revival of inspiring music of the masters as I've observed the expansion of this phenomenon from the time when my own international concerting began up through the present. During my high school years at age seventeen, I competed in a national music audition and was selected to participate with America's Youth in Concert, which provided my first performance opportunities at two of America's most prestigious venues—Carnegie Hall in New York City, and the Kennedy Center for the Performing Arts in Washington, DC—as well as several renowned concert venues in Europe. These thrilling performance experiences sparked my initial passion for travel and a ravenous desire to achieve a concert career as my life's profession.

My piano repertoire for the concerts at Carnegie Hall and the Kennedy Center included Beethoven's *Sonata op. 31, no. 3*, several Rachmaninoff *Preludes* from both *Opus 23* and *Opus 32*, and all of the Liebeslieder Waltzes of Johannes Brahms as accompanist for "America's Youth Choir"—exhilarating and uplifting performances for one so young!

Nostalgic memories of performing in the 2,804-seat, five-level Isaac Stern Hall, flood my mind still today. Forever uplifting to me was spending time walking through the horseshoe-shaped lobbies of all levels of this prestigious hall, perusing the walls adorned with autographed portraits and memorabilia of hundreds of the world's leading artists who had performed there. It was an inspiration to see the photos of Tchaikovsky, Paderewski, Rachmaninoff, Hoffman, Toscanini, Horowitz, Rubinstein, Cliburn, Caruso, Callas, Sills, Casals, Godowsky, and Kreisler. That occasion of being selected to perform on that stage steeped with such stellar musical history became, for me, a highly motivating and captivating honor.

A venerable and amusing story that has become part of the folklore of the hall is worthy of mention. Arthur Rubinstein, one of the greatest pianists in history, was once approached by a young man in the street near Carnegie Hall who asked, "Pardon me sir, how do I get to Carnegie Hall?" Rubinstein replied, "Practice, practice, practice!"

Equally encouraging and energizing was performing that same piano program at the Kennedy Center for the Performing Arts, located in our nation's capital on the Potomac River. This esteemed Center, which opened in 1971, continues today to produce and present theater, dance, ballet, orchestral, chamber, jazz, popular, folk music, and multi-media performances for all ages. From this illustrious performance beginning that exposed a young man to the exceptional power of music to uplift and enrich the soul, there is little wonder that I would continue the pursuit of a lifelong music career!

Music study can be a child's most important extracurricular activity, because it helps him in many facets of life. Along with music study in general, piano training builds physical skills and develops mental focus with an ennobling quality to uplift the spirit at the same time. In my opinion, therefore, there is no other activity that integrates all three aspects of humanness nor is there anything more effective than playing music to build wholesome, healthy, positive human beings. Of course, certain genres of music uplift the spirit more than do others. As an example, from my extensive background with classical music, it is rather easy for me to provide specifics within this style of music as examples of its capacity to uplift.

The prodigious music of Mozart is calm and elegant—masterful and heartening music to which to listen. Vivaldi also tends towards elegance, with occasional hints of Italian passion in this former monk's music. For those whose spirits are raised by drama, emotion, and romance, the music of Beethoven is unbeatable. Franz Schubert's music is rooted firmly in the Romantic period with superior and beautifully lifting melodies that easily produce moods of peace and comfort. Brahms and Wagner add to the scope, drama, and richness of the classical period, though listeners to Wagner will need more patience. Those whose spirits soar with the music of the Romantic period will find their spirits greatly elevated with the euphoric compositions of Frederic Chopin and Franz Liszt.

For me, the classy and gorgeous music of Tchaikovsky greatly raises my moods! His writing encompassed a fine line between his Romantic penchant for expression and the demands of classical structure. This delicate balancing act—between heart and head, emotion and reason, release and control, Russian expressive content and German Technique—is a key to his music that elevates the soul to heights of grandeur.

Twentieth-century classical music tends to be a bit more jarring and atonal. Consequently, it is not usually the type of music to which one would listen to improve the mood. Going back in time, surely the spirits of many individuals are raised while listening to the compositional genius of Johann Sebastian Bach with his patterns of sound, complicated melodies, and beautiful complexity. Naturally, that which has been mentioned here only scratches the surface of what is readily available musically to improve our lives and daily dispositions, but herein is an excellent start!

Speaking of music that is uplifting, I am reminded of another personal and inspirational happening that took place a few years ago during an extraordinary concert tour of Spain in the cities of Madrid, Barcelona, Granada, and Malaga. My concert in Madrid, however, was the tour highlight, as the aftermath in that new hall packed to the brim with a crowd of enthusiastic Spaniards is one I shall ever remember.

Months earlier, I had received an invitation from several of Madrid's city officials to present a concert celebrating that city's new contemporary concert hall, Fundación Canal de Isabel II. Here, for me, was vast artist exposure for the first time in this magnificent country. The performance, which included professionally printed programs as part of the city's "Cultural Arts Series," was also televised live throughout the country on its national television network.

It was an exhilarating feeling to watch as the highly energized audience poured into the hall and overflowed into standing room only—shoulder-to-shoulder in balcony aisles and into the venue's foyer, where the program could be viewed on a television monitor. During that evening concert, five television cameramen recorded the program from varied hall locations with some equipment in close proximity to the piano and angled toward the keyboard and performer—a situation that can sometimes be very nerve-racking!

Following my encores and an arousing piano quartet arrangement of Sousa's *Stars and Stripes Forever* performed on two seven-foot-long Yamaha grand pianos with three of my gifted students, the audience erupted into thunderous applause, with outbursts of praise from audience members and with ushers running to the stage to present gorgeous flower bouquets, all during a ten-minute standing ovation. The rush of adrenaline I felt during those moments not only caused my spirit to soar, but the concertgoers were ecstatic from the music! From the generous expressions of joy and enthusiasm for my performance shared by these passionate people, it became apparent that, of a surety, music does possess the magical power to lift, boost, and revitalize the soul of man.

In addition to this power of classical music, there is nothing like inspirational Christian music to uplift and empower mankind. There are times in our lives when only this music is able to reach the deepest, innermost part of our hearts. The influence of inspired music on society can be clearly seen from modern history. Journal entries indicate that only music could help Thomas Jefferson write the Declaration of Independence. At a time when he was having difficulty finding the right wording for a certain part of that text, he would play Christian music on his violin to receive inspiration. The music helped his mind to recognize the perfect words to use— removing them from his brain to the paper.

This reminds me of performance events that taught me this value of sacred and inspirational music. While serving as a young LDS missionary in the Pennsylvania Harrisburg Mission—which was presided over by the incredibly gifted Church leader and late general authority, Elder Hugh W. Pinnock—I learned early on of the power of music to uplift. On numerous occasions during that time, it was noticed while sharing such music that repeatedly tears would roll down cheeks—not because of pain but rather from joy. Inspiring, ennobling music has that special element that transports God's children to a much higher plane.

Following my classical recital at Pennsylvania State University, a physics professor, Dr. Phillip Zettler-Seidel, also an accomplished pianist, was quoted in the *DuBois Courier Express* the following day: "Of the many piano concerts of international artists to appear on this campus over the years, Elder Hatch's is one of the most impressive."

Fast becoming an excellent friend of mine, Dr. Zettler-Seidel, a German immigrant to this country, permitted me to practice on his grand piano at his home on my Monday preparation day each week. One morning, he entered the room where I sat drilling a Chopin Nocturne and flattered me with this high compliment, "Elder Hatch, yours is an impeccable musical style similar to the great Gieseking who I have heard many times in person!" Born in Lyon, France, in 1895, German pianist and composer Walter Gieseking was regarded as one of the finest interpreters of the music of Debussy and Chopin. I thanked the professor for his kind and generous words, though I certainly didn't agree!

Often visually touched by my music and enjoying our friendship over many months, the professor and his wife inquired about receiving the missionary discussions to learn more about our Church and the restored gospel! Although his wife died prematurely, Phillip, my newly found musical friend, later joined the Church, thrilled with the new spiritual life he had discovered in the restored gospel.

Shortly after that positive interaction and unique missionary opportunity in that part of the state, I received an invitation in a new area to participate in a concert event in the city of Kane, which became very enlightening. I was featured on a program with the newly crowned Miss Pennsylvania, Tina Marie Thomas of Lancaster, for an enthusiastic public crowded into the Kane High School auditorium. It was a successful musical evening of performances, and we both relished a most appreciative audience at the following reception. Learning from the press releases that I was a Mormon missionary currently serving in that area, several of the general public in that audience approached me and expressed how touched they had been with my music that evening. And, to my delight, several families personally invited me with my companion to teach our gospel message in their homes.

The following morning, a concert review in the local newspaper, *The Kane Republican*, read:

> David Glen Hatch stole the show Thursday evening in Kane Area Senior High School auditorium as the Kane Music Boosters Club presented its Second Annual "Evening of Music" Concert. Mr. Hatch, only 19 and a Mormon Elder, performed the brilliant Chopin Scherzo in B-Flat Minor, displayed an especially rousing rendition of the Sixth Hungarian Rhapsody by Franz Liszt, and finished with his own arrangement of Malotte's The Lord's Prayer each time receiving a standing ovation from the exuberant crowd. The current Miss Pennsylvania, Tina Marie Thomas, also performed well.

Miss Pennsylvania, a born-again Christian, sang several songs, including the one she had sung as a top-ten finalist in the Miss America Pageant that year: *Take My Hand, Precious Lord*. Having become good friends over a two-day period and learning backstage that evening of her devotion to her Protestant religion, I sent a referral—her name and address—to two of our fine Pennsylvania missionaries living in her area, who later taught her the discussions in her home. To this day, I have no idea the outcome of that missionary story, but I do know that before leaving Kane, Tina told me that from the power of my music that had lifted her spirit and filled her soul that night combined with my demeanor as a full-time ambassador for Christ, keen interest had been sparked within her to learn more about my church!

The power of music to uplift is genuinely magnificent! Not only can it elevate our moods, but it frequently provides unspoken sermons that touch us deeply. Those who listen to music that lifts will understand well the positive impact it has on the mind and spirit, as it will always bring with it joy and peace!

NOTES:

1. Karen Lynn Davidson, Our Latter-Day Hymns (Salt Lake City: Bookcraft, 1988), 57–58.

2. Jay E. Jensen, "The Nourishing Power of Hymns," *Ensign*, May 2007, 11–13.

3. *The Musician's Diary* (New York: McAfee Music, 1979), 213.

4. Michael Ballam, "Music's Great Power Can Uplift and Inspire—or Promote Evil," *LDS Church News*, August 10, 1991.

5. Boyd K. Packer, "Inspiring Music—Worthy Thoughts," *Ensign*, January 1974, 25, 28.

6. The Church of Jesus Christ of Latter-day Saints, "Music and Dancing," in For the Strength of Youth (Salt Lake City: Intellectual Reserve, 2001), 20.

7. Boyd K. Packer, "Inspiring Music—Worthy Thoughts," *Ensign*, January 1974, 28.

8. Helge Morklid, "Hatch Explodes at Stake Center," *Liahona*, December 2001, 15.

Chapter Eight

THE POWER OF MUSIC TO TEACH

"A song will outlive all sermons in the memory."

—H. Giles

From the beginning, my musical life as a young boy and up through the present has taught me two vital, eternal principles about music and teaching for which I'm grateful. First, music has power to teach in countless ways; and second, musicians have power to change lives through their inspired gifts of teaching.

My life has been blessed from being tutored from the lips of inspired master teachers. Many of them shaped my life and professional career in very meaningful ways. Over time, I learned firsthand the truth of the concept initiated by Plato, the classical Greek philosopher of centuries ago: "Music to the mind is as air to the body."[1] Helpful to this discussion will be providing information concerning my musical background, and particularly that of my exceptional musical genealogy in piano performance and pedagogy during the years of my career spent as a master teacher.

While in graduate school at the University of Missouri–Kansas City Conservatory of Music, I had the rare privilege of perfecting the *Brahms D Minor Piano Concerto* with my professor and piano chair, Joanne Baker. As one of the last living pianists with a direct pianistic line back to Brahms, each weekly lesson with Baker on this complex, exceptionally difficult, and stunning concerto for piano and orchestra was highly inspirational. Initially, however, a framework to this project is essential. After her college years, Professor Baker—who was teaching in Kansas City during 1948—auditioned and was accepted to study with master teacher Carl Friedberg, who served on the faculty of the Juilliard School in New York City, where he was recognized as one of the leading piano pedagogues in the world. That year, he had been hired by the University of Kansas City to work extensively with pre-selected, gifted students for summer study. Along with Baker, other important pianists chosen to study with Friedberg included Marian Jersild and Malcolm Frager, who became two of Friedberg's finest students.

Carl Friedberg (1872–1955) was internationally prominent as a concert artist and teacher in both Europe and America. A pupil of Clara Schumann and Johannes Brahms, Friedberg was known as a commanding link between the Classic-Romantic tradition and contemporary pianism. His superior intellectual accomplishments, combined with his artistic genius, provided an important source of inspiration, guidance, and encouragement for many pianists and teachers. Friedberg enjoyed teaching and coached many eminent pianists including Myra Hess, a famous international pianist, who was known to request lessons from Friedberg repeatedly during her visits to America.

As a gifted prodigy, Friedberg recalled his lessons with Clara Schumann and Johannes Brahms and shared exciting and specific musical information with my teacher, Joanne Baker. For instance, he disclosed to her that the Schumann home was frequently used for musical soirées, and described the joys of being there as a young man where he heard solo performances by Brahms and even served as page turner for the great composer/pianist during chamber music programs.

According to Baker, Friedberg possessed highly sensitive hearing, evoked creative interpretations through his use of imagery, and knew how to inspire confidence needed in performance. In general, his teaching incorporated the discussion of musical style, the production of beautiful tone and pianistic sound, meticulous technique, and the proper character required for each piece. This substantially valuable pedagogical information by Friedberg transferred beautifully to Baker's later teaching with her own students.

While I was working on the Brahms Concerto with Baker during various lessons, she would say to me, "David, in this particular passage, Friedberg told me that Brahms had envisioned the sound of light rain on a tin roof," or "Throughout this climax section, Brahms desired the sound of an army tank crossing a German border!" There were many times while working together on this magnificent composition that Baker would express disappointment that she hadn't written down all of Friedberg's reminiscences because she had forgotten many of the detailed instructions she had received from Brahms. However, she knew that she had absorbed many of these important pianistic traditions of this noble nineteenth-century pianism and passed them on to me and other students.

When I had mastered the rigorous composition after several months, Baker sent me to compete in various national and international concerto competitions, where I received numerous awards for my playing of Brahms. The most rewarding competition accolade came in being selected as a national finalist in the William C. Byrd Competition in Flint, Michigan. After my playing of those three significant movements, the adjudicators praised my exceptional Brahms interpretation and asked me to share with them more about Baker's extraordinary teaching techniques and of her impressive musical genealogy, since she was considered one of the finest piano pedagogues in the nation.

Decisively, my most thrilling performance of this concerto was with my hometown orchestra, the Utah Valley Symphony, after my return to Utah following those conservatory years in Kansas City. The reason is simple. While bowing to a standing ovation following the tempestuous last section and final chord of the third movement, my three adorable children at the time—Erika, age 7; Denise, age 6; and Ryan, age 5—hurried to the stage and greeted me with a bouquet of congratulatory balloons and hugs before the capacity audience. While adoring my small children during those special moments, I experienced an epiphany of sorts. A significant realization entered my mind that although our superior musical performances exhilarate, inspire, and move people emotionally, it is the gifted teaching and musical mentoring of the renowned and brilliant masters—performers, composers, and pedagogues of the past—that are to be revered.

Music is also used to teach the gospel and invites the Spirit into our most sacred meetings. The apostle Paul exhorted the Ephesian saints encouraging them to walk uprightly by "speaking to yourselves in psalms and hymns and spiritual songs, singing and making melody in your heart to the Lord" (Ephesians 5:19).

The power of music to teach the gospel is easily manifest through our hymns and other church music. Most importantly, music prepares our hearts and minds to hear, learn, and receive the gospel in our lives. Henry Wadsworth Longfellow once said, "Music is the language spoken by angels."[2]

The great hymn writers, particularly those who wrote of the restoration, provided lyrics that teach theologically and doctrinally sound principles. Similarly, music is powerful in teaching our children the gospel of Jesus Christ through inspired music for Primary and other youth meetings. It is always a moving experience to watch and listen to our little ones testify as they sing their music.

Sacred music has tremendous power to help us learn and live gospel principles. A sister was asked to talk to some youth in a seminary class about church music. Her first question to the youth was, "What were some of the lessons you were taught in Primary?" There was no response. Then she asked the students if they could remember any Primary songs. Many hands were raised, and the youth shared countless song titles. The sister wrote gospel principles on the chalkboard, and Primary songs and hymns were listed under each principle. Those young people quickly understood that music teaches the principles of the gospel, and songs and hymns—and the messages they teach—are remembered for years.

Last December, I experienced a similar occurrence, which demonstrated beautifully the power of music to teach. In fact, I was reminded that music can move us more than can the most powerful discourse. I had given a copy of my newest CD at the time, *My Redeemer Lives*—a compilation of my arrangements of the sacred Sacrament hymns of our Church associated with the Savior's life and atonement—to each of my current piano students as a Christmas gift.

It is recognized by many that pure and innocent little children often so close to the Spirit, will sometimes express personal feelings without reservation. A short time ago, the mother of two young prodigies of mine, who took this inspirational recording home from their Christmas performance class, shared with me an incident from their holiday season. The following is an excerpt taken directly from her journal:

> Tonight after I tucked Addie and Elle into bed, I turned on Dr. Hatch's new CD to help them go to sleep. Two children down, three to go! I went upstairs and was rocking Kate to sleep. Elle walked in and was really crying. She said, "Mom, I was just listening to that music and felt so warm in my soul. It really touched me and I just started crying and crying and can't stop. I looked over at Addie and just thought how I need to be nicer to her and be a better big sister." I held her and we talked about feeling the Spirit and how it motivates us to be better. I thanked her for sharing her sweet experience with me.

As Beethoven stated, "Music is a higher revelation than all wisdom and philosophy."[3] It is one of the greatest teaching tools! Music has been a source of inspiration, of protest, of wisdom, of intellect, and of emotion for millennia and touches every human being from infancy to adulthood. As has been explained in previous chapters, the power of musical sound can be the vehicle for expression of a wide variety of human emotions. But, not only does music move us emotionally, it also activates our intellect as a marvelous tool for learning.

Besides music's ability to teach the gospel in our homes and wherever Saints gather together, creating loving family relationships and feelings of togetherness as well as gospel fellowshipping, studies have shown that music possesses the power to develop the mind in numerous other matters of learning.

Certain types of music act directly on the body, prompting a calming state of mind that leads to faster learning. Music also stimulates the mind by increasing blood and oxygen flow to the brain and can reduce stress levels that inhibit learning. Music inspires emotion, which benefits long-term memory. And, as the universal language, music is uniquely adept at spanning cultural barriers and teaching ethnic traditions and values. Besides, it regularly takes on significant roles in teaching history, foreign language, sociology, political studies, geography, mathematics, science, body physiology and coordination, arts, and self-discipline. Music is invaluable to life's teaching process.

Specifically, music is math in its rhythmic aspects. Time is precisely subdivided into small increments that must be identified spontaneously from the musical notation. Music teaches foreign language. The international music language is, of course, Italian. However, other countries (such as France and Germany) publish musical terms in their own languages. Students are then exposed to foreign languages and learn many ways to express the same thing. It is a fact that text is more easily remembered when set to music. For example, virtually everyone knows the French version of *Are You Sleeping?* Here again it is stressed that music is the universal language communicating to the world at large.

Music teaches history. Human history and musical history co-existed through the ages with the following recognized musical periods: medieval (450–1450), renaissance (1450–1600), baroque (1600–1750), classical (1750–1810), romantic (1800–1890), and twentieth-century, which includes impressionism (1890 to present).The music of each period expresses the times of which it is born.

Music teaches geography and understanding of different cultures. The emotional makeup of a people is expressed in its music. Many classical composers produced music that exhibited specific feelings about their nationality by often incorporating existing folk music idioms in their writing.

Music also teaches scientific principles of acoustics, including sound intensity, tone quality, changes in volume, melody, and harmony. Each of these is related to its artistic implications. By learning to tune stringed instruments, for example, children learn about harmonic vibrations, the overtone series, and of those tighter, shorter strings that play higher pitches than looser, longer strings. Furthermore, they learn to calculate mathematically the relationship between the different lengths. While learning to play brass instruments, the student will learn about pipe length and how its pitch is affected by temperature. Physically, the study of music requires muscular coordination, agility, and motor control. Muscles of the hands, fingers, face, and diaphragm must work together with perfect timing. Kinesthetic senses develop as they relate to the sound that the ear hears and to an understanding of the mind.

Music not only teaches art, but it is art because it is human expression. It is a medium through which man can express beauty. Great music from all eras is marvelous, since it has power to humanize mankind. It assists individuals in becoming more feeling and sensitive. It can alleviate depression. It can provide lively impetus for action. It can poetically describe all ranges of human emotion.

With regard to music's ability to instruct, few things teach self-discipline as effectively as daily musical practice. The work is difficult, and tenaciousness is required to experience the rewards. David P. Gardner, president of the University of California, stated the case succinctly in an interview for the August 1984 issue of *BYU Today* magazine when he stated, "I think my capacity to concentrate and to be self-disciplined in my approach to problems was significantly helped by my training on the piano and pipe organ."

All of these show sufficient reasons to include the study of music in a child's or an adolescent's daily curriculum. Most definitely, music teaches, stimulates the thinking process, and is the driving force behind intuition. In actuality, most brilliant thoughts come from music. The Spirit, or light of truth, dwells in music that expands the human mind. Of a surety, God speaks and teaches through more than the scriptures; His voice is heard instructing through music.

During my six-stake musical fireside held at the Bracken Ridge Stake Center in Brisbane, Australia, everyone present felt the richness of the Spirit radiating throughout that building like a warm blanket enveloping each of us with love and validation. That evening, we learned that music's power to teach of spiritual things and the learning derived through the sensitivity and passion of inspired music is unusually profound.

To this day I recall spiritual promptings regarding the eternal blessings of missionary work that came to my mind that evening that were to be added to my prepared message concerning the blessings of music in our lives. The Spirit enhanced the music I performed so that it produced a tearful congregation. Never have I felt the sense of wonder and humility as at that time, while approached by one Stake President who said, "Brother Hatch, I feel impressed to tell you that you are, by far, the best and most effective missionary I've ever witnessed in action." I was stunned, and the realization of these words created within me a deep sense of gratitude for my Heavenly Father for providing me with these marvelous opportunities to share music and the spoken word that touches hearts and souls through the Spirit's teaching. For me, this fireside evening in Australia became one of the musically spiritual highlights of my life.

It is important to mention that not all performance opportunities are positive ones or as spiritually edifying. Sometimes, valuable perspectives of life can be taught through experiencing adversities—challenges of the profession. To me, it is imperative that students also acquire this understanding and training in their career development.

In the planning stages months prior to concert performances in Romania, I was delighted not only to schedule a one-day excursion for my students to Dracula's Castle of Vlad the Impaler (students also need "amusements" while on concert tours), in the wooded village of Bran (Transylvania), but to have effectively scheduled a concert date with the director of the distinguished Enescu Concert Hall, the most prominent performance venue in Bucharest. The hall was built in honor of the renowned Romanian composer, violinist, pianist, and conductor, George Enescu (1881–1955). Performing in this beautiful hall would certainly be an honor and privilege!

Regrettably, I received notice that my concert was canceled by the hall administration just four weeks prior to the performance date. Confused as to why this could happen, it came to my attention from reliable sources that all this time we had been working with "anti-Mormons". When the hall administration learned that I was a member of the Church, they promptly terminated our previous contractual agreement to perform in the prestigious hall. It is difficult to describe the disheartening feelings of being a recipient of this type of discrimination, and realizing that persecution against the Church and its members is yet a common practice in certain areas of our contemporary world!

With only one month until the tour, my contacts in Romania feverishly searched for an alternate venue with little success, since international concerts are generally scheduled at last one year in advance of the performance date. However, one remaining option was obtained—the dilapidated (though this information was not made known to us prior to our arrival), century-old Jewish Theater, which proved to be a fiasco!

Instead of a situation that could have become a tremendous debacle, a positive, indispensable learning experience resulted. This appalling occurrence relating to our music performances in that city allowed me a prime teaching moment with my students. We discussed valuable insights which included, "The test of a true artist is to keep an optimistic perspective even in the midst of difficulty," "It is the responsibility of the artist to strive always to give his best regardless the performance situation," and, "Even when encountering poor performance conditions, an effective, mature performer will exude confidence, enthusiasm, and love for the music while performing with technical and musical solidarity!"

It is manifest that through the power of music, teaching marvels occur daily in significant facets of life. Not only is it advantageous to recognize the formidable ability of music to teach, but it is also important to understand that inspired, effective music teaching is a skill that few individuals on earth have been gifted. It is prudent, therefore, that members of the Church and others seek out the best, most diligent and conscientious music training from these gifted and inspired teachers who have spent much of a lifetime cultivating these skills. Many in the Church who possess these God-given talents unselfishly and ungrudgingly render musical service, which becomes a blessing to all. In fact, according to some of the Brethren, these individuals were recipients of musical gifts in the premortal life because they proved most responsible in this vital stewardship. Authoritative thoughts on music's power to teach come from the inspired words of a modern-day Apostle, Elder Boyd K. Packer. In his remarks presented at a fireside at Brigham Young University, he said:

> I have been in places where I felt insecure and unprepared [to speak]. I have yearned inwardly in great agony for some power to pave the way or loosen my tongue, that an opportunity would not be

lost because of my weakness and inadequacy. On more than a few occasions my prayers have been answered by the power of inspired music. I have been lifted above myself and beyond myself when the Spirit of the Lord has poured in upon the meeting, drawn there by beautiful, appropriate music. I stand indebted to the gifted among us who have that unusual sense of spiritual propriety.

Go to, then, you who are gifted; cultivate your gift. Develop it in any of the arts and in every worthy example of them. If you have the ability and the desire, seek a career or employ your talent as an avocation or cultivate it as a hobby. But in all ways bless others with it. Set a standard of excellence. Employ it in the secular sense to every worthy advantage, but never use it profanely. Never express your gift unworthily. Increase our spiritual heritage in music, in art, in literature, in dance, in drama.

The Spirit of the Lord can be present on His terms only. God grant that we may learn, each of us, particularly those who are gifted, how to extend that invitation.[4]

One of the most incredible international concert tour experiences with my gifted, young student pianists occurred in Germany and Austria, the musical heartland of a significant number of the masters—J. S. Bach, Handel, Haydn, Beethoven, Mozart, Schubert, Czerny, Mendelssohn, Brahms, Schumann, Liszt, Wagner, Berlioz, Bruckner, and so many more. Unquestionably, these young musicians who were with me at this time learned first-hand of music's power to teach while exploring the historical and cultural background of the music of these master musicians from this superb and most beautiful region of the world.

The stimulating experiences and deep emotions associated with our visits to the birthplaces, homes, places of employment, performance venues, and graves of master composers were musically life-changing for each of us. Particularly instructive for my students historically and culturally were our many valuable instances of learning. We played Beethoven's piano in Bonn and visited Eisenach, the birthplace of J. S. Bach. Walking the streets of Halle, the city of Handel—which included the "Market Church" where he was baptized and entering St. Thomas' Church in Eisenstadt where Bach composed and performed for years—was awe-inspiring. Listening to a string quartet in the very Esterházy Palace where Haydn was employed as court composer and conductor for thirty years became highly tutorial and rewarding. Visiting the grounds of the homes of Wagner and Liszt in Weimar where much of their music was written, delighting in the spirit of Mozart's birthplace, "Mozartplatz" in Salzburg, and touring Schumann's home in Zwickau where frequent evening salon performances by Brahms and others were exceptionally educational activities! Learning about stunning musicality by listening to expressive live and electrifying performances in the great concert halls of the Munich Philharmonic and the Vienna Mozart Orchestras became unparalleled teaching moments that cannot be learned on the piano bench! Entering St. Stephens Cathedral where Mozart was married in Vienna and visiting the captivating and gorgeous Bavarian Alps where we learned about violin-making by the shop's expert craftsman in the tiny and charming village of Mittenwald also became for us highly educational opportunities. And, visiting the stunning nineteenth-century Neuschwanstein (New Swan) Castle, commissioned by King Ludwig II in homage to Richard Wagner as well as numerous other cultural and musical traditions in this geographical locality of gorgeous natural beauty motivated my group of young musicians to continue to learn all aspects of music of the masters with its power to teach and bless.

During this tour of exceptional music education, my students and I also learned valuable principles from our scheduled performances. Besides our concerts in Munich, Essen, and Vienna for appreciative and enthusiastic audiences, a life-changing, faith-promoting experience followed, relating to our outdoor performance at the Hellbrunn Palace gardens on the outskirts of Salzburg, Austria.

We awoke to a cold, windy, and stormy day. Thus, we became worried that our concert to be performed that afternoon on a rented Steinway grand placed adjacent to the *Sound of Music* gazebo behind the nineteenth-century Archbishop's summer home (filming locale of the famous movie) would be canceled. As a group, we prayed to Heavenly Father that He would remove the dark rain clouds from the concert area while providing a warmer temperature that June afternoon. Nervously, we watched for several hours without seeing improvement in the weather conditions. But, just when we decided to announce the concert cancellation to the tourists visiting the palace, a miraculous phenomenon occurred.

Precisely fifteen minutes prior to the performance start time of four o'clock, the black clouds dispersed, the wind and rain ceased, and warm sunshine appeared from a cloudless, blue sky. To me, this was no coincidence but instead a faith-promoting miracle of a loving Heavenly Father who had heard and answered our prayers.

With His help, the outdoor concert began on time, was successfully presented to an eager crowd of palace visitors, and all performers witnessed an amazing modern-day miracle! From this intense spiritual awakening associated with this musical happening in Austria, our minds were enlightened to the fact that music's power to teach is indeed monumental—especially when it teaches of God's all-powerful ways!

NOTES:

1. The Musician's Diary (New York: McAfee Music, 1979), 36.
2. Ibid, 281.
3. Ibid, 59.
4. Boyd K. Packer, "The Arts and the Spirit of the Lord" (Brigham Young University fireide, February 1, 1976).

Chapter Nine

MUSIC AND FAMILIES

"Music has boundless powers for moving families toward greater spirituality and devotion to the gospel. Latter-day Saints should fill their homes with the sound of worthy music."

—First Presidency Preface, *Hymns*, 1985, x

Our Heavenly Father has blessed each of us with an ability to enjoy musical creation and to use our spiritual judgment in selecting the best artistic atmosphere in which we become engaged. Our musical choices will either uplift us or move us slowly away from the Spirit. Parents, then, have a critical responsibility to make musical decisions for the home that are based upon educated, inspired understanding.

I was blessed with parents who love music. Appropriate, good music was playing almost constantly in our home or even on the patio speakers as we worked in our backyard on Saturday mornings. My parents were whistling, singing, or enjoying music all the time. If their house was devoid of tunes, then there was no one home. In a like manner, it is imperative that we do not allow our children to escape the influence of good music in their lives! When we seek after good, appealing, or inspired music, the Lord will bless our lives with a richness that can make our homes sanctuaries of peace, comfort, and joy. In addition, our families will begin to recognize the power of music, which is the language of the Spirit that will enrich our lives in immeasurable ways.

In discussing music and families, it seems relevant to share pertinent background information about our family and music in the Hatch home. More than any happiness that has come from numerous personal achievements, a vibrant performance career, abundant successes from studio teaching of prodigious young pianists over several decades, or various accolades from professional colleagues is the joy experienced during the years that my wife and I were raising our family of five gifted, intelligent children. We quickly learned that each child is born with unique gifts and abilities which should be carefully guided by supportive, perceptive parents. Unfortunately, from my many teaching years I learned that there are parents who are uninvolved or whose children are coerced to pursue paths chosen for them.

From the standard set by my intuitive parents, I learned that it is best to give children opportunities to explore personal interests and music during their formative years. Later, they can then choose to focus on one or two talents in which they excel. My wife, Paula, and I sought to follow this wise example in our home. To provide a better understanding of how parents might support their children's pursuits in the development of their individual gifts and talents, experiences from my upbringing may prove useful.

Interestingly, fundamental decisions concerning the direction my life would take came as a result of my father's valued support and influence. He has been an enormously talented athlete his entire life, winning the state marble championship in grade school, the state pole-vaulting championship in junior high school, awarded high school All-State distinction in three sports—baseball, basketball and tennis—and receiving honorable mention All-American status as one of the greatest collegiate pitchers from the state of Utah after receiving a collegiate basketball scholarship. In fact, he declined offers to sign with several professional baseball teams—including the Cincinnati Reds, the Baltimore Orioles, and the New York Yankees—in order to enjoy a more effective family life as a husband and father. While pursuing a coaching career in his degree program at Brigham Young University, Dad began playing a new sport—golf. Rapidly developing this skill, he began winning many Utah tournaments, turned pro for a time, and over the past forty years has become one of Utah's top golfers, several times winning the state amateur and senior championships.

For me, this athletic background of my father is vital to this discussion on families and music since it had become a self-induced hurdle in my life during my high school years that needed to be resolved in order for me to fulfill my life's dream. Being the oldest of my parents' five sons, I felt pressure to make my father proud by following in his athletic footsteps. Although I enjoyed participating in church sports teams and in city basketball and baseball leagues while also becoming a top bowler in my age divisions, actively engaging in these sports did not hold my interest long. After trying out for the high school basketball team and realizing the many required hours of daily practice at the school in addition to mounds of homework, three to four hours of daily piano practice, and teaching piano lessons to fifteen weekly students for income, I had to make an important decision, as there simply was not enough time to do it all! Eventually, I gathered the courage to discuss my dilemma with dad.

To my surprise, he immediately removed my concerns by voicing his strong support of my own particular talents and abilities. I'll never forget his astute comment during that discussion: "David, I would trade places with you in a heartbeat! There will come a time when I no longer am able to swing a golf club, shoot a basketball, or pitch a baseball game, whereas you'll always be able to inspire others with your beautiful music. Definitely, son, this is where you should devote your time and energy!"

My mother was equally gifted with domestic skills and other areas of accomplishment, while remaining supportive of her children's talents. She would, for example, frequently sit in the music room, enthusiastically encouraging me as she listened to my piano practice sessions for hours at a time. I am fortunate to have insightful, wise parents who understand that each of us comes to earth with our own unique gifts and talents. Because of this, I was able to pursue my own personal field of endeavor without the pressure of also balancing parental demands.

Likewise, our five children were born with their own wonderful, special abilities. In our home reside an accomplished singer, a talented dancer, fine pianists, and skilled athletes. Knowing that music study is vitally important to the advancement of young minds, their mother and I involved each of our children in piano instruction and other forms of music learning in an effort to enhance their educational and artistic development.

To be clear, I never expected our children to follow my career choice, but knowing the many advantages of music study, they worked until they reached a certain level of proficiency. Of course, it was difficult to wear two hats—father and piano teacher—but the rewards attained were immeasurable. The confidence, self-esteem, and pleasure our children gained from many years of music study, competition, and performance were well worth the effort. Though each has now chosen their own vocational pursuits, their study of and exposure to good music has been a tremendous advantage and blessing in their lives. Plus, I am convinced that, through our children, generations to come will be inspired by music!

In our society, there are many styles of music composed for different purposes and occasions which must be decided as appropriate or not for Latter-day Saints and their homes. Some types of music make us relax. After a stressful day at work, classical music, certain types of jazz, and even melodic ballads can distract our minds from the cares of the day for periods of time. Contrarily, loud, fast music with a strong beat can exhilarate or annoy us. We have all experienced music's physical and mental effects at one time or another. As an example, Beethoven, the classical master, became famous for creating specific emotions in his listeners by writing pieces such as his *Sonata, op. 81a*, which evokes joy, sadness, loss, and return. When we understand how strongly music can influence emotions, we can also recognize the difference it can make in the spirit of our homes.

Marden Pond, one of my dear friends and certainly one of Utah's premiere composers, shared this enlightened thinking:

> In our homes, where peace should be the norm, we are assaulted by music of the most raucous variety, either by the intrusion of the television or by our thoughtless selection of radio programming or recordings. Where we should be nurtured "out of the best books"

(including the best music), we may find our listening habits dominated by the most banal, or even spiritually-destructive, musical expressions. We cannot simply let the music in our homes "happen." Its use and value must be consciously and carefully considered, so that the spirit the music brings into our homes is uplifting and enriching. This doesn't mean that it must always be serious or pious. It can be lighthearted and entertaining as well. But it must be well chosen and be the best it can be, perfectly suited to the use we make of it.[1]

The following insight from Elder Russell M. Nelson is inspired counsel:

> Wherever we are we should carefully choose what we see and hear. We would not knowingly tolerate pornography in our homes, but if we are not careful, we may allow music into our lives that can be just as devastating.
>
> Many youth listen to music that can be described as loud and fast, becoming louder and faster. It aims to agitate, not to pacify; to excite more than to calm. Beware of that kind of music.
>
> As you know, continued exposure to loud sounds will, in time, damage delicate organs of hearing. In like manner, if you overindulge in loud music, you will more likely become spiritually deaf, unable to hear the still, small voice. A scripture states, "The Lord your God ... hath spoken unto you in a still small voice, but ye were past feeling, that ye could not feel his words" (1 Nephi 17:45).
>
> Do not degrade yourself with the numbing shabbiness and irreverence of music that is not worthy of you. Delete the rubbish from your minds and your MP3 players. Protect your personal standards! Be selective! Be wise!
>
> Do not allow unworthy, raucous music to enter your life. It is not harmless. It can weaken your defense and allow unworthy thoughts into your mind and pave the way to unworthy acts. Please remember: "That which doth not edify is not of God, and is darkness. That which is of God is light" (D&C 50:23–24).
>
> Fill your minds with worthy sights and sounds. Cultivate your precious gift of the Holy Ghost. Protect it as the priceless gift that it is. Carefully listen for its quiet communication. You will be spiritually stronger if you do. You know the proverb, "As [a man] thinketh in his heart, so is he" (Proverbs 23:7). As you control your thoughts, you control your actions. Indeed, worthy music can provide power and protection for the soul.[2]

Like many other facets of life, our musical interests are most often shaped by the atmosphere of the homes in which we grow up. Musical tastes are discovered and trained by the individual's experience and upbringing. It is within the family, therefore, that appropriate musical styles and traditions should be wisely planned and promoted. Our people ought to be surrounded by good music of all kinds. These may include a combination of folk, popular, jazz, show tunes, country, blues, patriotic, Christmas, hymns and inspirational music, stimulating classical music, and other worthy musical genres. Adopting uplifting music in our homes can create joy and optimism, which will in turn create happiness and encourage service to others as part of the gospel of Jesus Christ.

Some years ago, Sally Peterson Brinton—an acquaintance of mine, former Miss Utah 1972, a Juilliard-trained pianist, and mother of seven with a desire to provide an uplifting musical environment in her home—shared the following perceptive suggestions for all parents regarding the importance of listening to only good, quality music in our families:

> We are striving in our home to surround our children with beautiful music ranging from the classic composers to the rich heritage of Mormon hymns. What a thrill it was recently in family home evening to hear our two-and-one-half-year-old son sing the first verse of The Spirit of God Like a Fire Is Burning. Not all the words were correct, but he sang it with the spirit and fervor that he had heard so many times on a Mormon Youth Symphony and Chorus record as well as in our family home evenings and in sacrament meetings.
>
> How exciting it is to see our children choose the sacred hymns of the Church over songs heard on radio and television. As I watch our children gain appreciation for Beethoven and the other great masters, I'm convinced that it's not that they're musical geniuses, but simply that they are developing a love for this beautiful music through constant exposure. It is true that the more we become acquainted with good music, the more we can learn to enjoy and appreciate it. No one is too old or too young to learn to enjoy good music. Even a young babe loves the hum of a beautiful lullaby.
>
> We have discovered that listening to classical music during mealtimes adds a special spirit to our home. The children take their naps to the inspiring sounds of the Mormon Tabernacle Choir or the Mormon Youth Symphony and Chorus records. At night, mommy

and daddy sing the children's favorite Primary songs during "cuddle time." What a special time to teach our children the gospel through music! We can plant the tiny seed of testimony, the seed of love for our Heavenly Father and our fellowmen. We've found that our children delight in this and are responding positively to our efforts to instill a love and appreciation for that which is good and uplifting. . . . I believe that parents are the key influence in their children's attitudes toward music. It lies within their power to make music an investment their children will enjoy throughout their lives, providing beauty, variety, discipline, inspiration, and comfort.[3]

Because parents have a serious responsibility to introduce uplifting music in their homes, they must develop a musical awareness themselves. Although many other musical genres can and should be enjoyed, the power of classical music is often overlooked. Perhaps no other genre is more profound in its tendencies, more eloquent in its meaning and expression of eternal things, and more enduring through the centuries of time as is classical music. Although this type of music may be more difficult to initially appreciate and comprehend, it can eventually yield greater blessings. Rather than remaining satisfied with the most shallow music of our time simply because it is easily accessible, we can learn to find the great musical treasures of the earth that God has provided for our use through the musical geniuses He gifted on earth. And as we learn to develop a greater sensitivity to this music to which we choose to avail ourselves, we will discover that the great artistic creations are based on spiritual principles that are eternally lasting.

Attraction to and appreciation for classical music are best developed through the power and sensuality of the live sounds. Although we may listen to this great music at home or at the office, there is no replacement for live classical concerts. The excitement that ensues from the unpredictability and drama of these performances is comparable to watching spectator sports. While following a game on television is enjoyable, cheering at the stadium or sitting courtside is incomparable.

Other effective ways to gain an appreciation for this genre are available. Classical education begins with extensive exposure to this musical style whether in live concerts where printed programs provide background material or by listening to public, internet, or classical radio stations that feature this music with commentators who are usually well-trained in pertinent aspects of this music and provide knowledgeable information for each piece.

For some listeners, an appreciation of classical music will come almost immediately, in a crowded concert hall or perhaps while listening to a recording in a darkened room by themselves. For others, it may take time to acquire an understanding and approval for this remarkable musical style. Nevertheless, the more you learn about classical music, the more enjoyable it becomes. It has been said that classical music is one of the few living arts which continues to exist by being constantly re-created live, before an audience. It comes to life and envelops you in real time.

Although I personally developed a great love, respect, admiration, and understanding for this inspirational musical style over many years of studying and performing classical piano masterpieces, it was surprising that the following situation in my recent past could still create within me continued adulation and reverence for this music—beyond the vast appreciation I had experienced previously. But it happened!

The AUR record label commissioned me to record an album of international appeal titled *The World's Greatest Piano Melodies*, including both solo works and concerto excerpts with orchestra. I became very enthusiastic to learn that I would be performing with the famed Budapest Symphony Orchestra of Hungary under the baton of esteemed conductor Matyas Antal.

For months, I labored in my studio over the most significant and recognizable segments of five piano concertos by composers Edvard Grieg, Sergei Rachmaninoff, Peter Tchaikovsky, Wolfgang Amadeus Mozart, and George Gershwin in preparation for my recording sessions in the Hungarian Radio & Television Recording Hall.

In our first recording session with a gorgeous nine-foot Hamburg Steinway from Germany, the first notes of the orchestra in the opening measures of the Mozart were so astounding that the music gave me chills! Immediately, I realized that my performance must be elevated to match the exquisite musicianship and impeccable playing of this orchestra of Eastern European musicians, who obviously understood the performance style of this composer better than any orchestral group with which I was familiar.

The emotions I felt in those three four-hour recording sessions with this world-class symphonic organization are inexpressible. Rarely have I been as inspired by music and professional musicians as at that time during those crisp October days in Budapest, Hungary. The splendid music-making with this orchestra gave me a continued sense of extreme gratitude, appreciation, love, and humility for touching, inspired, classical music. There is no question that the time I spent in that beautiful country with this superb orchestra became one of the highlights of my life. Upon my return home, the realization came to me that from this brilliant experience, I had become a better person and a changed musician! In addition to this epiphany, that subsequent February I was reminded yet again of the value of hard work—that it generates success. In this case, the many months of rigorous labor at the piano preparing for this eventuality with this world-class symphony was well worth it as Mr. Antal and I were informed that our album had received two Grammy nominations.

TEACHING CHILDREN MUSIC

Of first importance is for parents to understand that teaching their children the value of singing hymns and listening to appropriate music throughout their lives begins at home. The First Presidency has reminded us:

> Latter-day Saints should fill their homes with the sound of worthy music . . . we hope the hymnbook will take a prominent place among the scriptures and other religious books in our homes. The hymns can bring families a spirit of beauty and peace and can inspire love and unity among family members.
>
> Teach your children to love the hymns. Sing them on the Sabbath, in family home evening, during scripture study, at prayer time. Sing as you work, as you play, and as you travel together. Sing hymns as lullabies to build faith and testimony in your young ones.[4]

Secondly, more than listening to it, one of the surest ways to begin a love-affair with classical music is in studying, learning, and performing it. Informed parents comprehend that a child's power of absorption in music study, especially between the ages of eight and twelve, is enormous! Studies show that music expands the mind and that piano lessons in particular help children develop essential skills for a lifetime. The human mind is a wonderful thing. For centuries, philosophers and scientists have puzzled over what it is, how it works, and whether it can be substantially improved. Now, as scientific researchers believe they are coming closer to the answers, one amazing fact is emerging: just as music educators have been asserting for some time, music actually enriches our mental faculties—especially in childhood. And piano lessons seem to do so even more than other disciplines.

All children are born with musical ability. Two-month-old infants have been known to match the pitch, intensity, and melodies for songs their mothers sing; at four months, infants can match rhythm as well. Yet, for neurological reasons, the older children get without exercising their musical aptitude, the more will be lost and never regained. More specifically, by approximately age eleven, the neuron circuits that permit all kinds of perceptual and sensory discrimination—such as identifying pitch and rhythm—become closed off.

Experiments at the University of Münster in Germany have found that exposure to music actually rewires neural circuits. Researchers used magnetic resonance imaging to examine the brains of subjects and discovered that brain areas that encode the sounds made by a piano are larger in musicians than in people who have never played a musical instrument. In other words, music expands the mind and augments brain power, some reasons why prudent parents everywhere—including Latter-day Saints—will involve their children in serious music study.[5]

When music is added to the school curriculum, mathematical skills also improve. Some of this finding comes from data compiled by the Music Educators National Conference from 1998 to present. Students with coursework and experience in musical performance scored fifty-one points higher on the verbal portion of the SAT and thirty-nine points higher on the SAT math portion than students with no coursework or involvement with music.[6]

Music professionals agree that the importance of music in education can be found by examining music itself. As any trained musician will admit, music is ultimately about communication. The only performance that is truly successful is one that says something! Music training, therefore, could be considered communication training. And it is interesting to note that musicians tend to do better on English and reading tests, which are mostly measuring the ability to communicate and to receive communication non-verbally.

This information also follows the findings of Frances Rauscher at the University of California at Irvine, who did tests of three year olds. After one year, those who had taken weekly piano lessons and participated in group singing scored eighty percent higher on tests of spatial and temporal reasoning, an ability that underlies many kinds of mathematics and engineering. What a travesty, then, that music programs are being slashed from elementary school curricula throughout the nation. In fact, when budgets are low, music courses are the first to go, as many administrators are uninformed of these studies and have little if any understanding of the extreme importance of music study as it relates to high achievement in serious academic curricula.[7]

Furthermore, there are obvious additional benefits to music study, and no other single instrument matches the piano for its broad application of musical concepts. Even if a child should choose to play another instrument later, the skills acquired with piano education form an unparalleled foundation. And, of course, music is a rich source of life-long joy, satisfaction, and accomplishment. In my teaching observations over decades, I have gathered a list of thirty reasons why every child should learn to play a musical instrument, especially the piano. They gain the following: achievement, enjoyment, self-expression, poise, confidence, perseverance, appreciation, pride, concentration, satisfaction, self-improvement, coordination, involvement, self-discipline, self-respect, comprehension, self-control, awareness, release, pleasure, patience, endurance, sociability, relaxation, alertness, fortitude, fun, intelligence, focus, and interaction.

All of these traits carry over into intellectual pursuits that lead to effective study and work ethic. Creating and performing music promotes self-gratification while giving pleasure to others. Music is about communication, creativity, and cooperation. If music students build on these skills, their lives will be enriched, and they will undoubtedly experience the world from a new perspective. As a consequence, it is imperative that Latter-day Saints and all good people the world over should foster good music in their homes, with parents encouraging their children in various aspects of musical training.

Not only did my parents support and encourage me through my years of music study, but expressions of confidence and encouragement from the lips of my inspired teachers also have continued to sustain me—often coming to me during today's performance career! Only a few years ago, for example, my very wise and accomplished first piano instructor sent me the following handwritten letter of reminiscences that became most meaningful at a difficult time. She wrote,

Dear David,

It was fun to have you as a piano student. I used to watch you out my window, clutching your books as you came up the sidewalk. You were always prepared and you also caught on easily to new concepts. There was that glimmer that let us all know you would become a superior musician as you have done. Your mother and I both cried when you played your concertos with the Utah Valley Symphony and other orchestras. Thank you for working hard so we can enjoy your wonderful arrangements, classical programs, and recordings. I listen to one or the other every day. Best wishes for continued success and happiness!

Love ya,
Barbara Elison

Young people who have learned how to concentrate through studying music are usually advanced intellectually beyond their years. Others, however, though talented—even gifted—students will often require a structured plan with parental expectations and support that engages effective focusing and the ability to remain on task for any length of time. Sometimes, undisciplined or uncooperative children can create frustration in the home. Parents of these types of personalities should not give up but know that the study of music has proven fundamentally important and indispensable to children's success in most other areas of academic pursuit! Realizing the magnificent rewards that come in the end, wise parents will remain strong in keeping their children actively involved with music no matter the child's provocations along the way! Throughout my teaching career, there have been many instances where a student will greatly challenge their parent's resolve in the process of continued music instruction. On a lighter note, I should also mention that many times a child's contrariness is even quite humorous! There are two accounts that are worthy of mention.

For one of my young female students, practice sessions were not always what they should have been, since her mother worked away from home and was not always there after school to oversee her daughter's practicing. Being on her own much of the time, my student confessed a few years later of a second hobby that had consumed some of her piano practice time. An avid reader, she loved books and often would surreptitiously have one open on the piano bench beside her as she practiced her scales and Hanon exercises. This way, the housekeeper did not know about the book reading trick and would later report to her mother, "Yes, Sally practiced a long, long time today and worked especially hard on her exercises."

Several years ago, one of my younger male students who disliked practicing the piano invented a creative scheme whereby he could satisfy his mother's wishes to do his practicing while simultaneously playing outside with his neighborhood friends. Having recorded one of his 90-minute practice sessions, he simply turned on the audio equipment that played the recorded practice while he quietly climbed through the front room window to the freedom of outside!

Hearing his practicing coming from the recording machine pleased his mother who was working in another part of the house. Thinking that Robert had been working at the piano the entire time, she decided to praise him for his diligence. When entering the piano room to the sound of the recording machine, there was no Robert. To her astonishment, she found the open window where he had escaped with the drapes blowing with the breeze! From these anecdotes about children with normal tendencies, it may be safe to say that I was one of the unusual few who actually enjoyed working at the piano.

To this day, I remember the first classical piece that touched my soul deeply—Chopin's *Piano Concerto no. 2 in F Minor*. I was a sixth-grader when my mother bought me the album. From that moment on, that magical music changed me forever, transporting me to another time and place. I played that classical music over and over again. I was hooked! The music expressed love, longing, despair, euphoria, and a depth of emotions I had never thought possible at that young age. What a blessing it was to come from a home that provided these incredible musical offerings through perpetual music education and enjoyment.

Astute parents and teachers are aware of the need for the best possible teaching early in life. The following idea is one often heard expressed by parents in this country, "Since my child is only a beginner, any teacher will do." This attitude has been the source of great laxity in American musical education. Correct learning during the formative years is crucial! In actuality, learning a musical instrument as a beginner is of such tremendous importance that only the best is good enough. This doesn't necessarily mean the most expensive teacher obtainable, but someone who is thorough, painstaking, conscientious, alert, and experienced. Everything during these early years must be solid, substantial, firm, and secure. Sometimes employing a teacher with a big reputation and exceptional skill, who would make an excellent teacher for an advanced student, might be incapable of laying a good foundation for the beginner.

In the process of teaching, when contemplating the growth of an aspiring musician, I appreciate the words of Timothy Gallwey in his book *The Inner Game of Tennis*:

> When we plant a rose seed in the earth, we notice that it is small, but we do not criticize it as "rootless and stemless." We treat it as a seed, giving it the water and nourishment required of a seed. When it first shoots up out of the earth, we don't condemn it as immature and underdeveloped; nor do we criticize the buds for not being open when they appear. We stand in wonder at the process taking place and give the plant the care it needs at each stage of its development. The rose is a rose from the time it is a seed to the time it dies. Within it, at all times, it contains its whole potential. It seems to be constantly in the process of change; yet at each stage, at each moment, it is perfectly all right as it is.[8]

How wonderful is the parent or music instructor who will teach young people to play music correctly and who will acquaint them with a variety of good music during their youth, always inspiring discipline, hard work and excellence in the development of these musical gifts and talents. To have such exposure to valuable music in one's life is a tremendous asset.

My foremost mentor to this day and illustrious, highly skilled—even gifted—piano professor throughout my teen years and undergraduate degree at Brigham Young University, gave me a hand-written letter just prior to my departure from Utah to Missouri for my new graduate school adventure. He was inspired in expressing the perfect message to encourage success in a most wonderful, albeit highly competitive, musical arena! He wrote,

> Dear David:
>
> Such a pleasure it has been as your teacher and colleague. I feel you are one of the most gifted and well-prepared graduates to leave BYU. You have splendid credentials to enter graduate school and a beautiful talent for performance. Go get 'em!!
>
> Convert your new friends to the Church and also to your special spirit of exciting living. Always radiate that wonderful joie-de-vivre. I am proud of your work and appreciative of your support, assistance, inspiration, and friendship.
>
> Best to you as ever,
> Paul Pollei

This kind of praise and reassurance from one of my superiors whose opinions I valued greatly at that time, remind me of the following thoughts and perspectives taught by President Kimball.

In February 1978, President Spencer W. Kimball wrote a First Presidency Message for the *Ensign* magazine, titled "The Gospel Vision of the Arts." He said,

> Members of the Church should be peers or superiors to any others in natural ability, extended training, plus the Holy Spirit which should bring them light and truth. With hundreds of "men of God" and their associates so blessed, we have the base for an increasingly efficient and worthy corps of talent . . . and if we strive for perfection—the best and greatest—and are never satisfied with mediocrity, we can excel.

President Kimball then nudges the Saints later in the article with specifics regarding the importance of discovering and training our children in the arts. He continued,

> And Niccolo Paganini, the Italian violinist (1782–1850)! Why cannot we discover, train, and present many Paganini's and other such great artists? And shall we not present before the musical world a pianist to excel in astonishing power of execution, depth of expression, sublimity of noble feeling, the noted Hungarian pianist and composer, Franz Liszt (1811–1886)? We have already produced some talented artists at the piano, but I have a secret hope to live long enough to hear and see at the piano a greater performer than Paderewski, the Polish statesman, composer, and pianist (1860–1941). Surely all Paderewski's were not born in Poland in the last century; all talented people with such outstanding recreative originality, with such nervous power and such romantic appearance were not concentrated in this one body and two hands! Certainly this noted pianist with his arduous super-brilliant career was not the last of such to be born![9]

In general, Latter-day Saints and good families universally are industrious, driven, and accomplishment-oriented. They desire to do good, to excel, and to provide lasting contributions for present and future generations. In Doctrine and Covenants 58:26–28 it reads,

> For behold, it is not meet that I should command in all things; for he that is compelled in all things, the same is a slothful and not a wise servant; wherefore he receiveth no reward.
>
> Verily I say, men should be anxiously engaged in a good cause, and do many things of their own free will, and bring to pass much righteousness; For the power is in them, wherein they are agents unto themselves. And inasmuch as men do good they shall in nowise lose their reward.

Thus, in addition to exposing uplifting and beautiful music in the home, wise parents, including Latter-day Saints, will be diligent in providing their families with excellent training in the development of the musical arts.

NOTES:

1. Marden Pond, *Virtuous, Lovely, of Good Report* (Provo: Music Enterprises, 1990), 43.

2. Russell M. Nelson, "The Power and Protection of Worthy Music" (Brigham Young University fireside address, May 4, 2008).

3. Sally Peterson Brinton, "Blessing Your Home with Music," *Ensign*, March 1983, 80–83.

4. Jay E. Jensen, "The Nourishing Power of Hymns," *Ensign*, May 2007, 11–13.

5. A. Wishey, Music as the Source of Learning (Baltimore: University Park Press, 1980), 198.

6. R. Sinatra, "Visual Literacy Connections to Thinking, Reading and Writing," Music Educators National Conference, Mar. 1986, 49.

7. Frances H. Rauscher, G. L. Shaw, & K. N. Ky, "Listening to Mozart Enhances Spatial-Temporal Reasoning: Towards a Neurophysiological Basis," *Neuroscience Letters*, Nov. 1995, 185.

8. Timothy W. Gallwey, *The Inner Game of Tennis* (New York: Random House, 1974), 176.

9. Spencer W. Kimball, "The Gospel Vision of the Arts," *Ensign*, February 1978, 1–2.

Chapter Ten

MUSIC AND ASPIRING MUSICIANS

M usic is one of the greatest gifts of deity—an eternal element which has always been and will always be! Humble master musicians and composers recognized that their musical genius was a divine gift bestowed by the God of heaven and earth to be a conduit of His presence and voice to the world.

Students of music should recognize that with their God-given gift, they have a critical responsibility to humanity. In the development of their gifts, musicians realize that truly great and inspired music emanates from God and creates unity and love, grace and kindness, truth and power, and that it is a powerful instrument of change and transformation. When people are singing, performing, or listening to music together, whether diverse individuals or languages—different nations and cultures—this demonstrates the power of bringing people together, allowing them to see God and the world in a new light. The purity of the instruments, the honesty of the lyrics, the rhythm, the chords, the harmonies, all clothe musicians' messages in compelling packages that can move audiences toward becoming more God- and Christlike.

Aspiring musicians who believe God created music in order for His children to express their varied experiences of life have a charge to create music that articulates all human emotions that communicate deeply to the soul. Furthermore, they recognize that music is an art that is fueled by passion, and passion that comes from positive influences in life can be expressed with focus on what is truly honest, noble, right, and pure.

Finally, musicians have an accountability to express gratitude to God for the musical gifts He has given them. The lack of gratitude is offensive to Him and the mark of a narrow and uneducated mind. With the bestowal of musical gift comes tremendous responsibility. This is a responsibility that does not treat the gift with indifference or selfishness, but that shares knowledge that this powerful force, music, is for change in our troubled world—a vehicle to connect, inspire and uplift the spirit of man. Felix Mendelssohn, early romantic German composer, pianist, organist, and conductor, once made a poignant statement. He said, "I know perfectly well that no musician can make his thoughts or his talents different from what Heaven has made them; but I also know that if Heaven had given him good ones, he must also be able to develop them properly."[1]

Larry Barkdull, in his book *Art and Writing*, provides pertinent observations regarding God-given gifts and talent:

> Innate Talent. Either you have it or you don't. Your talent, that spark of genius, was born with you. It is a natural part of you, an innate ability, although you may not have discovered it yet. If you think about this concept, you should immediately be able to think of some examples. For instance, you know many people who can sing, but some people can really sing. There are dancers, and then there are dancers.
>
> Go down the list: painters, sculptors, orators, teachers, administrators, businessmen … and writers. It is my belief that everyone in this world has been born with an innate talent or ability that they cannot—or should not—explain by their own hard work. I know this idea may fly in the face of our culture's cherished belief: "By hard work comes all good things." Sorry! It ain't necessarily so.
>
> Hard work DOES NOT create talent; hard work develops talent that already exists. Many good things—more than we may want to admit—are given to us; we cannot honestly point to cause and effect. These good things are inexplicable in everyday terms. They cannot be duplicated. Clearly, they are gifts. Once you accept that fact, you have to acknowledge the Source of your gift. By the way, it's not

arrogant to admit that you have a God-given talent—all the great artists I know humbly acknowledge that God is the Giver of their gift. In fact, it is the arrogant artist who claims that he alone is the author of his gift. Now, admitting such a gift can be as difficult as admitting a weakness—but both are intended to drive you to your knees. Why? Because once you admit that someone has singled you out and handed you a rare gift, you will be forced to ask yourself why? Why me? What is expected in return? If you are willing to put forth a concerted effort to get the answer, you will come to an interesting conclusion. I'll save you some time. The answer is responsibility and accountability. That's right. Responsibility and accountability accompany the gift of talent.

Let me clarify something before I go on: You may not have yet discovered your talent. You may need trusted parents, friends or teachers to help you recognize your potential and draw it out of you. Let them help, and don't get discouraged. Remember, Einstein started out by failing math.

Responsibility to develop your talent. The great artists of my acquaintance carry a burden. None of them take their gift lightly. They feel an obligation to work hard to develop their talent and fulfill the purposes for which it was given.[2]

Over many years, my piano performances have allowed me to individually relish the great music of the masters; to share beauty, passion, and spirituality with my international audiences; and to uplift hearts and minds to higher levels of existence. The performances we keep with us are those that speak to us in past experiences retold, in melodies that bring us to a secret place, in rhythms that capture our heartbeat, and in dynamics that reflect our passions. What amazing power music possesses to be able to emotionally transport us to places we otherwise would not go as part of a colorful, musical tapestry into which we are all interwoven.

It is my strong belief that a professional music career requires enormous work and preparation beginning during the formative years of one's life and is not a profession that can start with college study. Unfortunately, during the years of my university work and graduate schooling, I observed many students trying to succeed in this field without the necessary musical experience and understanding. Sadly, they had not realized the huge demands of this field of study—that taking piano lessons in their early years with a "neighborhood teacher" would not produce adequate preparation for such a professional career.

Often, music students desiring to become concert musicians enter the university level not knowing the extensive work that will be required of them. This is especially true of performers who haven't considered that to be a music major one must acknowledge the importance and comprehensiveness of music theory, music history, ear training, compositional harmony and analysis, conducting, piano proficiency, sight-reading aptitude, and other rigors of a collegiate music curriculum. Many students become discouraged when they're entrenched in cumulative music courses that span several years. Even some fine performers have trouble with many of these areas of study, but these concepts and areas of development are essential if students plan to teach or perform on a high or professional level.

Obviously, there is a large dropout rate with students who have been studying another career subject suddenly declaring themselves as music majors but failing their courses because they did not expect the rigorous academic work or did not have sufficient preparation. They had only thought this discipline looked appealing and fun. It is distressing to see these students fail because they did not anticipate the immense workload involved in becoming a professional musician—that it entails far more than simply playing an instrument or singing in an ensemble.

Although the classical arena is highly competitive, there has been no better time to pursue a music career. There is a current resurgence in the appreciation of this classical form with the number of concert venues, summer festivals, performing ensembles, and overall performances in classical music and opera increasing exponentially over the past three decades. Presently, there are nearly four hundred professional orchestras in America, according to the League of American Orchestras, while thirty years ago there were 203. There are over 500 youth orchestras, up from 63 in 1990. The number of orchestra concerts performed annually in the United States has risen 24 percent in the past decade to 37,000. Ticket-sale income from orchestra performances grew almost 18 percent to $608 million between the 2004 and 2005 seasons. The widening of interest in classical music isn't limited to our shores either, with Europe and Asia also increasing their classical music statistics.

Furthermore, unprecedented, easy access to the recorded treasures of classical music may have put an end to the commercial viability of recorded music, but there is a silver lining: it has inspired more people to go to live concerts. Recorded music now does what all reproductions should: it inspires the desire to experience the real thing, in real time and space! Hence, the positive ambiance of classical music throughout the world at the present time is alive and well!

Some present-day music researchers claim we are experiencing a serious talent crunch, that "great talent" is difficult to find. From what I have witnessed, though, this seems erroneous. In fact, many distinguished pedagogues agree that there is more talent in the performing arts area than ever before. So what we have is not failure of talent but perhaps failure to provide an environment where musicians understand the ramifications of value, productivity, and true worth. If there is a crunch, it is one not of talent but of perspective. We are not lacking people of talent and gift, but our society perhaps has not taught our people the principle of giving our all to the cause. As musicians, our true worth is determined by how much we give in value, never holding back.

From my perspective, there are three qualities that are absolutely essential in becoming a great musician: determination, excellence, and humility. The most important assurance of success is determination. When a person is determined to have something, they must have it, no matter the odds! Excellence is of a quality that surpasses ordinary standards in performance. Studies claim that achieving excellence as a performing musician requires practice of approximately 10 years of dedication, comprising approximately 10,000 hours of effort. Humility can be found in individuals who find joy from experiencing beautiful things because they realize they are part of something larger than self that gives meaning and goodness to the world. Here is a more extensive observation at each of these.

DETERMINATION

Determination is one of the greatest assets a person can possess. This attribute brings out the best in people and is a tool used to defeat discouragement. Determination builds character, a quality that drives individuals to succeed in their life's pursuits. It is the act of firmly achieving a desired end. As an example, Thomas Edison was a man who became successful in many fields of endeavor because he learned to master the art of determination. Having never given up after five thousand failed attempts to perfect the first light bulb, he succeeded.[3]

Determined individuals are positive in their attitudes and seem to know that there will be moments of disappointment in striving to attain goals. Sensible people understand that their mistakes, depressions, and problems seem to be a source of growth, and that they are actually necessary to success; therefore, they never give up!

Andreas Schachtner, a German poet, musician, and friend of the Mozart family, related in a letter how he and Mozart's father, Leopold, had once found the determined four-year-old Wolfgang writing a concerto! When the father examined it, he found it to be correct in musical form, but he told his son it would be impossible to play. But the energetic boy took the concerto and said, "No, Papa, that is why it is a concerto. You just have to practice until you get it right! This is how it goes." He then played it the best he could and showed that he knew what he wanted. "At that time," Schachtner wrote, "the little Wolfgang had the firm conviction that playing concertos and working miracles were one and the same."[4]

Determination is a must in achieving high levels of musical accomplishment. Most musicians would agree that the music field is a decidedly competitive and extremely difficult place in which to achieve major success. This is especially true in the classical music arena. To become a professional musician—including instrumental performers, singers, composers, conductors, theorists, therapists, technicians, musicologists, and applied music teachers—one must spend numerous years of academic study, research, practice, and performance to develop the required knowledge and mastery.

There are also many sacrifices along the way. For instance, many of my graduate student friends and budding professional musicians made meager incomes and, in a sense, starved to pay the bills in order to achieve their desired professional goals. Many of these young artists waited tables at night to finance their schooling and personal needs.

Success is a result of hard struggles, endless hustle, extremely long hours of study and practice, with determination to succeed, regardless! In the end, it was noticed that those who worked hardest and "paid the price" for success, were never disappointed. In every case, it was proven that the ultimate achievements were worth the large sacrifices!

Additionally, during my undergraduate years I gained fascinating insight while watching the work ethic of various students seeking a piano performance degree. Students who were not innately gifted but who possessed a tireless work ethic often succeeded far beyond the level of those who were blessed with natural technical facility and musical gift. To me, the reason for this phenomenon was simple: the naturally gifted student rarely worked hard since everything came easily to him.

It is most interesting to have watched the lives of these former students unfold. Those who were much less talented but greatly disciplined to achieve excellence through years of meticulous labor became well-known music professionals! In contrast, the naturally gifted, who remained indolent all that time, consistently struggled to attain promising careers that have not materialized to this day! This principle of success is a detectible fact in any undertaking of life.

To successfully complete his symphonies, songs, chamber music, piano concertos, and solo pieces from which he received both criticism and acclaim, Brahms acknowledged that both divine inspiration and intense work with creative genius were required. On one occasion he stated, "My compositions are not the fruits of inspiration alone, but also of severe, laborious, and painstaking toil. A composer, who hopes to write anything of lasting value, must have both inspiration and craftsmanship."[5]

Some musicians, including students, believe they will one day experience high levels of success without realizing the disciplined mastery required to prepare for such a future outcome! Preparedness is a key ingredient to diligence and accomplishment. Many people seem to pass the time until the "great opportunity" comes their way. But from my experience, opportunity never comes to the unprepared, careless individual.

Driven by perseverance, in his short thirty-five year life, Mozart composed more music than composers who have lived to be eighty-five! His prolific compositional output of symphonies, piano music, chamber music, masses, concerti, songs, and operas seemed to fly off his ink pad as a spindle with little effort. But his desire and determination to work hard was legendary. Stories are told of Mozart typically working long hours throughout the night, as was the situation when he wrote the overture to his famous opera *Don Giovanni.*

Mozart began this project after the body of the opera was written, for it was easier for him to weave all thematic elements of the opera into this introductory piece at the conclusion of the project rather than at the beginning. He had a deadline to meet, and because there had been so many other requests of him during this time, Mozart had not started writing the overture until the night before its first performance! The deadline to have the finished score to the copyist by 7:00 a.m. the next morning had to be met so that all instrumental parts could be copied during the day for the individual orchestra members to be able to perform it that evening with Mozart himself at the conductor's podium. Therefore, Mozart's wife fixed some punch and told him stories and jokes to keep him awake while he composed throughout the night. But in the wee early morning hours, Mozart began to doze. Constance decided not to wake him from his deep sleep until five o'clock—only two hours prior to the score's finish deadline!

Many other composers would have "thrown in the towel," so to speak. But not the determined Mozart! He worked fast and provided the finished composition of absolute musical genius to the copyist on time. Of course the ink on the manuscript paper for each individual part was barely dry by the evening performance, but all was completed.

After conducting the opera's premiere that evening to an very enthusiastic audience, Mozart was thrilled with the adequate sight-reading skills of the orchestra members. After the performance he applauded them with a "Bravo, bravo, gentlemen! That was excellent!" This narrative demonstrates a great lesson in determination![6]

Someone once said, "Success seems to be largely a matter of hanging on after others have let go." Truly a mature person, musician or otherwise, can gather internal strength to keep his or her self-control in a crisis situation. With musical determination, Bartok was driven toward, achieved, and maintained success few others have experienced. However, one's greatness is not defined merely by what one has achieved but by the obstacles one has overcome! Similar to Beethoven, then, who possessed an impressive tenacity in spite of the fact that he faced a musician's most horrific affliction—deafness—productive individuals, including musicians who are driven to succeed, will not give up but will constantly demonstrate firm resolve in the process. This remains the mark of the true achiever!

Tchaikovsky never feared difficult, mentally exhausting tasks. In fact, his impeccable work ethic reminds one of a passage in the Bible. On one occasion, the Master taught what some today consider "the extra mile principle" saying, "And whosoever shall compel thee to go a mile, go with him twain" (Matt. 5:41). A wonderful example of this is the story of Tchaikovsky's composition teacher, Nicolai Rubinstein, giving the class an assignment to write contrapuntal variations on a given theme. Expecting his students to write about a dozen each, Rubinstein asked for as many variations as possible for the next class period.

When the assignments were received, Tchaikovsky casually handed the teacher more than two hundred variations! This was characteristic of his productivity. An amazed Rubinstein claimed, "To examine all these would have taken me more time than it took him to write them."[7]

Accomplished musicians, therefore, do not make excuses for producing less than their best work, but instead are ambitious to succeed in reaching their full potential.

EXCELLENCE

Excellence is deliberate, not an accident we stumble upon. Excellence is a habit, an attainable goal for everyone by merely doing his or her best at every moment. The Greek philosopher Aristotle stated it this way, "We are what we repeatedly do; excellence, therefore, is not an act, but a habit." It is not about perfection, but rather demanding more of ourselves by becoming what we are capable of becoming. Those who stand on the sidelines and watch others succeed know what is required but are unwilling to devote the time and effort to improve themselves. Therefore, each of us has a decision to make. Will we become another statistic by merging with the mediocre majority, or do we desire to make a difference by embracing excellence?

The story is told of a man who visited a European performance hall in the final state of restoration where a German sculptor was making a statue of Beethoven. He noticed a similar statue lying in the wings nearby. Surprised, he asked the sculptor, "Do you need two statues of the same composer?"

"No," said the sculptor without looking up, "We need only one, but the first one got damaged at the last stage." The gentleman examined the previous statue and found no apparent damage.

"Where is the damage?" he asked.

"There is a scratch on the nose of the statue," said the sculptor, still busy with his work.

"Where are you going to install the statue?"

The sculptor replied that it would be installed on a pillar twenty feet high in the lobby. "If the statue is that far up, who is going to know that there is a scratch on the nose?" the gentleman asked.

The sculptor stopped his work, looked up at the gentleman, smiled and said, "I will know it!"[8]

With all of us, the desire to excel excludes whether someone else is appreciative or not. Excellence is a drive from within, not without—not for someone else to notice but for our own satisfaction and efficiency. Additionally, giving our best requires that we excel to please the Lord, not men!

Felix Mendelssohn, the great German composer and conductor was a perfect example of one who always strove for excellence in his work. His objective was always to provide the best possible product. As an example, his oratorio, *St. Paul*, is one of the best musical biographies in history of the conversion of Paul. A Jewish convert himself, this story must have been close to his heart.

Always a meticulous worker, Mendelssohn had expended much effort on this project. In one letter he referred to the composition, saying, "I must not make any mistakes." From historical journals we learn that in striving for perfection in this work, Mendelssohn researched everything available on Greek and church history and on first-century life in Palestine. This desire to achieve musical excellence in this composition contributed to Mendelssohn's becoming a master composer.

This, of course, is not to discount Mendelssohn's natural talent as a piano prodigy and musical genius. The story is told that one day a friend interrupted Mendelssohn when the composer was writing music. When the friend began to leave, Mendelssohn invited him to stay and visit, saying, "I am merely copying out." The friend was confused, as there were no notes being copied. Mendelssohn was obviously composing, but he treated it as simply writing down notes he had already completed in his mind. The result was his *Grand Overture in C Major.*[9]

Excellence is not perfection. Although many musicians are continually endeavoring for musical perfection, it is rarely achieved since it equates to "flawless—no mistakes, no blemishes." Instead, musical excellence is a talent or quality which is unusually good and so surpasses ordinary standards. It is also a desired goal for the standard of performance.

Speaking of excellence, in today's world most of us know the certain names associated with "quality" such as Cadillac, Hilton, Diamond, Steinway, and Stradivarius. Known as the most significant artisan in this field, Antonio Stradivarius (1644–1737) was the world's most-celebrated maker of stringed instruments—violins, violas, cellos, and basses.

Long before Mercedes Benz, the German manufacturer of automobiles, or Fazioli, the Italian piano manufacturing company that customizes high-quality products, Stradivarius was a synonym for superior craftsmanship. Antonio passed on his secrets to his two sons, and today the results of their superior work live on. Many of their instruments are still made and played in performances today—the standards of quality and excellence. In fact, after three centuries, these instruments continue to sell for hundreds of thousands—even millions—of dollars!

Over the years, research has been done and books have been written about what makes the Stradivarius violin completely magnificent. Many string experts today have sought the great secret that hundreds of string makers have tried unsuccessfully to copy.

Some speak of the special woods that had been used for the instruments, and some discuss the construction of larger instruments that produced substantially improved tone. But all the experts agree on one thing: there is extraordinary amount of care that went into each instrument—no sloppiness, no carelessness, nor cutting corners. From his desire to achieve pure excellence without flaw, this Italian master reached perfection in his art never to be surpassed.[10]

Thus, the same as with quality products, a certain excellence establishes one as a quality musician. To become a virtuoso requires excellence on many levels, not simply attaining mastery of an instrument and concentration as a performing artist. It necessitates a mastery of additional abilities of the human spirit—passion, communication, discipline, confidence, concentration, and creativity—to take a musician's skills to the next level of excellence.

The musician's quality of excellence will be attained through being responsible, setting and achieving goals, possessing a fearless work ethic, comprehensive knowledge of all aspects of music, becoming a critical listener, ego-free, and with a constant desire for further growth with a perpetual thirst for improvement.

PASSION, COMMUNICATION, DISCIPLINE, CONFIDENCE, CONCENTRATION, CREATIVITY

Passion is the beginning of all great musical accomplishment since it is impossible to express passion in music if it isn't felt deeply in the soul. Passion is the overcoming of senses by strong emotion. Musicians express passion in their music when they demonstrate great love for their work with excitement, enthusiasm, and compelling emotion in the process of musical creation.

Secondly, to **communicate** is the highest form of musical expression. If a performance does not communicate to the listeners, it is meaningless. Also, when two artists communicate by merging into one entity, there becomes a non-verbal principle that soloists, chamber musicians, and conductors use to attune to one another. It is never about one performer following another, but rather when the two or more artists respond to the music and communicate that which resides within each of them.

Another quality of excellence in the preparation of successful performances is **discipline**, which requires conscientious practice techniques and mental control. Achieving discipline in the process of learning music requires a person to develop good study and practice habits which lead to outstanding results. Therefore, highly skilled teachers spend much time disciplining good habits that will reduce and even eliminate problems normally acquired by music students.

Confidence is also a critically indispensable mental skill that a musician must possess to achieve musical success! From my experience in performance and teaching, self-doubt has been the main mental block to confident, enjoyable performances. A common challenge that musicians face is the ability to perform for others as well as they do for themselves during practice sessions. Much of this confidence comes from careful, thorough preparation and positive self "pep-talking" when approaching the performance stage. Automaker Henry Ford was once quoted as saying, "Whether you think you can or can't, you're right."[11] I believe strongly that this is true for performers as well. Therefore, it is imperative to me that my students identify and immediately discard thoughts that undermine confidence.

A useful illustration concerning this standpoint regarding genuine confidence comes from the life of Hungarian composer and pianist Bela Bartok, considered one of the most important composers of the twentieth century.

I learned of this anecdote while visiting Bartok's last residence (now a museum, Bartok Memorial House) in Budapest where he lived and composed from 1932 to 1940. Upon entering this former villa, visitors are greeted by a plaque inscribed with Bartok's magnificent quotation—his professed lifetime creed, "I am going to serve only one aim: the weal of the Hungarian nation and country."

Like many other musical masters, Bartok was a child prodigy, composing his first works at age nine. Through the years, he not only became a man of great acclaim but always exhibited a calm, steady demeanor, often pressing on in the midst of adversity with confidence and constant determination to succeed in his compositional pursuits. On one such trying occasion, Bartok's unruffled self-assurance was exemplary!

Disaster occurred at the premiere of his work *The Miraculous Mandarin*. This most-contemporary, innovative composition was denounced and "booed" by an audience throwing various items, including stink bombs, on stage. The crowd was so loud that the music could not be heard. Even the mayor demanded the conductor, Eugen Szenkar, to resign.

Bartok's reaction to this debacle is intriguing. Following that performance, he serenely entered the conductor's dressing room backstage, unperturbed by the rejection, and quietly said, "Eugen, on page 34, the second clarinet is marked mezzo forte. I couldn't hear it. Would you please mark it forte?" Furthermore, Bartok's secure nature assisted him in his final years when composing some of his greatest works while suffering silently from leukemia. He suppressed a fever for three years, at which time he composed his famous *Concerto for Orchestra*; no one ever heard him complain. With fierce determination, he worked until his last breath, finishing all but seventeen measures of his magnificent *Piano Concerto no. 3*, which some of his students later completed.

To achieve complete focus and the ability to channel nervous energy effectively requires well-developed **concentration**. Performance anxiety and inability to concentrate usually begin when performers are distracted or their minds wander. The results are nervousness, memory lapses, technical errors, and fear of performing. These problems are avoided when musicians genuinely realize that they've prepared to the best of their ability, are unconcerned with what audience members may think, listen to and incorporate all aspects of musicianship into the performance, and communicate to the listeners a love for the music.

Finally, **creativity** can become our inspiration in a musical world of constant discovery where we listen for our inner feelings or direction that provides insight. Creativity refers to the phenomenon whereby a person creates something new that has intrinsic value. Though highly desirable, creativity is often regarded as an elusive, subjective characteristic. My personal belief is that creativity is not just a gift simply sprinkled on a few musicians! Creativity is something that we each have imbedded within us, and it is our responsibility to unlock that creativity, whether in composing, performing, arranging, improvising, or teaching. Music enhances creativity.

In pursuing musical excellence, we must never express negativity or exhibit an attitude of self-deprecation. To be a provider of wonderful contributions, one must possess confidence to acknowledge high achievement. A simple "thank you," for example, is the appropriate response for a compliment.

In striving to attain musical excellence or any other type of excellence in our lives, we could specifically ask ourselves soul-searching questions such as, What is expected of me in this project? In what ways can I exceed these expectations? What will be required of me to do my very finest work? We must immerse ourselves in everything we do in producing our best—never settling for minimum efforts or holding back when we can give more—doing more than is expected. In essence, we need to be daily asking ourselves what tasks we are completing today that will enhance an effective, successful tomorrow. Herein lies our greatest fulfillment—where supreme self-satisfaction will be discovered.

When writing about musical excellence at this time, many of my prodigious students are somewhere feverishly practicing their technical drills for the day—Hanon, Philipp, scales, arpeggios, chords, octaves, and of course, Czerny exercises, determined to attain pianistic excellence. Generations of pianists have worked this regimen of daily keyboard technique composed by Franz Liszt's teacher and one of Beethoven's most famous students, the Austrian Carl Czerny (1791–1857).

Czerny was one of those rare individuals who never wasted time. In fact, dogged to work productively, he often labored on numerous projects simultaneously. Once, after having visited Czerny at his home, a European musician wrote in his diary of four desks, one in each corner of his study, upon which Czerny composed. He chronicled, "The first desk contained a long list of national tunes to be arranged for D'Almaine and Co. At the second, there was an unfinished arrangement of Beethoven symphonies (piano, four hands) for Cocks and Co. The third desk contained his new edition of Bach fugues, and at the fourth was a Grand Symphony Czerny was composing."[12]

In his day, this composer, who has challenged piano students for over one hundred and fifty years, was known as an example of legendary productivity and excellence. Czerny composed hundreds of pieces, including concertos and sonatas, but is remembered most for his études, including his famous *The School of Velocity*. Also one of Europe's finest editors and publishers, he published the ominous first complete edition of all the keyboard music of J. S. Bach. It is intriguing to note that he never employed a copyist but instead wrote out every note himself!

From this valuable example of quality work and creative ingenuity, an evaluation of our present levels of efficiency and excellence may foster increased desire for improved productivity—like the hundreds of tenacious piano students in my and other piano studios across the world who, still today, continue laboring over Czerny's piano exercises, striving to achieve proficient technical and musical excellence!

Musical excellence, then, should be the prime objective of every serious musician. In achieving this worthwhile goal, important elements of musicianship must be developed—mastering musical concepts of proficiency, refinement, and artistic communication through ease of playing, expressiveness, accuracy, rhythmic vitality and stability, beautiful tone, focused attention, and positive attitude. When producing our best musically, whether through teaching or performing, we are considering the true character of music that the true musician will always strive, with every fiber of their being, to grasp and share. And what marvelous sentiments of fulfillment are gained in the process!

HUMILITY

Having a reverence for music is an essential part of creative growth. In discussing humility in music, one must understand the fine line between confidence and egotism. The best and most successful musicians are those who exude confidence, yet possess genuine humility for great music, a humility that stems from many years of graciously appreciating the work of master composers of the past as well as fellow artists, while humbly learning all that is possible from them. After all, a true musician is never bigger than the music itself!

One mature and accomplished musician once commented to me that he had been playing the violin for over thirty-five years and still could not perform well in public. He continued, "I'm actually very good when I play for myself but get too distracted when others are listening. After speaking with a professional orchestra musician, I came to realize that this deficit in my playing is because I lack humility. I am too focused on myself instead of the music. I become an obstacle!"

When a musician is humble, he or she possesses a modest view of his or her own importance, a defining characteristic of an unpretentious person and someone who does not think he or she is better or more important than others or than the music itself. It is the opposite of aggressiveness, arrogance, boastfulness, and vanity. Beethoven once said, "Humility is the only true wisdom by which we prepare our minds for all the possible changes of life."[13]

A wonderful example of this can be related from the life of Felix Mendelssohn. Mendelssohn knew he was extraordinarily talented, yet he never flaunted it, always preferring in genuine humility to elevate and encourage those around him. On one occasion, when he was to be the pianist in a piano-cello-violin trio, his piano score for the musical ensemble went missing. Of course, he didn't need his music (being able to play his part from memory), but, not wishing to embarrass the cellist and the violinist who needed their music, he placed any music he could find upside down on the piano (so as not to distract himself), and then had a friend turn pages throughout the performance![14]

On a personal level, several years ago I was invited to be one of three adjudicators at a regional piano competition in Arizona. One of the contestants, a brilliant technician from the East Coast, exuded arrogance from the outset. Each contestant was required to perform three pieces of contrasting styles. After concluding a fine performance of the first piece, a highly taxing Prokofiev sonata, this young man made a scene of exaggerated proportions. He removed his sport coat and threw it on the floor; then while wiping his brow, jumped off the stage and grabbed and began to drink one of the three water bottles on the judges' table, acting as if his repertoire was more difficult than any of other contestants' that day. But it was his attitude regarding certain musical interpretation I had questioned him about following the competition that distanced me from him as the possible winner.

In the Prokofiev score, the composer writes "*ffff*" (quadruple forte) over a series of notes. When this performer arrived at this passage, rather than playing *ffff* he played *pp* (pianissimo). When I asked him why he had made this change in dynamics from the written score, he answered, "Oh, I feel that passage should be played pianissimo!" Now, for one who believes in following a composer's score with honesty, I was not amused with this blatant lack of humility toward the composer's intent. This, coupled with the prior affectation of his stage presence following the sonata, caused our judge's panel to award another contestant first prize.

A certain level of self-confidence is essential as a driving force toward accomplishment. Humility doesn't come from lack of confidence! Instead, confidence and humility work together. Pride is very different from self-confidence. Pride is having feelings of extreme self-worth, whereas self-esteem can be synonymous with healthy confidence. Hence, self-worth is a normal personal trait that all people possess and does not necessarily equate to pride. If a person is contentious with others to simply prove their point, that is pride. When a pianist performs well for others, they exhibit high self-esteem. Pride is the need to brag about personal strengths. Self-worth is finding ourselves acceptable but not having to express that fact to everyone! Furthermore, self-esteem is intrinsic and not related to material possessions. Fame and fortune may fluctuate, but strong self-worth is constant, enhanced by a life lived with strong personal values.

Confident performers strive to communicate the musical language by deciphering and conveying the message of the composer with honesty and humility. Ideally, all musicians throughout the world will put the purity of their art at the service of mankind in an effort to unite all people in fraternal ties. Let each of us contribute as he is able until this standard is attained in all its glory.

In speaking personally about developing humility as an artist, I need to briefly share the background of my earliest musical beginnings. My maternal grandparents were largely responsible for the discovery of my musical gifts. They owned a large commercial building south of Brigham Young University campus in Provo, Utah, where various businesses rented space. The very large top floor area was rented by a professional dance studio, comprising several classes of over one hundred students.

At age three, I recall entering this room with my grandparents one afternoon during a dance class. We sat for a few minutes and observed while the students rehearsed to music from a blaring radio. When the music concluded and the teacher announced the end of class, the young students began leaving the building while I walked over to the old upright piano against a wall. To the astonishment of my grandparents, I climbed on the bench with my short legs dangling high above the floor, and with both small hands began playing the melody "by ear" of the music we had just heard on the radio. Uncommon for one so young, this happening was the catalyst that initiated my private piano instruction with a wonderful teacher during those significant, earliest years of my childhood.

Subsequently, during my teen years when I began winning and receiving honors and awards in various local, state, regional, national, and international competitions, my maternal grandfather consistently cautioned me to stay humble. He would say to me, "Now, David, don't get the big head!" At first, I felt he wasn't pleased with my achievements and my work. My mind often questioned why he would, rather than praise me, always take this opposing approach—"Don't get the big head!" It wasn't until years later that I began to fully understand his intuition, eternal perspective, and special pride and love for me, his grandson. In my opinion, his example taught me that the humble musician does not regard his musical gifts, possessions, or accomplishments as his own, but as gifts of God to whom all appreciation and honor is given!

Some of the prominent musicians of the world, past and present, also realize that their musical strength comes from humility. Those who sought divine guidance in their musical creations always recognized the true source of their inspired work. Recorded in diaries of the day, it is said that Bach composed as if God were directing him. Some of the church hierarchy often noticed that when he began filling in notes on a new page of manuscript paper for the next Sunday service, he often initialed the blank manuscript "J. J." which stood for *Jesu Juva*, meaning "Help me, Jesus." After finishing a composition, he frequently initialed the last page with "S.D.G." denoting *Seli Deo Gloria*, or "To God Alone the Glory."[15] This spiritual composer was well aware of God directing his work, and because of this, his compositional accomplishments reached a new zenith.

In our own day, I have appreciated artists who demonstrate unassuming dispositions in their work. A few years ago, Itzhak Perlman, a world-renowned violinist, came on stage to give a concert that I attended at Avery Fisher Hall at the Lincoln Center in New York City. For Perlman, getting on stage is no small achievement. Stricken with polio as a child, he wears braces on both legs and walks with the aid of two crutches.

To see him walk slowly across the stage, one step at a time, is an unforgettable sight. Humbly, he walks painfully, yet majestically, until he reaches his chair. He sits down, slowly places his crutches on the floor, undoes the clasps on his legs, tucks one foot back, and extends the other foot forward. Then, he bends down and picks up the violin, puts it under his chin, nods to the conductor, and proceeds to play.

But this time something went wrong. Just as he finished the first few bars, one of the strings on his violin broke. You could hear it snap—it went off like gunfire across the room. There was no mistaking what that sound meant and what he had to do. The audience that night thought to themselves, "He will have to get up, put on the clasps again, pick up the crutches, and limp his way off stage to either find another violin or find another string for this one." But he didn't. Instead, he waited a moment, closed his eyes, and then played with such passion, such power, and such purity as this audience had ever heard. Of course, anyone knows that it is impossible to play a symphonic work for violin with just three strings. We all know that, but that night, Itzhak Perlman refused to know that!

You could see him modulating, changing, and recomposing the piece in his head—a true genius with such humility, yet with such strength and conviction. When he finished, there was an awesome silence in the room. The people rose and cheered. There was a display of tremendous emotion and an extraordinary outburst of applause from every corner of the auditorium. Everyone was on their feet, screaming and cheering and doing everything they could to show how much they appreciated what he had done.

He smiled, wiped the sweat from his brow, raised his bow to quiet the audience, and then he said, not boastfully, but humbly in a quiet, pensive, reverent tone, "You know, sometimes it is the artist's task to find out how much music you can still make with what you have left." This powerful statement has remained with me ever since that night. I believe this is the way of life—not just for artists but for all of us. So perhaps, for those of us who are musicians, our task in this shaky, fast-changing, bewildering world in which we live is to make music, at first with all that we have, and then, when that is no longer possible, to humbly make music with what we have left.

Humility requires sincerity and honesty. Any self-conceit, whether nurtured by superior intelligence, wealth, high position, or the praise of others, is an obstacle on the path. It requires a constant willingness to deny oneself, to be critical of oneself, and to be open to heaven's guidance, especially when it differs from one's own pre-conceived concept. Although you and I will most likely not produce the world's next great musical piece, each of us can always listen to the voice of God as He speaks directly to our spirits through music, through the scriptures, through magnificent opportunities presented us, and through our family and friends. Then we, too, in humil-ity might produce masterpieces from gifts with which we've been blessed in our own realm of influence, as we walk humbly with faith, remembering the Lord's promise, "And thine ears shall hear a word behind thee, saying, this is the way, walk ye in it." (Isaiah 30:21).

As Haydn gained wealth and fame amid the high-society atmo-sphere of his time, he remained content to dress as a peasant, to mingle with the common folk, and to downplay his musical status. Once he responded to an admiring fan, "Do not speak so to me. You see only a man whom God has granted talent and a good heart." And in his later years, he acknowledged, "I have associated with kings, emperors, and many great gentlemen and have heard many flattering things from them; but I do not wish to live on an intimate footing with such persons, and I prefer people of my own status."[16] It is said of Haydn that simplicity, generosity, and humility exemplified his life to the very end.

J. S. Bach acknowledged, "The final aim and reason of all music is nothing other than the glorification of God and the refreshment of the spirit."[17] Others have remarked that adulation can be poison! History indicates that most individuals are incapable of managing fame or fortune successfully or with spiritual maturity. The Italian composer Giuseppe Verdi seemed to be one of those significant few.

The story is told of the 1887 premiere of perhaps Verdi's greatest opera, *Otello*, at Milan's gorgeous opera house, La Scala. At the conclusion of this mesmerizing performance, the enthusiastically cheering audience, including patrons from throughout Europe, gave Verdi an unprecedented twenty curtain calls. Even after Verdi left the opera house, fans were shouting his name and followed after his carriage as it wheeled away. At five o'clock the next morning, some were still screaming in the streets, "Viva Verdi!"

Though the attention Verdi received following this historic performance was considerable, his reaction to all of this uproar is rather fascinating. Bowing graciously, Verdi seemed embarrassed by the commotion. Showing little if any pride, he humbly received the praise with appreciation, for he had already learned an important lesson of life—that one should live life to the best of his or her ability, with or without triumph. Like many of us, Verdi had previously experienced both success and failure and realized that neither mattered much nor endured long. Yet from spiritual wisdom comes an appropriate response to thunderous applause or accolades of men for a job well done, never pride and arrogance! Verdi understood that the vanity often associated with triumph is capable of destroying the humility that God desires each of us to possess.[18]

Gifted musicians are born with a special ability—with music in them; that is all. No special credit or treatment is due. The only recognition we claim is for the use we make of the talent we are given. That is the reason why musicians must never be vain, because they've been blessed with talent. We are not responsible for that; it is not of our doing. What musicians do with their talent is what matters. This gift must be cherished, never wasted. Instead, we must work—work constantly and nourish it! An artist of our time understood these conceptions completely.

One of the greatest cellists ever, Pablo Casals, taught the tw^{entieth}-century world much about humility with regard to musical appreciation. Throughout his long life, the driving force behind Casals was to make men understand each other. As a man, he was seemingly small, and yet he was a giant in beauty and spirit. Though tender and apparently fragile, delicately tuned to every whisper of sound and thread of loveliness, he had within him an indomitable strength. Those who knew him closely felt the special qualities of his personality—his warmth, his optimism, his understanding, his boundless humanity, and his humility. He had a radiance and magnetism that affected all around him.

Casals once shared this perspective: "An artistic performance is the blending of intelligence and intuition. We must look for the meaning of music and this is only to be found when the performer approaches it with honesty and humility." Throughout his life he maintained, "I am a man first, an artist second. As a man, my first obligation is to the welfare of my fellowmen. I will endeavor to meet this obligation through music—the means which God has given me—since it transcends language, politics, and national boundaries. My contribution to world peace may be small, but at least I will have given all I can to an ideal I hold sacred."[19]

PERSPECTIVES ON COMPETITIONS

During no time in the history of instrumental performances has the phenomenon of competition among performers been keener or more apparent than now. Of course, we live in a world of vast competition in every arena of life. Dr. Paul C. Pollei, founder and artistic director of the Gina Bachauer International Piano Competition, stated:

> One of the most telling activities of music-making in the last part of the twentieth century has been the increase on the part of teachers and parents to provide opportunities to demonstrate that the musical gifts and art of the past have not diminished with time. In no other activity has this become more obvious than in the increase of music competitions throughout the world.
> The diminution of cultural boundaries and the ability for speedy interchange from country to country and culture to culture have

augmented the instructional possibilities, and increased the need for displaying excellence in the form of winning performances. Most cultures and countries identify their best citizens by the number of accolades and promotions earned. This has become highly evident in the classical music world through the phenomenon of music competitions.

At competitions some parents, teachers, and students are so obsessed with the goal of winning that it becomes a singular goal of the studio and home to prepare students to participate and hopefully win the next competition. Teachers even accept students and plan curricula, with only one goal in mind—entering students into competitions to win.

Never would my colleagues in the music world suppose that I, a founder of an international competition, would speak, in disfavor of competitions . . . I have no dislike of the competition procedure, only a plea to treat the situation and the opportunity with dignity and honor, thereby allowing young pianists the privilege of avoiding the onus of failure by declaration."[20]

Ours is a time that has been saturated with the stunning technical wizardry of young pianists who accomplish the most amazing feats in a very short time frame, thereby qualifying them as young, high-ranking winners of national and international fame and stardom. Unfortunately, with the widespread notoriety attained by such accomplishments, the technical approach to music-making has often replaced the more important aspects of musical communication.

It is apparent from my experience that many music students who are subjected to this kind of music tutoring have been exposed chiefly to music which will dazzle the judges for the moment. As a consequence, there is no substance in their background, due to a lack of fundamentals as part of their training. It has been too often the case to have students audition for my studio who can play a virtuosic étude but not able to sight-read the most simple hymn or elementary teaching piece. Music is and must be more than this!

Teachers and parents would be wise to understand the musical void that can sometimes be created by introducing a competition repertoire and a flavor to win in favor of the skills necessary to build a long-lasting contribution to personal musical satisfaction. Personally, I have seen far too many young musicians who are fed a false sense of what music means by memorizing lengthy, difficult works, in an attempt to impress judges at the expense of a natural progression of solid building blocks which would endure for a lifetime.

It is not requisite to win a competition to be considered an accomplished, inspiring musician! Comprehensive musical training and musical communication are key. More important than winning competitions is that communication always remains the prime concern and obligation of a performer. An effective performer communicates most successfully when he or she is humble enough to demonstrate artistic integrity by deciphering and following the musical score with honesty, by making a sincere effort to grasp the intent of the composer, and by conveying a designated message to the listener. To flaunt unnecessary histrionics and technical prowess without carefully and sensitively preparing repertoire of thoughtful and meaningful communication is an artificial approach to impressive musical performances.

Personally, it is a sad scenario to witness competitors, parents, teachers, and colleagues who, for one reason or another, malign others in the competition process. Unfortunately, they sometimes revel in the misfortune—mistakes, memory slips, and other troubles—of those with whom they are competing. But it is my conviction that when failure is wished upon others, everyone loses. Actually, my frequent exposure to this tactic has taught me that it is always manufactured by personal insecurity! Some strive to belittle others as a way to provide for themselves feelings of superiority though this never produces those results. Rather, it delivers false confidence for a time but is never long lasting. A true principle of life is that when we build others, we are built! There is never a need to become a destroyer or to spend time with those who strive to demean.

During my competition years, I discovered that contestants were often interested only in themselves and their own personal agendas, objectives, and achievements. On one occasion during a prestigious international piano competition in which I advanced from the preliminary round of 130 contestants from various countries, to thirty-four quarterfinalists, and finally to one of the remaining sixteen semifinalists, I experienced firsthand this self-absorption among competitors.

At the very moment I was introduced to walk out from behind the curtain to the piano on stage to perform my repertoire, I was tapped on the shoulder from behind. Turning around, the Russian contestant who had also advanced to this round of competition, stood there beaming. In his broken English, he said to me, "David, I heard your quarterfinal round of competition yesterday and thought you played like a pig!"

Had I psychologically internalized his rude, insensitive comment, it could have resulted in a problematic, even disastrous performance. But understanding his malicious intent saved for that very instant, coupled with my persistent nature to always do my best, I refused to be affected by it. Determined to keep that secure frame of reference throughout my playing, I produced a stunning performance that propelled me into the semifinal round. Incidentally, the Russian contestant did not advance.

Although there are negatives or downsides of competitions, much good can come from them. Competitions can provide constructive, positive elements for musical development. Specifically, competition preparations will often generate favorable conditions for learning and growth, provide students and teachers with great opportunities to explore and master significant repertoire, assist in meeting deadlines, encourage students to be driven to excel, develop strong self-discipline, establish vigorous attitudes for accomplishment, and create experiences of motivation and fulfillment by refining the musical presentations to a superior level where artistic communication between the performer and listener is successful. Competitions provide opportunities to see what other students are achieving through sufficient effort, and teachers can benefit from judges' feedback, which typically encourages and provokes ideas for enhanced teaching.

Sometimes, however, competitions teach hard lessons. On occasion, I have witnessed competitions where politics played a significant role in the adjudication process and outcome. In some of my participations with competitions, there have been times when the "legitimate" winner didn't win! From these difficult learning experiences, however, one can develop a high quality of character and spiritual maturity, in addition to reaping blessings in disguise. At one competition in particular, one of my fifteen-year-old male high school students, a gifted, intelligent, young musician and pianist, encountered a most difficult and life-changing experience while participating in the challenging Four Corners Regional Piano Competition, which comprised contestants from Utah, Colorado, Arizona, and New Mexico.

After advancing to the final round of competition, it was apparent that he was nervous to be performing in the large concert hall on the university campus for the older, more experienced competitors and the audience of piano aficionados present. Before we approached the stage at his appointed time, he told me that he had prayed for comfort and peace to play his best and that he had received a spiritual confirmation that all would be well with his performance.

The meticulous concerto ensemble that afternoon between the solo piano part (performed by my student) and the orchestral reduction of the Grieg *Concerto* (performed by me) was "awe-inspiring," according to numerous audience members. Furthermore, a spiritual power enabled my student to perform with beauty and accuracy beyond any previous performance he had given. Following the final chord of his musical and flawless playing, audible gasps came from members of the audience. Afterward, he was greeted by many individuals, some with tears dribbling down their cheeks, who thanked him for his inspiring performance. For the vast majority, it was by far the superior playing of the competition that afternoon!

After an unprecedented two hours of deliberation, the adjudicators returned to the hall to announce the final results of the competition. Many in the audience were shocked and dismayed, as were we, to hear that my student, the youngest of the four finalists, had received fourth place in this final round of competition! Although competitions are often subjective, many voiced the blunder of this outcome. Then, later that evening, we acquired a better understanding of this injustice.

Unethically, one of the jurors spoke to my student in private that evening, telling him that he knew nothing about real music-making. The juror further informed him that his musical training (my teaching) had mistakenly led him to believe that his conception of musical beauty and technical proficiency was in fact only stiff, non-musical playing, and that he should find a competent teacher immediately! His careless words left my teenage student crushed and absolutely devastated.

Directly upon hearing of this conversation, I recognized where this problem had originated. The previous evening, this particular juror had given a solo recital for the public and competition participants. Upon hearing his Mozart sonata (the same sonata my student performed the next morning in the preliminary round), I became concerned, as his rendition of the sonata was far inferior to the performance my student delivered! How embarrassing, even intimidating, it must have been for him. Accordingly, in an effort to save face, this juror made an attempt to hide his unprofessional manipulation and political indiscretion with false pride by challenging my young student's obviously stellar competition performances.

Sadly, this man's actions destroyed much of my student's self-confidence for a long time and caused him to question himself, his pianistic abilities, and whether or not he had really received the previously mentioned spiritual confirmation from the Lord. It took months to put my young student back together emotionally! These many years later, when discussing this adversity from the past, this gifted young pianist shared with me valuable lessons he had learned from this experience:

> Dr. Hatch, I learned that we should always put our trust in the feelings the Lord has given us first before we trust in the words of men. I also realized later that at that stage of my life, had I won that competition, I would likely have taken the glory to myself and not given it to the Lord. I now know that the performance the Lord helped me give was not really for me, but for Him to touch the hearts of audience members through this beautiful music. This was actually a far better reward than a gold medal or monetary prize! In every ordeal we encounter here on earth, there are important lessons to be learned that will help shape our lives and benefit us eternally.

There are other times when competitors prepare repertoire according to what they've heard in the interpretations of world-class artists. Many of the world's greatest musicians believe that young musicians should learn and strive for much more than to merely imitate other well-known performers—that they must find themselves and recognize their own personal performance strengths and abilities in an appropriately creative process. Each performer must bring the spiritual, emotional, musical, technical, and intellectual aspects of music together, combined into one. Intellect and mind is only the control, not the guide. Similar to what was mentioned earlier in this chapter, Vladimir Horowitz, the world-renowned Russian pianist claimed, "The first point of music is control of emotion and communicating to the listener!"[21] Rarely is this the case in the competition format, hence the reason Horowitz gave for disliking instrumental competitions.

Each student musician is unique in their abilities and ideally should only be in competition with self. They need to understand and achieve confidence by applying productive mental inquiries to their lives: Am I improving? Am I performing better than I was one year ago? Am I achieving my desired personal goals? Also, musicians will become genuinely confident when, with sensibility, they discover correct perspectives of life that relate to their career work such as: If another musician performs brilliantly, this doesn't mean I perform poorly, or When a colleague is an excellent teacher, that does not make me an inferior teacher. When someone in this profession does well, this results in the rest of us advancing in the process. Positive musical influence is infectious!

There was a time when my self-confidence and level of excellence in my pianistic abilities were challenged. At age twelve, after working for many years with my exceptionally skilled first piano teacher, my parents and grandparents decided that I should audition to study with a university professor who could guide me along my career path to becoming a professional artist/teacher.

The Christmas prior to this audition time, one of the gifts from my parents was a classical album of pianist Byron Janis, a prodigious graduate of the Juilliard School. I still remember the album cover, a picture of Janis reaching down to accept flower bouquets from the front row audience members at his Moscow debut performance. There was a particular piece on this recording that gave me goose bumps each time I listened to it and with which I fell in love. I knew from the outset that I had to learn it—the *Sixth Hungarian Rhapsody* of Franz Liszt!

Scheduled auditions with two professors were held in the new year. From these experiences I learned a valuable lesson about teaching that would remain with me throughout my life. Some teachers are optimistic. Others are not. Some teachers build while others discourage and frustrate!

After my playing in the first audition, I explained to the professor that a great desire of mine was to learn Liszt's Sixth Rhapsody. He laughed and said, "David, you cannot learn that piece at this time for it is far too difficult. In fact, you may never be able to develop the required technical facility during your lifetime." This response to an energetic, driven young man was demoralizing. Although he agreed to accept me as a new student, he had made me feel inferior—that I wasn't good enough—that perhaps I may never be the accomplished pianist I dreamed of becoming.

Contrarily, the second audition was exhilarating! After playing for the second professor, who had reacted very favorably to my musical talent, I eagerly sought his reaction to my same request to learn that *Hungarian Rhapsody*. To my surprise his response was clearly encouraging from that of the previous teacher. He said, "David, that rhapsody is a most difficult showpiece. With your exceptional musical talent, it would be my pleasure to assist you in developing the necessary technique to perform it well! This is an outstanding personal goal!" I was elated! In my view, here were two dissimilar teachers—one positive, one negative—one builder and one destroyer.

Incidentally, I learned the *Sixth Hungarian Rhapsody* at that young age and have since performed it hundreds of times for audiences throughout the world as one of my "signature pieces." My thanks to Byron Janis for introducing to me this captivating masterpiece and for unleashing within a young boy perpetual performance excitement and musical determination toward my chosen career!

Finally, one of the most difficult, soul-searching, and possible career-altering occurrences in my life relating to competitions was experienced in the fall of 1976, the bicentennial year of our nation's birth. Never before or since have I faced such harsh reality in my musical pursuits. Still vivid in my mind today is the heartbreak of that time and the pit in my stomach that occurred following a deeply-troubling musical challenge. Rather than experiencing euphoria after winning first place in the collegiate division of the Utah State Fair piano competition, I was left devastated for months afterward. It was only through the continual support and encouragement of my piano professor, parents, and kind friends and associates that I was lifted beyond the misfortune into a realm of thoughtful, mature understanding.

My greatest musical goal, for which I had worked for years, was to perform with the Utah Symphony in the Annual Salute to Youth concert. For years, select winners from three age divisions of this Utah State Fair music competition were invited to perform in this prestigious concert the Wednesday evening prior to Thanksgiving. From the previous twenty seasons, it was common knowledge that the first-place piano winner of the collegiate division was the concluding concerto soloist on those programs. Needless to say, I was thrilled to have become that year's collegiate winner as my dream would come true—performing as a concerto soloist with the Utah Symphony. But it didn't happen!

One week after the competition, I returned to Salt Lake and performed my winning concerto in an audition for the conductor, Maurice Abravanel, and those few professional musicians assisting him that afternoon. All first-, second-, and third-place winners in each of the three instrumental and piano competition divisions had been invited to play for the conductor from which a well-balanced Salute to Youth program would be selected. Since the collegiate piano winner would end the concert, it was explained to me that my audition for the conductor was only a matter of protocol.

We learned that the names of the soloists and concert programming would be announced in the arts section of the *Deseret News* the following afternoon. My remarkable piano professor and I had driven together to Salt Lake that next day for another musical event and excitedly picked up a copy of the newspaper to read the announcement before returning to Provo. What occurred at that time was absolutely shocking!

Never will I forget the devastation while reading that announcement of winners to perform in that season's Salute to Youth concert only to find my name omitted from that list! Frantically, my teacher and I read the article repeatedly, trying to find my name. It was not there! At last we began to accept the sad reality that I would simply not be performing on that prominent program.

The forty-five-minute drive home on I-15 South was the longest, hardest drive of my life. As my teacher drove, I stared out my side window. Not a word was spoken by either of us. We were both despondent. For months we had worked tirelessly for this success, but in a flash this opportunity was gone forever. In desperation we decided there must be an error—a reason why I hadn't been selected. Perhaps my name had been inadvertently omitted from the news release. Should we call and double-check? What had happened?

For several days I felt severe depression and a lack of desire to persevere. As I was not rebounding well after several days, my astute father made a telephone call to one of the committee members involved in the Symphony auditions to seek clarification. Simply, his question was, "Why had the collegiate piano winner become the first in two decades to be denied that performance opportunity?"

To our bewilderment, we learned that the audition committee had selected the third-place winner of my division to perform on that program since he had performed a concerto written by Samuel Barber, an American composer. To them, this choice was the appropriate work for this year's special bicentennial program. But even with this logical explanation, still I felt less than comforted and questioned my pianistic abilities!

At the risk of appearing arrogant, I can admit that I was being a self-absorbed young adult, wanting this magnificent opportunity for myself. When it didn't come, I began to entertain thoughts such as, "If I had been truly phenomenal, they would have chosen me for the Salute to Youth program despite the American concerto." In fact, this trial caused me to perceive myself as a failure and produced doubt in my mind about my talent and ability to truly achieve a successful career as a professional pianist.

In subsequent weeks, I began to heal emotionally through a barrage of praise and encouragement. Specifically, my parents, grandparents, and university instructor all expressed pride in my impressive accomplishment. Other competitors, pianist friends, and a couple of General Authorities of the Church—friends of mine—conveyed their love and deep respect and admiration for me and my work.

Clearly, that affection and sincere reassurance from many significant people in my life restored hope and a firm desire within to forge ahead with all of my professional ambitions.

Although competitions can sometimes be cruel, musical motivation in our lives should deepen our thoughts and feelings toward virtue and beauty and make us more sensitive to others, to ourselves, and to the Spirit. Good, influential music can encourage receptivity to the light of Christ, the source of all righteous inspiration. Additionally, the illumination of great music, which is an expression of God's love, will never let us down; I've learned that, regardless of the outcome of competitions, the beauty of music transcends time and space and encourages the best in people.

NOTES:

1. Heinrich E. Jacob, *Felix Mendelssohn and His Times*, trans. Richard Weston and Clara Weston (Westport: Greenwood Press, 1973), 213.
2. Larry Barkdull, "Some Observations on Art and Writing," http://ldsmag.com/books/book-reviews/article/8186?ac=1.
3. Matthew Jospehson, *Edison: A Biography* (New York: McGraw Hill, 1959), 242.
4. Alfred Einstein, *Mozart: His Character, His Work* (New York: Oxford University Press, 1945), 5.
5. Joseph Machlis, *The Enjoyment of Music* (New York: W.W. Norton and Co, 1955), 84.
6. Patrick Kavanaugh, *Spiritual Moments with the Great Composers* (Grand Rapids: Zondervan Publishing, 1995), 98.
7. Gerald Abraham, ed. *Tchaikovsky: A Symposium* (London: Drummond, 1946), 221.
8. Arthur Rubinstein, *My Many Years* (New York: Alfred A. Knopf, 1980), 243.
9. Eric Werner, *Mendelssohn: A New Image of the Composer and His Age*, trans. Dika Newlin (New York: Free Press, 1963), 167.
10. Patrick Kavanaugh, *Spiritual Moments with the Great Composers* (Grand Rapids: Zondervan Publishing, 1995), 52.
11. Henry Ford, *My Life and Work* (Lawrence: Digireads.com Publishing, 1996), 73.
12. Albert Dreetz, *Czerny and Beethoven* (Leipzig: Kistner and Co., 1932), 45.

13. *The Musician's Diary* (New York: McAfee Music, 1979), 111.

14. Eric Werner, *Mendelssohn: A New Image of the Composer and His Age*, trans. Dika Newlin (New York: Free Press, 1963), 289.

15. Albert Schweitzer, *J. S. Bach*, trans. Ernest Newman (Boston: Humbphries, 1964), 96.

16. Rosemary Hughes, *Haydn* (New York: Collier, 1962), 192.

17. The Musician's Diary (New York: McAfee Music, 1979), 133.

18. Patrick Kavanaugh, *Spiritual Moments with the Great Composers* (Grand Rapids: Zondervan Publishing, 1995), 69.

19. Fritz Henle, *Casals* (New York: American Book Publishing, 1975), 46.

20. Paul C. Pollei, "What is Right with Competitions?" *Clavier*, Dec. 1989, 43.

21. Reginald R. Gerig, *Famous Pianists & Their Technique* (New York: Robert B. Luce, 1990), 466.

Chapter Eleven

MUSICAL COMPOSITIONS
FOR THE HOME

Fundamental masterpieces of music from the lives of faith and
inspiration of master composers, listed by stylistic period

I n selecting these composers and their important compositions, I
was clearly restrained by all that exists and by what groupings
might constitute a relatively balanced and complete chapter on
major composers and their works. I trust that readers will find this
representative listing valuable for excellent family listening, although
it is certainly not exhaustive.

Furthermore, I've provided short narratives of select composers to enlighten the reader with reflections, insights, and inspiration
from their lives; demonstrations of faith in their work; and the creative genius that sometimes involved spiritual motivation in their
musical endeavors.

There is strong evidence that most of the composers cited in this
book were professed Christians who glorified the Lord. It would
be prudent to learn from their experiences, from their works and
inspiration, and from the spiritual promptings they encountered
throughout their musical lives.

As human beings, these composers each possessed temporal challenges, adversities, weaknesses, and difficulties throughout their lives. However, they were highly motivated to develop their innate, God-given musical gifts, to compose music that uplifted and inspired others, and to communicate divine truths and spiritual understanding within their compositions of beauty and intellect. Thus, it is remarkable to consider the spiritual inspiration of much of their work during a time when none of them had been introduced to the restored gospel!

BAROQUE (1600–1750)

GEORG PHILIPP TELEMANN (1681–1767), GERMANY

Key factors in Telemann's rise to power and wealth as the most famous musician in Germany of his time were his sense of humor and likable personality. He was always admired and envied, rather than resented, for his relentless pursuit and acquisition of major court and church positions throughout his life. Although his Lutheran family (his father was a clergyman and his mother, the daughter of a clergyman) disapproved of music, such resistance served only to reinforce his determination to persist with his musical studies. With exceptional musical gift mastering the violin, flute, zither, keyboard, and early composition by the age of ten, Telemann developed a self-confidence and productivity that were extraordinary by any standard.

Telemann was a prolific composer, who provided an enormous body of sacred and secular work. He was also commercially active in publishing and selling his musical compositions. His good friend, George Frederic Handel in Halle, once jokingly related that Telemann "could write a church piece in eight parts with the same expedition another would write a letter!"[1]

Living his later years in Hamburg until his death, Telemann filled the coveted post of Kantor, a position which included teaching responsibilities and directorship of the city's five principal churches. Also, he was over-optimistic in becoming actively involved in the Hamburg Opera, for there was strong opposition to his participation by the city council. Telemann reacted characteristically by threatening to resign and applying for the post of Kantor of the Leipzig

Thomaskirche. He was chosen over Bach and four other candidates. This caused the Hamburg Council to more readily appreciate his gifts as they refused to grant his release, improved his salary, and withdrew their objections to his association with the opera company. By the end of his life, Telemann had become one of the greatest composers of the baroque era.

Significant Works by Georg Phillip Telemann
   Trumpet Concert in D Major
   Viola Concerto in G Major
   Tafelmusik
   Suite for Two Flutes
   Darmstadt Overtures (Suites) in G Major, C Major,
      and A Minor
   Suite La changeante

Johann Sebastian Bach (1685–1750), Germany

A religious man, J. S. Bach was a humble composer and organist whose music wasn't widely distributed during his lifetime. He was a career church musician who was well aware of God directing his work as he composed. Only ten of his original compositions were published in his day, with his music being performed for people who seldom knew great works from poor ones and often by mediocre musicians who were unable to showcase his work. However, he gathered all of the musical ideas and techniques of his era, perfected them, and elevated baroque music to a new pinnacle.

In time, performances of his music generally ceased, and precious manuscripts were lost, thrown away, or sold for a few cents. Some of his music copies were even used as wrapping paper by local merchants and butchers! Subsequently, today's musicologists and classical music lovers have become discouraged, as many of his works were lost forever. We are indebted to Felix Mendelssohn of the nineteenth century, who rediscovered and promoted the valuable musical output of this baroque-period genius.

Significant Works by J. S. Bach

Brandenburg Concertos nos. 1–6

Chaconne in D Minor for Unaccompanied Violin, from Partita
no. 2, BWV 1004

Clavier Concertos – F Minor, D Minor, G Minor

Organ Chorale Preludes

Organ Toccata, Adagio, and Fugue in C Major, BWV 564

Passacaglia in C Minor, BWV 582

Preludes and Fugues, Vol. I and II from the Well-Tempered
Clavier

St. Matthew Passion

The Musical Offering, BWV 1079

Two & Three-Part Inventions

Vocal Cantatas – no. 51, no. 53, no. 158

GEORGE FRIDERIC HANDEL (1685–1759), GERMANY

Although his early life was one of poverty and failure, it is what
Handel's life became that is significant. Unlike many of his contem-
poraries, Handel was internationally renowned during his lifetime,
with his fame never being eclipsed in succeeding generations. By the
end of his life, he had become wealthy from his diligent, continuous
work and from the acceptance of an adoring public.

There were no musicians in Handel's family, but the boy's talent
was so pronounced in his early years that his father grudgingly
allowed him to take organ lessons and to study composition from the
director of music in the principal church in Handel's native town of
Halle in Saxony. Handel became an accomplished organist and harp-
sichordist, studied violin and oboe, received a thorough grounding
in counterpoint, and became familiar with contemporary German
and Italian composers by the usual and effective method of copying their scores. During many early decades, he had struggled musically and financially but as a successful, older man, Handel chose to
use his affluence to help others less fortunate. The well-known story
behind his magnificent oratorio, *Messiah* (shared in chapter two of
this book), demonstrated his abundant generosity.

Significant Works by George Frederic Handel

Messiah
Overture to Agrippina
The Faithful Shepherd: Suite
Water Music

ANTONIO VIVALDI (1678–1741), ITALY

Known by the nickname "Red Priest" because of his red hair, Vivaldi battled acute bronchial asthma throughout his life. He trained to be a priest for three years and was ordained in 1703 at age twenty-five, at which time he was taught to play violin by his father. His earliest known performance was in 1696. Following his ordination, he put an end to saying Mass, claiming "his chest was too tight" due to his asthma, although many believed he quit because he was forced to become a priest against his wishes.

During his life, the prolific Vivaldi wrote approximately five hundred concertos, along with a wealth of opera and religious-themed pieces. In 1723, he composed *The Four Seasons*, which is undoubtedly his most famous piece of work—a set of four violin concertos, each section having been composed to resemble its respective season. While something of a musical genius, he was also said to be somewhat cocky. He once claimed he could compose a concerto in all its parts faster than it could be copied. Like Mozart, Vivaldi died in poverty in 1741 and was buried in an unmarked grave.

Significant Works by Antonio Vivaldi

The Four Seasons

CLASSICAL (1750–1810)

LUDWIG VAN BEETHOVEN (1770–1827) GERMANY

Born in Bonn, Germany's beautiful Rhineland, young Ludwig was a victim of child abuse. Although he had a kind, loving mother, his father, a musician and drunk, was often severe with his young son. From the ongoing cruel mistreatment by his father, young Ludwig learned to be brash and headstrong.

No doubt inspired by the triumphs of the child-prodigy Mozart, which were then well known in that region, Ludwig's father was ambitious for his own son to win equal fame. However, Ludwig's talents as a musician were not to appear at such an early age. Even so, his father worked him extremely hard and presented him in public concerts when he was only eight, though advertising the boy as six.

Beethoven's childhood was most difficult, with circumstances not changing much by his early adult life. By seventeen, Beethoven was an accomplished pianist and excellent composer and went to study with Mozart in Vienna, the great musical city of Mozart and Haydn. However, the proposed lessons were shattered by the news that Ludwig's mother was seriously ill. He returned home in time to be at her side when she died. Since his father was unemployed from his drunkenness that had become progressively worse, the heavy responsibility of supporting the family now fell squarely on Beethoven's shoulders. Now, at eighteen, Beethoven was drawing a larger salary, which he needed to feed his father and two brothers.

Beethoven later returned to Vienna to study with Haydn, though not successfully, as the rapport between teacher and student was less than ideal. Over the next few years, his fame grew, as did his adversities, for he began to lose his hearing. Over time, the harsh, rebellious, and stubborn nature of the master composer who eventually became a recluse—shunning people almost entirely—began to change. He became passionately fond of nature, and his compositions began taking on new dimensions of love and emotion.

Having been reared in the Catholic faith, Beethoven was continuously a religious man, though not in the confessional sense. Just weeks prior to his death, in the midst of a tremendous thunderstorm on the evening of March 26, 1827, surrounded by close friends and presents from admirers, Beethoven evaluated his life in this manner:

> I was formerly inconsiderate and hasty in the expression of my opinions, and thereby I made enemies. Now I pass judgment on no one, and indeed, for the reason that I do not wish to do any one harm . . . with tranquility, O God, will I submit myself to changes, and place all my trust in thy unalterable mercy and goodness. . . .

I must confess that thou didst try with all thy means to draw me to thee. Sometimes it pleased thee to let me feel the heavy hand of thy displeasure and to humiliate my proud heart by manifold castigations. Sickness and misfortune didst thou send upon me to turn my thoughts to my errantries. One thing, only, O Father, do I ask: In whatsoever manner it be, let me turn to thee and become fruitful in good works.[3]

Significant Works by Ludwig van Beethoven

Concerto in C Major for Violin, Cello, and Piano, op. 56

Overtures, op. 43; op. 72a, no. 3; op. 62; op. 84; and op. 117

Romance in G Major for Violin and Orchestra, op. 40

String Quartets, op. 18, no. 1; op. 59, no. 8; op. 130, no. 13; op. 131, no. 14; and op.135, no. 16

The Five Piano Concertos

The Nine Symphonies

The Thirty-two Piano Sonatas

Violin Concerto in D Major, op. 61

FRANZ JOSEPH HAYDN (1732–1809), AUSTRIA

One of the most important classical composers, Franz Joseph Haydn possessed an optimistic disposition and love for life. Even in the midst of tremendous personal challenges, he caught the attention of Prince Anton Esterházy, one of Austria's richest nobles. As the Prince's Kapellmeister was growing old, he engaged Haydn as an assistant at his estate in Eisenstadt, not far from Vienna. Life there was such bliss for Haydn that he remained with the Esterhazy's for the rest of his life.

Haydn had been at Eisenstadt for only a year when Prince Anton died. The Prince's brother, Nicolaus, who succeeded Anton, was even more enthusiastic about music and built a fantastic fairytale palace, which was modeled after Versailles in France. He called the palace Esterház; it included buildings of all kinds—an opera house, a puppet theatre, temples, and summerhouses; in all, it contained one hundred and twenty-six magnificent rooms.

Haydn and the prince became excellent friends, and he was paid a comfortable yearly income. Finally appointed Kapellmeister, he was expected to write novel music for every occasion. Consequently, Haydn was a prolific composer of symphonies, string quartets, piano sonatas, numerous concertos, operas, oratorios, and compositions for liturgical purposes.

During the first half of his life, Haydn rarely ventured far away from Esterház. His name, nevertheless, spread throughout most of Europe. He was known in Russia, for whose grand duke he wrote his Russian Quartets, and publishers in London and Paris were clamoring for the honor to print his works.

Always good-natured, Haydn wrote a symphony that would keep the audience from falling asleep during the slow movement. Calling it the *Surprise Symphony*, he interspersed it with sudden loud passages. And a surprise it was for the unsuspecting many during its first performance!

Prince Nicolaus enjoyed life at Esterház so much that he disliked leaving it or allowing the musicians to leave to visit their families in Vienna. To remind the prince that it was time to give them a break to go see their families, Haydn composed his *Farewell Symphony*, in which, at the end the instrumentalists stop playing one by one and walk out with the music under their arms until no musicians are remaining. The prince took the hint and gave them a holiday!

His last time in public, Haydn attended a performance of his monumental masterpiece, *The Creation*, one of his last major works. When the choir sang, "And there was light," at one moving moment during the work, Haydn pointed to the heavens and exclaimed, "It came from thence."[4]

Significant Works by Franz Joseph Haydn

Concertos for Violoncello in C Major and D Major
Concerto for Trumpet in E-flat Major
Piano Concerto in D Major
Piano Sonata no. 57 in F Major, Hob. XVI/47
Piano Sonata no. 62 in E-flat Major, Hob. XVI/52
Symphonie Concertante in B-flat Major

Symphonies no. 88 in G Major; no. 92 in G Major ("Oxford");
    no. 99 in E-flat Major; no. 104 in D Major ("London")
The Seasons
The Seven Last Words of Christ (Vocal)
Variations in F Minor for Piano
Variations in C Major for Piano

WOLFGANG AMADEUS MOZART (1756–1791) AUSTRIA

As great as they were, many composers (including Haydn,
Beethoven, Chopin, Brahms, and Debussy) composed their works
slowly and arduously. Mozart, however, was blessed with a prodigious gift for writing masterpieces with astounding speed, frequently
within a few hours. Oftentimes, the music was perfectly composed
in his mind, and he simply drew bar lines on manuscript paper and
filled in the measures. What is impressive is that Mozart had a reputation of using this remarkable ability to serve others.

On one occasion Mozart helped a friend in need—Michael
Haydn, brother of the famous Franz Joseph Haydn. Needing money,
Michael Haydn was relieved when he received a financially attractive
commission to write duets for tenor and violin. But, the writing was
to be completed in a very short time period and, at that same time,
he was too ill to write the compositions. When Mozart learned of
his friend's dilemma and that he would lose that income, he visited
Haydn, who lay weak in bed, and commenced writing the pieces
himself while disregarding protests from Haydn that he do this. The
duets were completed masterfully, on time, and not known to the
public until years later to have been composed by Mozart. Listed
today as K. 423 and K. 424, it is admirable that Mozart had insisted
the pieces take Haydn's name and that Haydn receive the income.

This charitable act by Mozart is deemed meritorious, as this kind
of generosity is not common even in our day. Mozart simply filled
a gap by stepping in to help a friend at a difficult time. People can
learn a great lesson from this Christian deed.

Significant Works by Wolfgang Amadeus Mozart
Concerto for Flute and Harp in C Major, K. 299

Concerto for Three Pianos in F Major, K. 242

Concerto for Violin no. 5 in A Major, K. 219

Eine Kleine Nachtmusik

Fantasia in C Minor, K. 396

Fantasia in D Minor, K. 397

Overture to The Marriage of Figaro, K. 492

Concerto for Piano and Orchestra in D Minor, K. 466

Concerto for Piano and Orchestra in A Major, K. 488

Concerto for Piano and Orchestra in C Minor, K. 491

Concerto for Piano and Orchestra in C Major, K. 503

Concerto for Piano and Orchestra in D Major, K. 537 ("Coronation concerto")

Concerto for Piano and Orchestra in B-Flat Major, K. 595

Piano Sonata in A Minor, K. 310

Piano Sonata in D Major, K. 311

Piano Sonata in C Major, K. 330

Piano Sonata in A Major, K. 331

Piano Sonata in F Major, K. 332

Piano Sonata in B-flat Major, K. 333

Piano Sonata in C Major, K. 545

Piano Sonata, K. 576 in D Major

Rondo in A Minor, K. 511

Sinfonia Concertante for Violin and Viola in E-flat Major, K. 364

String Quartet no. 15 in D Minor, K. 421

String Quartet no. 17 ("Hunt") in B-flat Major, K. 458

String Quartet no. 19 ("Dissonant") in C Major, K. 465

Symphony no. 36 ("Linz") in C Major

Symphony no. 38 ("Prague") in D Major

Symphony no. 40 in G Minor

ROMANTIC (1800–1890)

JOHANNES BRAHMS (1833–1897) GERMANY

Throughout his life, this modest German composer was universally loved. A life-long bachelor who had been a quiet benefactor of the poor, who loved children, and who made friends easily, Brahms became one of the most renowned composers of the nineteenth century. To successfully complete his symphonies, songs, chamber music, piano concertos, and solo pieces from which he received both criticism and acclaim, Brahms acknowledged that both divine inspiration and intense work with creative genius were required.

Unassuming about this unsolicited fame and most revealing of his characteristic humility are comments he often made comparing his music to that of other musical geniuses. Concerning Mendelssohn, Brahms said, "I'd give all my compositions if I could have written such a piece as the *Hebrides Overture.*" After playing a Bach sonata, he threw a copy of his own sonata on the floor saying, "After that, who could play such stuff as this?" And, at a dinner party during which his host was about to toast "the health of the greatest composer," Brahms interrupted by standing with glass in hand and shouted, "Quite right! Here's to Mozart's health!"

Prior to his death, the highly spiritual Brahms shared insights into the sources of his creative intellect. Among many explanatory comments he claimed, "the Spirit speaks when the creative urge is upon me . . . and the ideas flow directly from God."[5]

Significant Works by Johannes Brahms

    Academic Festival Overture, op. 80

    Concerto for Piano and Orchestra no. 1 in D Minor, op. 15

    Concerto for Violin and Orchestra in D Major, op. 77

    Intermezzos for Piano, op. 76; op. 116; op. 118; and op. 119

    Liebeslieder Waltzes for Voice and Piano

    Serenade no. 2 in A Major, op. 16

    Sonata for Piano and Clarinet (or Viola) in F Minor, op. 120, no. 1

    Symphony no. 1 in C Minor, op. 68

    Symphony no. 2 in D Major, op. 73

    Symphony no. 3 in F Major, op. 90

    Symphony no. 4 in E Minor, op. 98

    Variations on a Theme by Joseph Haydn, op. 56A

    Variations and Fugue on a Theme by Handel, op. 24

FREDERIC CHOPIN (1810–1849), POLAND

On a beautiful Paris morning, Tuesday, October 30, 1849, throngs of people filled the square in front of the Church of the Madeleine. The approximately four thousand invited guests were attending the funeral of one of the greatest romantics of the nineteenth century, Frederic Chopin. Interestingly, the shy, reserved poet of the piano disliked large crowds but, leaving his homeland of Poland in search of a musical career in Western Europe, he became very famous—especially with the Paris high society—as a brilliant performer, composer, and teacher. During his life, he gave to the world a vast amount of uplifting, touching, and elegant music.

Although reared in a devoutly Christian home, Chopin became accustomed to living a life of luxury and status. His morals deteriorated and he yielded to many temptations of the flesh, including several unhealthy relationships. It seems he was not spiritually equipped to manage a life of fame and fortune. After suffering for years with tuberculosis, which finally took his life at a young age, Chopin turned away from his destructive influences and reaffirmed his faith in God.

On his deathbed, Chopin pressed a crucifix to his heart amidst the many people in the room and shared these last words, "Now I am at the source of Blessedness." The prodigal son finally returned and expressed joy and gratitude to God, the very giver of his enormous musical gifts.[6]

Significant Works by Frederic Chopin

    Andante Spianato and Polonaise in E-flat Major, op. 22
    Ballade no. 1 in G Minor, op. 23
    Ballade no. 2 in F Major, op. 38
    Ballade no. 3 in A-flat Major, op. 47
    Ballade no. 4 in F Minor, op. 52
    Barcarolle, op. 60
    Berceuse, op. 57
    Concerto for Piano and Orchestra in E Minor, op. 11
    Concerto for Piano and Orchestra in F Minor, op. 21
    Études, op. 10 & op. 25

Fantaisie in F Minor, op. 49

Impromptu in C-sharp Minor, op. 66, no. 4

Mazurkas

Nocturnes

Polonaise no. 3 in A Major, op. 40, no. 1 ("Military")

Polonaise no. 5 in F-sharp Minor, op. 44

Polonaise no. 6 in A-flat Major, op. 53

Polonaise-Fantaisie in A-flat Major, op. 61

Sonata no. 2 in B-flat Minor, op. 35 ("Funeral March")

Sonata no. 3 in B Minor, op. 58

Scherzo no. 1 in B Minor, op. 20

Scherzo no. 2 in B-flat Minor, op. 31

Scherzo no. 3 in C-sharp Minor, op. 39

Twenty-four Preludes, op. 28

Waltzes

ANTONIN DVOŘÁK (1841–1904) CZECH REPUBLIC

Czech composer Antonin Dvořák was a spiritual man who had deep love for God and his fellowman. He also appreciated animals, games, the outdoors, ocean liners, and trains. But of his many passions, the enthusiastic Dvořák most adored his children and recognized that strong family relationships are most important in the eternal scheme of things.

Dvořák's father was always proud of his son's musical gifts but felt that he should pursue a profession that would guarantee an adequate income for his family. In spite of his father's concerns, however, Dvořák worked tenaciously to perfect his musical talents and enjoyed a celebrated music career while prospering in his chosen vocation. It was said of him that he favored being with his family rather than dignitaries and loyal fans with whom he associated throughout the world. In fact, when the internationally renowned composer traveled away from home, he always sent loving letters to his children reminding them to "pray fervently" and to "attend church regularly." Oftentimes, when composing most genres of music—from concertos to chamber music, from solos to symphonies, from oratorio to opera—he worked at the kitchen table while his wife cooked or baked bread and his children played noisily around him. There was immense grief and sadness, therefore, when he lost three children within a short time. His deep sorrow caused Dvořák to write his greatest work, the lovely *Stabat Mater*, which related personally to his family. Based on a poem by Jacopone da Todi, this composition portrays the grief of Jesus's mother at her son's death.

Among his significant symphonic works given to the world is Dvořák's *Symphony no. 9 in E Minor*, known as *The New World Symphony*, which was composed in 1893 while he was visiting the United States. It is one of his most famous compositional masterpieces and surely one of the most popular symphonies in the modern repertoire. Shortly after his enjoyable visit to the States, the Bohemian composer moved to New York City to spend his final years.[7]

Significant Works by Antonin Dvořák

Mass in D Major
Piano Trio no. 4 ("Dumky"), op. 90
Requiem, op. 89
Stabat Mater
String Quartet ("The American"), op. 96
Symphonic Poems
Symphony no. 9 in E Minor ("New World")
Te Deum

EDVARD GRIEG (1843–1907) NORWAY

The *Piano Concerto in A minor, op. 16*, was the work with which Edvard Grieg achieved international stardom. In fact, even today this concerto, which was composed during the summer of 1868 in a secluded country cottage in Denmark when Grieg was only twenty-five, is possibly the most frequently performed concerto of any in the standard repertoire today.

Desiring the renowned pianist's input, Grieg was benefited by the advice of the intimidating Franz Liszt, who was thirty years his senior. He was hopeful that if Liszt approved of his piece, the news would travel abroad and Grieg's career could be launched for good.

Liszt welcomed the young composer and asked him to play the work for him, but the anxious Grieg hadn't practiced. So Liszt himself sat down and sight-read the entire concerto with great dexterity and panache. His enthusiasm was apparent from the first note as the encouraging Liszt made positive comments throughout significant sections of the work, though he suggested some changes, which Grieg incorporated before publishing the score in 1872. Finally, Liszt handed the manuscript back to Grieg following the triumphant conclusion and said, "Keep steadily on! I tell you, you have the capability, and do not let them intimidate you!"[8]

Grieg never forgot these words of encouragement from the piano master, and in that same spirit, he himself later became an encouraging support and mentor for younger composers. The acceptance and acknowledgement by the formidable Liszt gave Grieg the confidence to carry on throughout his life. He later wrote, "This final admonition of Liszt was of tremendous importance to me. There was something in it that seemed to give it an air of sanctification."[9]

Of interest is that Liszt may have been this positive force in Grieg's life, having experienced a similar affirmation during his own early years! As a boy of twelve, he played the piano at a concert attended by the renowned classical master, Beethoven. In the midst of the applause, the great Beethoven arose, approached the stage, and blessed him by kissing his cheek—a blessing Liszt could now pass on to another remarkable talent younger than he.

Significant Works by Edvard Grieg

    Lyric Pieces, Book I, op. 12
    Gynt Suite
    Concerto in A Minor, op. 16 Sonata in E Minor, op. 7

FRANZ LISZT (1811–1886), HUNGARY

The life of Liszt is a biographer's dream or nightmare. Outrageously gifted from birth and clearly destined to dazzle and astound, he also exhibited deep internal conflict that attracted a no less divided opinion of his life and works.

Franz Liszt was believed by many to be the world's greatest pianist of the nineteenth century. That his vastly energetic work and lifestyle should cost him incalculable pain is an ironic travesty. Although true of many artists that we admire countless years later, often the culmination of intense personal suffering represents a peculiar case with Liszt. His lifelong vacillation between worldly acclaim and spiritual seclusion and the constant friction between the personal and public sides of his nature were invariably at the center of many predicaments of his famous life.

Also known as one of the finest piano pedagogues of his time, the aristocracy wanted their children to study with him due to his huge reputation. On one occasion, a young performer invented a story to attract a larger audience for her concert in Berlin. She advertised that she was a "pupil of Liszt," whom she had never met!

On the morning of the publicized performance, the newspapers announced that Liszt had arrived in town. She was horrified and decided to find him at his hotel and ask his forgiveness for this offense. To her surprise, Liszt asked what pieces she would be performing on that evening's program. Then, he chose one of the pieces and asked her to perform it for him, after which he gave her a lesson with several helpful musical suggestions. He then dismissed her with a smile saying, "Now, my dear, you may call yourself a pupil of Liszt." What a powerful, charitable lesson this young woman received from the seemingly humble, forgiving piano master![10]

Significant Works by Franz Liszt

Annees de Pelerinage, Books I & II
Concerto for Piano and Orchestra no. 1 in E-flat Major
Concerto for Piano and Orchestra no. 2 in A Major
Dante Sonata
Hungarian Fantasia for Piano and Orchestra
Nineteen Hungarian Rhapsodies
Liebestraume no. 3
Mephisto Waltz
Paganini Étude no. 6 in A Minor
Sonata in B Minor
Three Concert Études

Totentanz for Piano and Orchestra
Twelve Transcendental Études

FELIX MENDELSSOHN (1809–1847), GERMANY

Mendelssohn is regarded by some critics as the nineteenth-century equivalent of Wolfgang Amadeus Mozart. Whether he was born with his incredible talent or became a product of a wealthy, artistically-and intellectually-inclined family will remain a mystery, but like all prodigies, Mendelssohn showed signs of true genius from childhood. He played the piano, violin, and organ and studied composition, painting, and languages. During the years that followed, he composed several master works for the piano and many different combinations of instruments and voices.

Born to a religious family, Mendelssohn's parents baptized their four children into the Lutheran Church—they were a Jewish family converted to Christianity and the Lutheran faith when they moved from French-occupied Hamburg to Berlin. Here, Mendelssohn studied at Berlin University where he decided on music as his chosen vocation. Although he experienced occasional setbacks, the happily-married Mendelssohn remained optimistic, confident, and cheerful throughout his life. Ignoring the possibility of failure, he always expected the eventuality of success and was rarely disappointed.

In time, Mendelssohn traveled and performed all over Europe, finally settling in Leipzig where he became conductor of the Leipzig Gewandhaus Orchestra, performing mostly works by Bach and Beethoven. It is Mendelssohn to whom we owe homage for reviving the masterful and spiritual music of J. S. Bach. Mendelssohn revered the great composer so completely that he used his own popularity and four hundred singers and soloists of the Singakademie to help renew interest in the baroque master's works. He even made his debut as a maestro being the first to conduct Bach's *St. Matthew Passion* since the composer's death in 1750 and, more important, one hundred years after Bach's own premiere performance of the masterpiece. Mendelssohn also founded and directed the Leipzig Conservatory, which remained one of the most prestigious music institutions in Germany for over half a century.

Significant Works by Felix Mendelssohn

Capriccio in F-Sharp Minor, op. 5
Capriccio brilliant for Piano and Orchestra, op. 22
Concerto for Piano and Orchestra in G Minor, op. 25
Concerto for Piano and Orchestra in D Minor, op. 40
Concerto for Violin and Orchestra in E Minor, op. 64
Overture to A Midsummer Night's Dream
Overture in B Minor, The Hebrides ("Fingal's Cave"), op. 26
Overture to Ruy Blas in C Minor, op. 95
Rondo Brilliant for Piano and Orchestra, op. 29
Scherzo a capriccio in F-sharp Minor
Songs without Words
Symphony no. 3 in A Minor ("Scottish"), op. 56
Symphony no. 4 in A Major ("Italian"), op. 90
Variations Serieuses in D Minor, op. 54

ALEXANDER SCRIABIN (1872–1915), RUSSIA

Scriabin was a Russian composer and pianist who initially developed a lyrical and idiosyncratic tonal language inspired by the music of Frederic Chopin. He developed an increasingly atonal musical system, and although the process of innovation was somewhat gradual, he may be considered to be the main Russian Symbolist composer.

Scriabin was one of the most controversial of early modern composers. The Great Soviet Encyclopedia said of Scriabin that, "No composer has had more scorn heaped or greater love bestowed." Leo Tolstoy once described Scriabin's music as "a sincere expression of genius."

With regard to his religious tendencies, Scriabin, for some time before his death, had planned a multimedia work to be performed in the Himalaya Mountains, that would bring about the Armageddon, "a grandiose religious synthesis of all arts which would herald the birth of a new world". This piece, titled Mysterium, was never realized. [11]

Significant Works by Alexander Scriabin

Preludes

Études

Sonata no. 4

SERGEI RACHMANINOFF (1873–1943), RUSSIA

Sergei Rachmaninoff was perhaps the most controversial figure among the composers of his generation, with his truest and most powerful medium of expression in the piano—both as a pianist and as a composer. In both capacities, he was indeed an innovator and a revolutionary. He wrote practically all his most important works between 1901 and 1917, and the remainder of his life was devoted primarily to international concertizing.

One of the greatest, if not the greatest pianist of his time, Rachmaninoff created an entirely new style and sound of piano playing within the framework of an enormous work ethic. He became a brilliant performer, composer, and conductor through long hours of daily discipline and dedicated effort. His early lyrical approach gave way to a steely, dramatic concept of sharply sculptured lines. He was perhaps the first to fully exploit the magnificent percussive potentialities of the instrument within poignant expression and coloristic effects. Whether it was in his rapid chord technique or in his dry percussive staccatos, in his brilliantly intricate passage work or in the musical elegance of his lines and astonishing vitality and incisiveness of his rhythm, it was a new way to play the piano—a new way to make the piano sound.

Rachmaninoff's supreme knowledge and understanding of the instrument bears witness to lifelong thinking and feeling in terms of the piano. His phenomenal command of the instrument led him to explore unknown sonorities and colors; he created an entirely new "symphonic" concept of piano music that deeply influenced an entire generation of pianists!

Although history marks Rachmaninoff as not being particularly religious, it is clear from his letters to friends and colleagues, and from the nature of his work *The Liturgy of St. John Chrysostom,* written in 1910, the first of his three major choral works that he intended it to be used in church rather than just as a concert piece. Rachmaninoff's written postscript on the manuscript ("Finished, thanks be to God, 30 July 1910, Ivanovka") would seem to confirm that he did feel spiritual motivation and inspiration.[12]

Significant Works by Sergei Rachmaninoff

    Concerto for Piano and Orchestra no. 1 in F-Sharp Minor, op. 1

    Concerto for Piano and Orchestra no. 2 in C Minor, op. 18

    Concerto for Piano and Orchestra no. 3 in D Minor, op. 30

    Concerto for Piano and Orchestra no. 4 in G Minor, op. 40

    Études Tableaux, op. 33 & op. 39

    Piano Sonata in B-Flat Minor, op. 36

    Preludes, op. 23 & op. 32

    Rhapsody on a theme by Paganini, op. 43

    Symphony no. 1 in D Minor, op. 13

    Symphony no. 2 in E Minor, op. 27

    Symphony no. 3 in A Minor, op. 44

    Vocalise

FRANZ SCHUBERT (1797–1828), AUSTRIA

Scholars and fans of Franz Schubert's music continue to debate the nature of his religious beliefs, but most recognize that Schubert was a devout Christian from listening to his many sacred works, especially his *Mass no. 5 in A-flat major*.

In musical history, Schubert stands with others at the beginning of the Romantic Movement, anticipating the highly personal approach to composition of later composers but lacking the forcefulness and the creative means to experiment with instrumental music that Beethoven displayed.

Many of Schubert's large-scale instrumental pieces were unknown until after the middle of the nineteenth century. He was never a conductor or virtuoso performer and did not achieve considerable public recognition during his lifetime. However, there is a lasting quality to Schubert's work that few composers have matched. He is recognized as the foremost composer of "melody," having created hundreds of songs during his short lifespan.

Significant Works by Franz Schubert

Fantasy in F Minor for Piano, Four Hands, op. 103

Impromptus, op. 90 & op. 142

Moment Musicaux, op. 94

Oratorio: Lazarus

Piano Sonata in A Major, op. 120

Piano Sonata in C Minor (posthumous)

Piano Sonata in B-Flat Major (posthumous)

Select Song Cycles: Erikoenig, Heidenroeslein, Winterreise, Gretchen am Spinnrade

String Quartet no. 13 in A Minor ("Rosamunde")

Symphony no. 8 in B Minor ("Unfinished")

ROBERT SCHUMANN (1810–1856), GERMANY

It is easy to criticize another's work in an effort to build one's own self-importance and ego. How elevating then, when striving to promote the fine work of his fellow composers, Robert Schumann became the editor of an important music publication, *Neue Zeitschrift für Musik*. A few examples of his support of others' work include the following.

Acknowledging the exceptional musical gifts of Chopin, Schumann carried a Chopin piano score to a meeting of other musicians and declared, "Hats off, gentlemen—a genius!" He claimed Mendelssohn to be "the Mozart of the 19-century, the most brilliant musician, the one who sees most clearly through the contradictions of this period, and for the first time reconciles them." And, regarding the extraordinary compositional gifts of the almost obscure Schubert, he wrote, "It would require whole books to show in detail what works of pure genius his compositions are."[13]

A great lesson can be learned from Schumann's good will and of his striving to help establish healthy camaraderie among master musicians by frequently putting his personal reputation on the line through positive reviews and public recommendations for younger composers and complete unknowns. By doing so he did not diminish his own personal worth or musical greatness. He simply understood the brotherhood of man.

Significant Works by Robert Schumann

Abegg Variations, op. 1
Carnival, op. 9
Concerto for Piano and Orchestra in A Minor, op. 54
Davidsbundlertanze, op. 6
Fantasia in C Major, op. 17
Fantasiestuke, op. 12
Faschingsschwank aus Wien, op. 26
Kinderszenen, op. 15
Kreisleriana, op. 16
Papillons, op. 2
Piano Sonata in F-Sharp Minor, op. 11
Select Lieder
Symphonic Études, op. 13
Symphony no. 2 in C Major

PETER ILYITCH TCHAIKOVSKY (1840–1893), RUSSIA

From the outset, Tchaikovsky was considered a perfectionist. Starting his music career late in life, he entered the St. Petersburg Conservatory to become, as he phrased it, "a musician," after having already received a law degree at St. Petersburg School of Jurisprudence at age nineteen.

Although plagued with depression, self-doubt, and other personality difficulties, Tchaikovsky frequently sought personal self-worth and achieved extraordinary sensitivity and beauty in his musical creations. He became well known in Europe and America for his numerous art songs, solo pieces for piano, chamber music, operas, his famous *Piano Concerto in B-flat Minor*, and his *Violin Concerto*. Furthermore, from his strong attachment to the beauty of Russian Orthodox worship, he composed the magnificent *Liturgy of St. John Chrysostomos*.

His fourth, fifth, and sixth symphonies are standard repertoire for major symphony orchestras, and his three ballets—*Swan Lake, Sleeping Beauty*, and *The Nutcracker*—are considered in the world of ballet, standard classics of the form. His music has always been beloved universally. [14]

Significant Works by Peter Ilyitch Tchaikovsky
> Ballets: Swan Lake, Sleeping Beauty, and The Nutcracker
> Concerto for Piano and Orchestra in B-flat Minor, op. 23
> Manfred Symphony, op. 58
> Overture "1812," op. 49
> Symphony no. 4 in F Minor, op. 36
> Symphony no. 5 in E Minor, op. 64
> Symphony no. 6 in B Minor ("Pathetique"), op. 74
> Violin Concerto in D Major, op. 35

GIUSEPPI VERDI (1813–1901), ITALY

The music of Verdi served the audience of the mass public rather than that of the musical elite. The subjects of his works, Verdi said, should be "original, interesting...and passionate; passions above them all!" His most mature works, except for *Falstaff*, were serious and ended tragically. These fast-paced works dealt with emotional extremes, and the music emphasized the dramatic situation.

In performance, it is the expression of the melodies given to the singers that represents the expressive spirit of Verdi's work. He used duets, trios and quartets along with significant and memorable passages for chorus. As he aged, his works became increasingly unconventional with the orchestration becoming more imaginative with richer accompaniments. His final work, the comic *Falstaff*, presents this with its carefree finale: a fugue declaring "All the world's a joke!" [15]

Significant Works by Giuseppi Verdi
> Select Operas:
> Aida
> Falstaff

Il Trovatore
Otello
Rigoletto

Richard Wagner (1813–1883), Germany

Wagner was a German composer, conductor, theatre director, and writer, primarily known for his operas (or "music dramas", as they were later called). Wagner's numerous compositions, particularly those of his later period, are notable for their complex texture, rich harmonies and orchestration, and the elaborate use of leitmotifs, musical themes associated with individual characters, places, ideas or plot elements. Unlike most other opera composers, he wrote both the music and words for all of his stage works.

Parsifal of 1882 was the last opera by Wagner, who described it a sacred festival play which was produced in a religious atmosphere. Since he died in 1883, the belief is confirmed by many that, feeling the approach of death, Wagner returned to the religion of his youth, Lutheran, but his stay in Catholic Bavaria had affected him for most of his life.

Wagner returned to his spirituality despite a life characterized, until his last decade, by political exile, turbulent love affairs, poverty and running from his creditors. Interestingly, his second marriage to Cosima Liszt, the great pianist's daughter, was successful. His argumentative personality and often outspoken views on music, politics and society made him a controversial figure during his life. But, the impact of his musically brilliant ideas can be traced in many of the arts throughout the twentieth century.

Significant Works by Richard Wagner
   Rienzi: Overture
   Tannhäuser: Overture & Bacchanal
   Tristan and Isolde: Prelude & Liebestod

TWENTIETH CENTURY (1890–PRESENT)

BÉLA BARTÓK (1881–1945), HUNGARY

From 1899 to 1903, Bartók studied piano under István Thomán, a former student of Franz Liszt, and composition under János Koessler at the Royal Academy of Music in Budapest. There, he met Zoltán Kodály, who influenced him greatly and became his lifelong friend and colleague. And although Bartók was not conventionally religious, he was a nature lover—always mentioning the miraculous order of nature with great reverence.

When visiting a holiday resort in the summer of 1904, Bartók overheard a young nanny, Lidi Dósa from Kibéd in Transylvania, sing folk songs to the children in her care. This sparked his lifelong dedication to folk music. From that time forth, he spent much time in gathering the tunes of Hungarian gypsies which began to appear in his compositions.

In 1907, Bartók began teaching as a piano professor at the Royal Academy. This position freed him from touring Europe as a pianist and enabled him to work in Hungary. Among his renowned students were Fritz Reiner, Sir Georg Solti, György Sándor, Ernő Balogh, and Lili Kraus.

Significant Works by Béla Bartók

Allegro Barbaro
Concertos for Piano and Orchestra, Nos. I & II
Concerto for Orchestra
Duke Bluebeard's Castle
Music for Strings, Percussion & Celeste

CLAUDE DEBUSSY (1862–1918), FRANCE

French composer Claude Debussy is considered one of the most admired and influential composers of the twentieth century, though he wrote some of his most important compositions before the turn of the century. During his formative years, he studied and assimilated many diverse musical idioms. Yet from an astonishingly early period, his music began to show a striking originality and has become part of the world's cultural heritage. It has been one of the original factors affecting the creative directions taken by many composers since his time. Some of the most important composers of our time show conclusively in their music how penetrating and pervasive Debussy's influence has been. But it took courage on Debussy's part to chart this new course for the future direction of music.

Debussy started piano lessons at age four, and his talents soon became evident; by age ten he entered the Paris Conservatory, where he studied for eleven years. From the start, though clearly gifted, Debussy was argumentative and experimental, challenging the rigid teaching of the Academy by favoring instead dissonances and intervals, which were frowned upon at the time. Concurrently, he became a brilliant pianist and sight reader who could have had a professional performing career had he not experienced consistent depression and a difficult, even turbulent private life.

Eventually, Debussy decided to move beyond the compositional techniques of the past, never feeling a need to adhere to the rules of the day. He was a man who would not be stopped in his quest for new, innovative ideas. Specifically, his harmonies, considered radical in his day, were influential to almost every major composer of the new century, especially the music of Ravel, Stravinsky, Messiaen, and Bartók as well as the leading Japanese composer Tōru Takemitsu. He also influenced many figures in jazz, most notably Bill Evans, Thelonious Monk, and Duke Ellington.

Significant Works by Claude Debussy

    Arabesques in E Major & G Major
    Children's Corner
    Danse
    Estampes
    Pelleas et Melisande
    Petite Suite for Piano, Four Hands
    Prelude a l'apres-midi d'un faune
    Preludes, Books I & II
    Suite Bergamasque
    Symphonic Suite: La Mer

SERGEI PROKOFIEV (1891–1953), RUSSIA

One of the leading pianists of his time, Prokofiev was one of the most prolific composers of contemporary piano music, although he became a comprehensive composer with all forms of writing—ballets, symphonies, concerti, chamber music, opera, and children's music. Even his contemporary, the famous Stravinsky, described Prokofiev as the greatest Russian composer of his day. But, over the course of his stormy life, it didn't begin that way.

For years his music was misunderstood. Even into his adult life, European and American audiences failed to respond to it. Of his earlier years, the story is told that his mother turned to him in exasperation at one period and exclaimed, "Do you really understand what you are pounding out of that piano of yours?"[16]

But in today's world, Prokofiev became known as a twentieth-century sensation! Prokofiev displayed unusual musical abilities by the age of five and from there studied piano, organ, and composition at the St. Petersburg Conservatory, where, becoming a formidable pianist equipped with the necessary theoretical, musical and technical tools, he began experimenting with dissonant harmonies and unusual time signatures, laying the basis for his own musical style.

After a life of poverty, illness, rejection, discouragement, and unsettling family life, with his music often being interpreted as representing "venting his anger and frustration with the Soviet regime," his work was finally rewarded. His premieres became instant sell-outs, international audiences became great fans of his output, and Prokofiev became one of the most outstanding composers of the century.

Significant Works by Sergei Prokofiev

Concerto for Piano and Orchestra no. 1 in D-Flat Major, op. 10

Concerto for Piano and Orchestra no. 2 in G Minor, op. 16

Concerto for Piano and Orchestra no. 3 in C Major, op. 26

Peter and the Wolf

Romeo and Juliet

Sonata for Piano, no. 3 in A Minor, op. 28

Sonata for Piano, no. 6 in A Major, op. 82
Sonata for Piano, no. 7, op. 83
Toccata, op. 11

MAURICE RAVEL (1875–1937), FRANCE

Ravel was born in the Basque town of Ciboure, France, near the border with Spain. His mother, Marie Delouart, was of Basque descent and grew up in Madrid, Spain, while his father, Joseph Ravel, was a Swiss inventor and industrialist from French Haute-Savoie. Both were Catholics and they provided a happy and stimulating household for their children. Joseph delighted in taking his sons to factories to see the latest mechanical devices, and he also had a keen interest in music and culture. Ravel verified his father's early influence by stating later, "As a child, I was sensitive to music—to every kind of music."[17]

Ravel was very fond of his mother, and her Basque heritage was a strong influence on his life and music beginning with his earliest memories of Spanish folk songs she sang to him. The family moved to Paris three months after his birth and at age six, Maurice began piano lessons with Henry Ghys and received his first instruction in harmony, counterpoint, and composition with Charles-René. His earliest public piano recital was in 1889 at age fourteen. At that time Ravel's parents continued to encourage him in his musical pursuits by sending him to the Paris Conservatory, first as a preparatory student and eventually as a piano major where he received a first prize in the piano student competition in 1891.

Though obviously gifted at the piano, Ravel demonstrated a preference for composing. He was particularly impressed by the new Russian works conducted by Nikolai Rimsky-Korsakov at the Exposition Universelle in 1889. That year Ravel also met Ricardo Viñes, who would become one of his best friends, one of the foremost interpreters of his piano music, and an important link between Ravel and Spanish music.

Significant Works by Maurice Ravel

Bolero

Concerto for Piano and Orchestra in G Major

Daphnis and Chloe: Suite no. 2

Jeux d'eau

La Valse

Le Tombeau de Couperin

Miroirs

Rapsodie espagnole

Sonatine

String Quartet in F Major

Valses nobles et sentimentales

Symphonic Poem: Don Juan, op. 20

Symphonic Poem: Thus Spake Zarathustra, op. 30

Symphonic Poem: A Hero's Life, op. 40

IGOR STRAVINSKY (1882–1971), RUSSIA

Considered one of the outstanding composers of the twentieth century, Stravinsky was born in St. Petersburg, Russia, into a musical family. He received international recognition mostly for his ballets, *Firebird*, *Petrushka*, and *The Rite of Spring*, commissioned by the Russian impresario, Serge Diaghilev. Since Stravinsky converted to Christianity, it is ironic that these ballets were written with secular—even pagan—content, with no intimation regarding his newfound faith in Christ that would later play a major role in his work. For example, *The Rite of Spring*, with its radical and vicious approach to musical style and choreography, created a riot among members of the audience in its premiere performance.

Soon after his conversion, Stravinsky was interviewed in Belgium, where he declared, "The more one separates oneself from the canons of the Christian church, the further one distances oneself from the truth . . . Art is made of itself, and one cannot create upon a creation, even though we ourselves are graftings of Jesus Christ." Interestingly, the Symphony of Psalms, his next major work, he dedicated "to the glory of God."

From the Christian beliefs and doctrines he espoused for the rest of his life, Stravinsky became a highly religious musician who possessed many strong spiritual convictions. Although he followed his creative imagination and established a new direction for music composition, he remained fearless when receiving severe criticism for much of his work. Others' adverse opinions did not affect him, as he always claimed to work for a "higher audience."

On one occasion he exclaimed, "Music praises God. Music is as well or better able to praise Him than the building of the church and all its decorations; it is the church's greatest ornament." And when asked if one must be a believer to create sacred music, Stravinsky insisted, "Certainly, and not merely a believer in 'symbolic figures,' but in the person of the Lord, the person of the Devil, and the miracles of the church." Finally, considering his own compositional genius, Stravinsky asserted, "Only God can create. I make music from music. . . . I regard my talents as God-given, and I have always prayed to Him for strength to use them."[18]

Significant Works by Igor Stravinsky

Ballet: Petrouchka
Histoire du Soldat
Petrouchka Suite: Three movements for Piano (transcription)
Rite of Spring
Symphony of Psalms
The Firebird Suite

Additionally, the following master composers contributed meaningful works that are highly recommended for the home and family.

BAROQUE

DOMENICO SCARLATTI (1660–1725) ITALY

Keyboard Sonatas

CLASSICAL

MUZIO CLEMENTI (1752–1832) ITALY

Gradus ad Parnassum
Piano Sonatas

ROMANTIC

HECTOR BERLIOZ (1803–1869) FRANCE

Symphonie Fantastique

GEORGES BIZET (1838–1875) FRANCE

Carmen

CESAR FRANCK (1822–1890) FRANCE

Piano Quintet in F Minor
Prelude, Chorale and Fugue for Piano
Select Organ Works
Sonata for Violin and Piano in A Major
Symphony in D Minor

EDWARD MACDOWELL (1860–1908) USA

Concerto for Piano and Orchestra no. 2 in D Minor, op. 23
Ten Woodland Sketches, op. 51

GUSTAV MAHLER (1860–1911) AUSTRIA

Symphony no. 1 in D Major ("Titan")
Symphony no. 4 in G Major ("Humoresque")
Symphony no. 6 in A Minor ("Tragic")
Symphony no. 8 in E–flat Major ("Symphony of a Thousand")
Modest Mussorgsky (1839–1881) Russia
Boris Goudonov
Night on Bald Mountain
Pictures at an Exhibition

GIACOMO PUCCINI (1858–1924) ITALY

> Select Operas:
> La Boheme
> Madame Butterfly
> Tosca
> Turandot

NIKOLAI RIMSKY-KORSAKOV (1844–1908) RUSSIA

> Symphonic Suite: Scheherezade, op. 35

CAMILLE SAINT-SAËNS (1835–1921) FRANCE

> Concerto for Piano no. 2 in G Minor, op. 22
> Concerto for Piano no. 4, in C Minor, op. 44
> Concerto for Piano no. 5 in F Major, op. 103
> Carnival of the Animals
> Danse Macabre
> Le Cygne
> Opera: Sampson and Delilah
> Symphony no. 3 ("Organ")

TWENTIETH CENTURY

SAMUEL BARBER (1910–1981), USA

> Adagio for Strings
> Piano Sonata in E-Flat Minor, op. 26
> Violin Concerto

BENJAMIN BRITTEN (1913–1976), GREAT BRITAIN

> Holiday Diary for Piano
> Young Person's Guide to the Orchestra

AARON COPLAND (1900–1990) USA

> Appalachian Spring
> Billy the Kid
> Fanfare for the Common Man

Piano Variations
Rodeo

FERDE GROFÉ (1892–1972), USA

Grand Canyon Suite

GEORGE GERSHWIN (1898–1937), USA

Piano Concerto in F Major
Porgy and Bess
Rhapsody in Blue for Piano and Orchestra
Three Preludes for Piano

GUSTAV HOLST (1874–1934), GREAT BRITAIN

The Planets

CARL ORFF (1895–1982), GERMANY

Carmina Burana

OTTORINO RESPIGHI (1879–1936), ITALY

The Pines of Rome

ARNOLD SCHOENBERG (1874–1951), AUSTRIA

Pierrot Lunaire, op. 21

DMITRI SHOSTAKOVICH (1906–1975), RUSSIA

Concerto for Piano and Orchestra no. 2
Symphony no. 1, op. 10
Symphony no. 5, op. 47
Symphony no. 7, op. 60 ("Leningrad")
The Nose, op. 15

RICHARD STRAUSS (1864–1949), GERMANY

Der Rosenkavalier
Fantastic Variations: Don Quixote, op. 35
Salome

NOTES:

1. Steven Zohn, *Music for a Mixed Taste: Style, Genre, and Meaning in Telemann's Instrumental Works* (New York: Oxford University Press, 2008), 349.

2. Paul Henry Lang, *George Frideric Handel* (New York: Norton, 1966), 262.

3. George Mare, *Beethoven: Biography of a Genius* (New York: Funk & Wagnalls, 1969), 149.

4. Karl Geiringer, in collaboration with Irene Geiringer, *Haydn: A Creative Life in Music*, 2nd ed., rev. and enl. (Berkeley: Univeristy of California Press, 1968), 386.

5. Peter Latham, *Brahms* (New York: Collier, 1962), 79.

6. Benita Eisler, *Chopin's Funeral* (New York: Vintage Books, 2003), 183.

7. Alec Robertson, *Dvořák* (New York: Collier, 1962), 137.

8. David Monrad Johansen, *Edvard Grieg*, rans. Madge Robertson (Princeton: Princeton University Press, 1938), 117.

9. John Horton, *Grieg* (london: J. M. Dent, 1974), 89.

10. Patrick Kavanaugh, *Spiritual Moments with the Great Composers* (Grand Rapids: Zondervan Publishing, 1995), 136–137.

11. Arthur Loesser, *Men, Women and Pianos: A Social History* (New York: Dover Publications, 1954), 593.

12. Robert Matthew Walker, *Racmaninoff* (London and New York: Omnibus Press, 1980), 219–220.

13. Gerald Abraham, ed., *Schumann: A Symposium* (New York: Oxford University Press, 1952), 168.

14. Edwin Evans, *Tchaikovsky*, rev. ed. (New York: Farrar, Straus, & Giroux, 1966), 303.

15. Carlo Gatti, *Verdi: The Man and His Music*, trans. Elisabeth Abbott (New York: Putnam, 1955), 169.

16. Claude Samuel, *Prokofiev* (London: Faber and Faber, 1971), 93.

17. Arthur Loesser, *Men, Women and Pianos: A Social History* (New York: Dover Publications, 1954), 498.

18. Patrick Kavanaugh, *Spiritual Moments with the Great Composers* (Grand Rapids: Zondervan Publishing, 1995), 158.

Summary

Throughout history, the unspoken but exceedingly inspirational language of music has exerted powerful influence on individuals and societies alike. Felix Mendelssohn once remarked that music is more specific about what it expresses than words written about those expressions can communicate. That music has the power to express, convey, and elicit strong emotions is without question.

Musicians create and perform music that enhances and manifests emotion; is used as a carrier of information, a method used to teach information by all cultures; and is effectively used in science and therapy. Dedicated musicians devote most of their time creating music and to perfecting their instrument and artistry. Music itself requires these kinds of artistic and committed people to sustain and spread its creation.

Of course, there is much more regarding music and musicians that makes a difference in the world. The study of music, as well as the psychology of music, has become increasingly more extensive, allowing new appreciation of the recurring presence and power of music. Disciplines such as music therapy strategically utilize music to benefit people physically, cognitively, socially, or emotionally, thereby demonstrating overwhelmingly the powerful effects of music and its role in today's world.

It has become evident that, in the twentieth century, the condition of serious music in Western culture has undergone a change that few could have imagined one hundred years ago. The reasons for this transformation are many and varied, including the influence of technology, the media, and the resultant exposure to new cultures and ethnic traditions, commercialism, the increased emphasis on visual media and various cultural, ideological, and social changes.

Additionally, religion for so long has been the "moral compass" of society. Certainly, then, the inherent beauty of praiseworthy music can itself draw us to Christ. On numerous occasions in diverse parts of the world, I have listened to the testimonials of people who, upon hearing inspirational music or compositions of the masters, were suddenly aware of their need for God or to draw closer to God—a marvelous example of how music can be used to glorify the Lord.

Within the contents of this book, *Praiseworthy Music and Spiritual Moments*, we have considered the power of music to unite, bless, heal, empower, inspire, praise, uplift, and teach. I have submitted that music is a source of power, inspiration, and expression that speaks when words fail, connects the world, relieves stress, calms, and heals. But music does much more than this!

Music can be profoundly evocative with deep resonances, without being familiar, and without calling up specific memories. All of us have had the experience of being transported by the sheer beauty of music—suddenly finding ourselves in tears, not knowing whether they are of joy or sadness, suddenly feeling a sense of the sublime or a great stillness within. Though difficult to characterize these transcendent emotions, they can still be evoked. Music can bring them, if only for a short time, a sense of clarity, joy and tranquility.

As William Congreve put it, "Music hath charms to soothe a savage breast, to soften rocks, or bend a knotted oak."[1] Music has the power to transform the way we feel, both physically and mentally. It can bring to life happy memories and cause the painful ones to fade away.

Sometimes in our society of distractions, to the chagrin of professional music teachers and performers, music and other arts options tend to be seen as curriculum frills, activities that are nice for students and the populace to engage in but have little or nothing to do with serious matters of life.

Yet Aristotle, in Politics, made the following provocative statement about music: "It is not easy to distinguish what power it neither has, nor for the sake of what one ought to partake of it whether for the sake of play or relaxation or because . . . it is in some respect directed to virtue and . . . is capable of right enjoyment."[2] Praiseworthy music is spiritual, the language of God and the angels. Its power and influence is beyond understanding but its power in all forms is perhaps the most magical and meaningful creation in humanity since the world began.

Eagerly, I anticipate this enriching career of mine that has spanned decades of profuse musical involvement to be ongoing. It is my passion to spread righteous influence through music's inspiration by weaving an expansive panorama of intriguing music-making and colorful contributions to the musical life of our time.

NOTES:

1. *The Musician's Diary* (New York: McAfee Music, 1979), 156.
2. Aristotle, *Politics*, 1339a 14–26.

Bibliography

JOHANN SEBASTIAN BACH

Geiringer, Karl. *Johann Sebastian Bach—The Culmination of an Era*. New York: Oxford University Press, 1966.

Schweitzer, Albert. *J.S. Bach*, trans. Ernest Newman. Boston: Humphries, 1964.

LUDWIG VAN BEETHOVEN

Kerst, Friedrich and Krehbiel, Edward. *Ludwig van Beethoven: The Man and the Artist, as Revealed in His Own Words*. Compiled and annotated. New York: Dover Publications, 1964.

Marek, George. *Beethoven: Biography of a Genius*. New York: Funk & Wagnalls Company, 1969.

JOHANNES BRAHMS

Evans, Edwin. *Handbook to the Works of Johannes Brahms*. New York: Lenox Hill, 1970.

Latham, Peter. *Brahms*. New York: Collier, 1962.

CARL CZERNY

Dreetz, Albert. *Czerny and Beethoven*. Leipzig, Germany: Kistner and Company, 1932.

FREDERIC CHOPIN

Eisler, Benita. *Chopin's Funeral.* New York: Random House, 2003.
Hedley, Arthur. *Chopin*, ed. and rev. Maurice J. E. Brown. London: J. M. Dent, 1974.

CLAUDE DEBUSSY

Fulcher, Jane, ed. *Debussy and His World.* Princeton: Princeton University Press, 2001.
Oscar, Thompson. *Debussy: Man and Artist.* San Diego: Tudor Publishing Company, 1940.

ANTONIN DVOŘÁK

Hughes, Gervase. *Dvořák: His Life and Music.* New York: Dodd, Mead, 1967.
Robertson, Alec. *Dvořák.* New York: Collier, 1962.

EDVARD GRIEG

Horton, John. *Grieg.* London: J. M. Dent, 1974.
Johansen, David Monrad. *Edvard Grieg*, trans. Madge Robertson. Princeton: Princeton University Press, 1938.

GEORGE FRIDERIC HANDEL

Abraham, Gerald. *Handel: A Symposium.* London: Oxford University Press, 1954.
Lang, Paul Henry. *George Frideric Handel.* New York: Norton, 1966.
Young, Percy M. *Handel*, rev. ed. New York: Farrar, Straus & Giroux, 1965.

FRANZ JOSEPH HAYDN

Geiringer, Karl, in collaboration with Irene Geiringer. *Haydn: A Creative Life in Music*, 2nd ed., rev. and enl. Berkeley: University of California Press, 1968.
Hughes, Rosemary. *Haydn.* New York: Collier, 1962.

FRANZ LISZT

Morrison, Bryce. *Liszt*. New York: Omnibus Press, 1989.

Sitwell, Sacheverell. *Liszt*. New York: Dover, 1967.

Walker, Alan. *Franz Liszt, the Man and His Music*. New York: Taplinger, 1970.

FELIX MENDELSSOHN

Jacob, Heinrich E. *Felix Mendelssohn and His Times*, trans. Richard Weston and Clara Weston. Westport: Greenwood Press, 1973.

Radcliffe, Philip. Mendelssohn, rev. ed. New York: Collier, 1967.

Werner, Eric. *Mendelssohn: A New Image of the Composer and His Age,* trans. Dika Newlin. New York: Free Press, 1963.

WOLFGANG AMADEUS MOZART

Einstein, Alfred. *Mozart: His Character, His Work,* trans. Arthur Mendel and Nathan Broder. New York: Oxford University Press, 1945.

Landon, H.C. Robbins, ed. *The Mozart Companion*. London: Oxford University Press, 1956.

SERGEI PROKOFIEV

McAllister, Rita. "Sergey Prokofiev" in *The New Grove Dictionary of Music and Musicians*. London: Macmillan Publishers, 1980.

Prokofiev, Sergei. *Prokofiev by Prokofiev: A Composer's Memoir*, trans. Guy Daniels; ed. David H. Appel. New York: Doubleday, 1979.

Samuel, Claude. *Prokofiev*. London: Faber and Faber, 1971.

SERGEI RACHMANINOFF

Harrison, Max. *Rachmaninoff: Life, Works, Recordings*. London and New York: Continuum, 2005.

Maes, Francis, trans. Arnold J. Pomerans and Erica Pomerans. *A History of Russian Music*. Berkeley, Los Angeles, and London: University of California Press, 2002.

Matthew-Walker, Robert. *Rachmaninoff*. London and New York: Omnibus Press, 1980.

FRANZ SCHUBERT

Abraham, Gerald, ed. *The Music of Schubert*. New York: Norton, 1947.

Brown, Maurice J. E. *Schubert: A Critical Biography*. London: Macmillan, 1958.

Hutchings, Arthur. *Schubert*, rev. ed. New York: Octagon, 1973.

ROBERT SCHUMANN

Abraham, Gerald, ed. *Schumann: A Symposium*. New York: Oxford University Press, 1952.

Chissell, Joan. *Schumann*, rev. ed. New York: Collier, 1967.

IGOR STRAVINSKY

Kavanaugh, Patrick. *Spiritual Moments with the Great Composers*. Grand Rapids: Zondervan Publishing House, 1995.

Vlad, Roman. *Stravinsky*, trans. Frederick Fuller and Ann Fuller, 2nd ed. New York: Oxford University Press, 1967.

White, Eric Walter. *Stravinsky: The Composer and His Works*. Berkeley: University of California Press, 1966.

PETER ILYITCH TCHAIKOVSKY

Abraham, Gerald. ed. *Tchaikovsky: A Symposium*. London: Drummond, 1946.

Evans, Edwin. *Tchaikovsky*, rev. ed. New York: Farrar, Straus, and Giroux, 1966.

GEORG PHILIPP TELEMANN

Petzoldt, Richard. *Georg Philipp Telemann*, trans. Ernest Benn. New York: Dover, 1974.

Zohn, Steven. *Music for a Mixed Taste: Style, Genre, and Meaning in Telemann's Instrumental Works*. New York: Oxford University Press, 2008.

GIUSEPPE VERDI

Gatti, Carlo. *Verdi: The Man and His Music*, trans. Elisabeth Abbott. New York: Putnam, 1955.

About the

AUTHOR

D istinguished international concert and recording artist and
master teacher of piano David Glen Hatch enjoys an active
performance career in prestigious venues on five continents including
the Church of the Madeleine in Paris, Rome's Basilica di Mecenzio,
Shanghai's Conservatory Recital Hall, New York's Carnegie Hall,
the Kennedy Center in Washington, DC, and the Bass Concert Hall
in Dallas, Texas.

Dr. Hatch has recorded a wide variety of repertoire on over
thirty CDs. His Sony/BMG *Living with the Classics, Vols.1 and 2*
are being marketed internationally in over forty countries.

Hatch's recordings have been Grammy nominated, received
Pearl Awards from the Faith-Centered Association, and garnered
commissions, including *Smitten with Britten*, the first-ever recording by an international artist of the complete published solo piano
music of British composer Benjamin Britten. In addition to receiving the 2002 Best of State Award as Utah's Best Instrumentalist,

Dr. Hatch—a previous winner of state, regional, national, and international piano competitions—is a frequent competition juror, lecturer, and master class presenter at renowned conservatories, music schools, and Annual World Piano Conferences in Novi Sad, Serbia, sponsored by the European Piano Teachers Association. He was also selected as one of the 1984 Outstanding Young Men of America, and nominated by numerous United States Senators as one of the Ten Outstanding Young Men of America for 1985.

Dr. Hatch received the master teaching certificate from the Music Teacher's National Association (USA) in 1994, was named one of the Best Teachers in America in *Who's Who Among America's Teachers 1998*, is listed in *International Who's Who in Music 2000*, *Who's Who in American Education 2006*, *Who's Who in America 2007*, and *Who's Who Among Professionals, 2008 Honors Edition*.

In 2004, Hatch was invited to perform in Kiev, Ukraine, with the National Symphony Orchestra of Ukraine under conductor Vladimir Sirenko at the Mariinsky Palace concert commemorating the one hundredth anniversary of the birth of Russian-born pianist, Vladimir Horowitz. Several of his live and recorded performances and interviews have been aired on National Public Radio, classical radio stations, and affiliates of PBS television in the United States, TVE National television in Madrid, the BBC in the United Kingdom, Bulgarian National Classical Radio, and on classical radio stations in Copenhagen, Hong Kong, Sydney, and Oslo.

Dr. Hatch has published six volumes of piano arrangements with Sonos and Jackman Music Corporations, is published in *Clavier* (an American keyboard magazine), and has served as a member of the Board of Trustees of the Gina Bachauer International Piano Foundation and Competitions.

David and his wife, Paula, are the parents of five children and reside in Orem, Utah.